THE TRUE S

The True Story of
Lu Xun

David E. Pollard

The Chinese University Press

The True Story of Lu Xun
  By David E. Pollard

ISBN 962–996–060–5 (paperback)
      962–996–061–3 (hardcover)

THE CHINESE UNIVERSITY PRESS
The Chinese University of Hong Kong
SHA TIN, N.T., HONG KONG
Fax: +852 2603 6692
      +852 2603 7355
E-mail: cup@cuhk.edu.hk
Web-site: www.chineseupress.com

Printed in Hong Kong

Contents

Illustrations

Preface

The question of nationhood did not arise in China until near the end of the nineteenth century. The name of the state that we know as China was taken from the ruling dynasty up until 1912, when the last dynasty was overthrown and the title of Republic of China (Zhonghua minguo) was adopted. For the previous two and a half centuries the state was known as the Great Qing Empire. Ethnically speaking, the great majority of the population were Han Chinese, but the ruling Qing dynasty itself was Manchu, the Manchus being a tribe from the northeast borderlands that ruled by right of conquest. The empire also embraced Mongolians, Tibetans, and many other minorities in the west. Obviously it would have been impolitic to base a notion of 'Chinese' identity on ethnicity under the empire. In fact it was not necessary to ask what it meant to be Chinese at all then, as the rest of the world did not count very much. A people only feels the need to define itself in order to differentiate itself from other peoples, and until the second half of the nineteenth century other peoples were no more than aliens (or 'barbarians') to be kept their side of the frontiers of the empire. The personal ideal, therefore, was not to be a good Chinese (as others might aspire to be 'a fine American'), but simply to be fully human, because Chinese equalled human.

The distinction of being fully human was achieved by embodying the tradition and culture of China. The Manchu rulers themselves preserved their authority after military conquest by demonstrating allegiance to that heritage. Culturally that full humanity was realized through mastering the history, literature and arts of China, and in the moral and behavioural sphere it meant living out the doctrines of the great sage Confucius. The values of Confucianism under-pinned the laws and practices of the state, and permeated society from top to bottom. The administrators who ran the empire all underwent lengthy examination in the Confucian books, hence the description of them in Western writings as 'scholar-officials'. As Confucianism was by no means an ignoble philosophy for a semi-feudal empire, there was little or no objection to it being taken as orthodox. For the spiritual needs it did not satisfy, there was always Taoism and Buddhism, which had their recognized place. As long as the world about them did not change, the Chinese could be contented with their way of life, indeed feel so superior to other peoples that they could ignore them. The trouble was, the world did change.

From being the dominant power in its part of the world, China declined in the nineteenth century to be 'the sick man' of East Asia. Internal rebellion, brought about by natural disasters, bureau-cratic corruption and inefficiency, combined with inability to match the military might of the European powers to undermine the Chinese faith in their system and in themselves. Most devastating of all was China's defeat in 1895 by a fellow Asian country, Japan, in a war that ceded Taiwan to Japanese rule. In the space of fifty years, unchallenged Chinese superiority gave way to indisputable inferiority. Inevitably that led to them asking what was wrong with themselves. It was in those circumstances that the subject of this biography grew up, and that question that he sought to answer.

At first the Chinese leaders thought that survival could be secured by copying the armaments and manufactures of the West without affecting the established Chinese way of life, but more enlightened thinkers came to realize that basic change was needed, because industrial strength rested on a very different kind of educational base from the traditional one, and the resources of the nation could not be mobilized under the semi-feudal system that they had. Political reform therefore came onto the agenda too. Han Chinese put the blame on the reactionary nature of Manchu rule, and a rising tide of antagonism eventually toppled the dynasty in the rebellion of 1911. The progressive intellectuals were able to provide the political model for the new republic, and a nominal national government came into being, but the armed forces largely remained under the control of the former military governors, who now set themselves up as regional warlords. Most of the warlords and a large proportion of the civilian population were conservative in outlook, so the stage was set for a confrontation between the old and new social forces, the latter being led by the younger generation who had been educated abroad or in the new modern schools in China. Essentially they wanted to establish the civil liberties and humanitarian values currently respected in the West. That meant dethroning Confucius and dismantling the social hierarchy which gave superior classes and senior family members authority over inferior ones. This ideological struggle was fought out in the magazines that flourished in the 1920s and 1930s, and was the implicit background to most of the creative literature of the time. Lu Xun played a prominent part both as a social critic and as a writer of fiction.

Though new standards of liberty, equality and tolerance were set in civil society, the nation's destiny was still in the hands of the groups that commanded armies. Among those, the Guomindang

(Nationalist Party) led by Sun Yatsen offered the most hope, as it had an egalitarian socio-economic policy and promised eventual full democracy, although in the first stage of its rule the country would come under the party's 'tutelage'. To wide rejoicing the Guomindang did succeed in uniting China under one flag in 1928, but the alliances and compromises it made to gain support for that victory soon diminished its prestige and adulterated its policies. The comparatively small but ideologically pure Chinese Communist Party therefore grew in numbers and influence, despite ruthless suppression by the Guomindang and allied warlords. The war against Japan from 1937 to 1945 gave the Chinese Communist Party the chance to build up its battered armies, and when all-out civil war came the Communists swept to victory in 1949.

With the defeat of Japan in 1945 China regained its self-respect as a military power — the Chinese saw it as *their* victory — but the question of its civilization remained. The Communist line was that the 'old society' was thoroughly bad, but if all traces of the past were stamped out, the country would be left blank and character-less, without a distinctive culture. That prospect was very nearly realized in the years of the Cultural Revolution from 1966 to 1976, when vast quantities of books and historical relics were destroyed. Fortunately China has recovered from those excesses, the past has been retrieved, including the more recent past in which Lu Xun lived, and the danger its culture faces is similar to that of all countries in the world, namely mass ignorance and triviality of pursuits.

That then is the broad context for the life and after-life of our hero, Lu Xun. His biography is of general interest because he lived through a period of spectacular transformation, and changed along with his country's changes. Having been born and grown up in a provincial town, his early youth was of unquestioning observance of the established norms and order of the old empire. Then he converted to a 'modern' education, discovered the wide world outside, and was caught up in the quest of his generation to save his country. He witnessed the creation of a new republic, but felt that the political revolution had left the moral fabric of the nation unreformed. After having resigned himself to obscurity when his first attempts to make a difference failed, he answered the call of the New Culture movement in 1918, and emerged to become the most prominent of China's dissident intellectuals. His personal importance was that he contributed as much as an unempowered individual could to the direction his country took.

Lu Xun was not a politician. He did not make a blueprint for a model society. He did not promote culture heroes. He wrote much more about things that he was against than what he was for. Above all he was a moralist who made it his task to satirize and castigate bad Chinese characteristics, customs and practices. Chinese characteristics were considered positive in the Chinese Communist Party formulation of 'socialism with Chinese characteristics' in the 1980s, but in Lu Xun's day they were very suspect. 'Social Darwinism' was in the air then: Darwin's notion of 'the survival of the fittest' in natural evolution was applied to human societies and nations, and China seemed to be in danger of going under as 'unfit'. Lu Xun looked for the causes of Chinese weakness in his compatriots' ingrained habits of mind and behaviour, relating contemporary abuses that came to his notice to historical vices. He aimed his arrows at so many targets that to attempt to represent them all would turn this small book from a biography into a general history of modern China. There is space only to deal with a few campaigns he conducted. One point that should be made here, though, is that despite his unremitting criticism of the Chinese, Lu Xun never pretended that he was anything but a Chinese himself.

Except for a brief spell on his return from study in Japan he never wore Western suits, as did many of his contemporaries. In family matters he honoured his mother and generously supported his brothers. In personal relations he likewise accepted the customary obligations. He wrote poems in classical Chinese to mark occasions in the time-honoured fashion. And though urged to go abroad in later life for his own health and safety, he never did. He thought of himself as a true patriot.

Particularly since his preeminence was proclaimed by Chairman Mao, there has been a veritable industry of 'Lu Xun studies' in China, and until very recently all accounts had to be laudatory. These accounts have to be read, but obviously cannot be taken at face value. Even the purely biographical material presented has to be treated with some scepticism. I have tried to strike a balance, offering neither a flattering view, nor in reaction an unduly negative one. Studies of Lu Xun's life and works in English and other European languages, which are also fairly numerous, are not so biased, but there is to date no reliable full-length biography. This is an attempt to provide one. The difficulty is that without sufficient detail the biography would read too blandly; with too much detail, especially as it relates to a culture unfamiliar to most readers, it would be indigestible. Again I have tried to strike a balance, but cannot hope to satisfy everyone. I make my apology in advance.

Perhaps the majority of biographies of writers are based on the presumption that readers will be familiar with their writings, and hardly more than a bare mention of titles is needed. If, to the contrary, extensive description and analysis is included in the biography, you not only end up with a thick book, but also continually break the thread of the historical narrative. In Lu Xun's case I cannot presume great familiarity, but neither can I afford to try the reader's patience too far with unhistorical digressions. The compromise has been to provide some thumbnail sketches of his literary works in an appendix which readers can refer to if and when they feel the need.

Finally, readers of this book may notice occasional lapses from the austere language of scholarship into the common speech of normal human beings. These I attribute wholly to the influence of Lu Xun, for good or ill.

Since the events described in this book took place, spelling conventions for Chinese place names have changed. Somewhat arbitrarily, we retain the old spelling for Peking (now Beijing) and Nanking (now Nanjing), but adopt the new spelling for other places, including Guangzhou (formerly Canton) and Xiamen (formerly Amoy).

Lu Xun Outline Chronology

Year	Family/person	Nation
1881	Born into gentry clan in Shaoxing, Zhejiang province. Name at birth Zhou Zhangshou. First son of Zhou Boyi, who held the first degree of *xiucai* (comparable to bachelor degree). Mother Lu Rui, from rural gentry. Grandfather an official in Peking.	*Following defeats in wars with European powers, the ruling Qing dynasty has allowed foreign businesses and missions to operate in China, and has given the administration of zones in major ports over to foreign countries (the so-called 'foreign concessions').*
1887	Started education under home tutor.	
1892	Entered local private school and began formal classical education.	
1893	Grandfather imprisoned. Lu Xun sent to mother's family in country to escape trouble.	
1894	Resumed school. Father fell ill.	
1894– 1895		*War with Japan, resulting in cession of Taiwan to Japan.*
1896	Father died. Lu Xun now nominally head of family.	

Year	Family/person	Nation
1898	Entered Nanking Naval Academy. Changed name to Zhou Shuren. Passed first round of state examination. Did not enter further rounds.	*Reform movement supported by reigning emperor suppressed by Empress Dowager Cixi.*
1899	Changed to School of Mines and Railways.	
1900		*Anti-foreign Boxer Rebellion leads to siege of foreign legations in Peking. An international relief force occupies Peking for some months.*
1902	Graduated and selected for further study in Japan. Entered Kobun Academy in Tokyo to learn Japanese.	
1903	Translated Jules Verne novels from Japanese.	
1904	Went on to study medicine at Sendai University.	
1906	Withdrew from Sendai, returned to Tokyo to study German. In June returned briefly to Shaoxing to perform marriage ceremony with Zhu An, as arranged by mother. Returned to Tokyo, accompanied by brother Zhou Zuoren. Later made abortive attempt to launch magazine.	
1909	Published collection *Stories from Abroad*, translated with Zhou Zuoren. Returned to China to teach at Hangzhou Normal College.	

Year	Family/person	Nation
1910	Took new post at Shaoxing Prefectural Middle School as dean of studies.	
1911	Lu Xun appointed Principal of Shaoxing Normal College. Wrote first short story, in classical Chinese.	*National revolution overthrows the Qing dynasty.*
1912	In February joined new Ministry of Education in Nanking. In May moved with ministry to Peking.	*Republic of China proclaimed. Veteran revolutionary Sun Yatsen appointed provisional president, but yields presidency to army commander Yuan Shikai.*
1917	Brother Zhou Zuoren joined him in Peking.	
1918	Published first short story in *New Youth* magazine, entitled "Diary of a Madman". Used the penname Lu Xun.	
1919	Purchased large compound in Badaowan Lane, brought whole family (mother, wife, brothers with wives and children) to live there.	*May Fourth patriotic movement gives boost to 'New Culture'.*
1920	Appointed part-time lecturer at Peking University and other schools. Continued to publish fiction, essays and translations.	
1921		*Founding of Chinese Communist Party.*
1923	Rupture with brother Zhou Zuoren, moved out of Badaowan compound. Published first volume of *A Brief History of Chinese Fiction.*	

Year	Family/person	Nation
1924	Moved to small house near Fucheng Gate (the site of present Lu Xun Museum) with wife and mother.	
1925	Began correspondence with student Xu Guangping, and supported student struggle against principal at her college, the Women's Normal College. In August dismissed from post at Ministry of Education. In November completed second collection of short stories.	*Death of Sun Yatsen.*
1926	Post at Ministry restored by court order in January. Following 18th March shooting of students at demonstration, Lu Xun wrote articles in condemnation. Later put on blacklist by government, went into hiding. In September left Peking to take up post as professor in School of Chinese at University of Xiamen. Xu Guangping left Peking with him, but went on to Guangzhou to teach school.	*Launch of Guomindang (Nationalist Party) Northern Expedition from Canton, led by Chiang Kai-shek and supported by communists.*
1927	Transferred to Sun Yatsen University in Guangzhou, reunited with Xu Guangping. In April resigned post because of internal disagreements and failure of university to support students arrested in purge by Guomindang authorities. Moved to Shanghai and began openly cohabiting with Xu Guangping. Thereafter gave up teaching, apart	*Nanking made capital of Guomindang government.*

Year	Family/person	Nation
1927 (*cont'd*)	from invitation lectures, and earned his living by editing magazines and publishing essays and translations.	
1928	Began to buy and read Marxist books on being attacked by young firebrands as feudal in his thinking.	
1929	Son Haiying born.	
1930	Joined League of Leftwing Writers and other communist front organizations. Writings increasingly politically committed.	
1931		*Japanese occupy Manchuria.*
1932		*War in Shanghai: Chinese city invaded by Japanese marines.*
1934–1935		*Long March of Red Army from south-east to north-west China. Mao Zedong becomes leader of Chinese Communist Party.*
1930–1936	Reigned as grand old man of letters in Shanghai, the scourge of the authorities and all 'proper gentlemen', and patron of radical youth. But chafed under the 'foremen' of the Communist Party who attempted to whip him into line, and never became a party member.	
1936	Died of tuberculosis on 19th October.	

Year	Family/person	Nation
1937–1945		*Sino-Japanese War.*
1949		*Foundation of People's Republic of China.*

Plate 1. Lu Xun in Japanese kimono. Tokyo, 1909.

Plate 2. Lu Xun in Western suit. Hangzhou, 1909/1910.

Plate 3. Lu Xun in Shanghai, 1927.
Front row (from right to left): Lu Xun, Xu Guangping, Zhou Jianren.
Back row (from right to left): Sun Fuyuan, Lin Yutang, Sun Fuxi.

Plate 4. Lu Xun with Yao Ke in 1933.

Plate 5. Lu Xun with wife and child in 1931.

Plate 6. Lu Xun lecturing at Peking Normal University, November 1932.

Plate 7. Lu Xun and Feng Xuefeng, each with wife and baby, 1931.

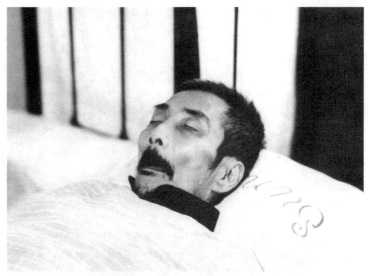

Plate 8. Lu Xun in death, October 1936.

Plate 9. Part of Lu Xun's funeral cortège.

Plate 11. Zhu An

Plate 10. Scroll presented by
Lu Xun to Qu Qiubai, 1933.

Plate 12. Zhou Zuoren

1

Lu Xun: Family and Childhood

Like so many other troublesome intellectuals of the past and present, Lu Xun was born into a prominent family that was in the stage of decline. His clan genealogy traced its origins back to the Song dynasty (A.D. 960–1279). Driven south from Henan by barbarian invasions, it settled in Shaoxing, a sizeable town in Zhejiang province, situated on a plain intersected by rivers and canals, not very far from the provincial capital of Hangzhou. The surrounding countryside produced an abundance of 'fish and rice', and the town itself was a centre for handicrafts, pottery and textiles, besides the distilleries that produced the famous Shaoxing rice wine. Material prosperity commonly brings with it high culture. The south-eastern seaboard as a whole had the highest success rate in the nationwide civil service examinations, and Shaoxing in particular was famous for its *shiye*, the secretaries in government offices who were expert in legal, tax, and other administrative areas. The Zhou clan, to which Lu Xun belonged, had its share of such higher and middle ranking bureaucrats over the centuries to stiffen its fabric. According to Lu Xun's grandfather, the Zhou clan reached the height of its prosperity in the Qianlong period (eighteenth century), owning ten thousand *mu* (roughly 1,500 acres) of agricultural land, and some dozen pawnshops besides other businesses in town. By the nineteenth century the subdivisions of the Zhou clan, called 'houses' (*fang*), occupied three mansions in town, all within a stone's throw of each other. The New Mansion (Xintaimen) where Lu Xun was born accommodated six such houses.

Expanding numbers of family members who were successful neither in scholarship nor in enterprise but still were accustomed to living in gentry style gradually reduced the family fortunes. In that it conformed to the usual pattern. But in the middle of the nineteenth century came an unexpected blow. Shaoxing was caught up in the Taiping Rebellion, which devastated the southern half of the empire. The town itself was occupied from 1861 to 1863. The destruction of war and the taxes exacted by both government and rebels to pay for the war impoverished the region and further depleted the clan's resources. The Zhou clan nevertheless emerged intact, and with enough property to support itself at a modest level. It was still able to celebrate festivals in a proper manner and observe traditional rituals and ceremonies as befitted its superior class. Its members maintained their dignity by not working with their hands, and were able to employ adequate numbers of live-in servants. If the men left the house after dark they were preceded by a manservant with a lantern bearing the name of the clan.

At this point Lu Xun's grandfather comes into our story. Zhou Fuqing (1838–1904) was a man of strong will and autocratic tendencies. He came out of the hard times of the Taiping Rebellion determined to succeed in life and raise the fortunes of his branch of the clan. After some reverses he managed to pass the highest examination in the empire, conducted in the imperial palace in Peking, and was appointed a Hanlin scholar in 1871. This achievement, announced in Shaoxing by six special runners from the capital all banging gongs, brought great glory to his house. Unfortunately, a brilliant career did not follow for Zhou Fuqing.

He had to study three years in the Hanlin Academy for a post, which turned out to be a minor one as a magistrate in Jiangxi province. There his prickly character did not make him popular, and he was sacked after three years for insubordination. He then returned to Peking and bought himself the position of Intendant Official (i.e. candidate for a regular posting) in 1879. A substantive appointment as secretary in the Grand Secretariat (*neige zhongshu*) did not come along until 1888, and that was still a lowly post. In the meantime he sold off land to support himself.

In the course of his life Zhou Fuqing had two wives and three concubines. The first wife bore him a son, Lu Xun's father Zhou Boyi, in 1861, but died in 1865. His second wife, née Jiang, bore him a daughter. This wife was with him while he was a magistrate in Jiangxi, but was sent home to Shaoxing when Zhou Fuqing went back to Peking, and hardly saw her husband again until 1893. In the family there she enjoyed the full status of and honours due to the patriarch's wife, and was treated as mother by her stepson and as grandmother by his children. To those children, born in the 1880s, she was indeed the only grandmother they ever knew, and they all remembered her fondly as a kind person, who entertained them with children's stories.

Away from home much of the time though he was, Zhou Fuqing vested high hopes in his son, Zhou Boyi. He ensured for him an education that would enable him to climb the ladder to officialdom, and indeed Zhou Boyi did pass the local level examination to earn the first degree commonly known as *xiucai* ('outstanding talent') in 1881. But Boyi failed to improve on that by passing the provincial level examination, despite repeated attempts. To the end of his life — he died in 1896 — he had no employment, and lived on the rents from the house's land. In the 1880s his house owned 40 to 50 *mu* of paddy fields, which yielded 4,000 or so catties of cereals per year, enough to comfortably sustain a family of ten. Other houses were worse off. The richest house in the clan, who lived in another mansion, owned around 500 *mu*, but that was fast dissipated. In fact very few of Lu Xun's father's generation had secure incomes; ill health and early death were common, and addiction to opium not unusual. As a result the clan's land bank gradually drained away.

At the beginning of the 1890s, however, the long-term prospects of Lu Xun's house were good. Zhou Boyi's wife had delivered three sons, Shuren (Lu Xun) in 1881, Zuoren in 1885, and Jianren in 1888, all of whom were bright lads, and promised to be eminently educable. Zhou Boyi himself, though a disappointed man, was still a responsible father. But in 1893, the year in which a fourth son was born, there came a bolt from the blue. In February Lu Xun's great grandmother Dai died, at the age of seventy-nine, and her son Zhou Fuqing had to retire from office in Peking to observe the statutory twenty-seven months of mourning. He arrived back in Shaoxing in March, bringing with him a concubine and young son, born of a previous concubine. This son, Zhou Fengsheng, was thus uncle to Lu Xun, though one year younger than him. In the autumn of the same year the thunder broke. One day two runners from the local yamen (magistrate's office) turned up at the mansion door yelling "Arrest the criminal official Zhou Fuqing!". In an instant, everyone within earshot knew that the pillar of the house had fallen: overnight its chief asset had become its chief liability. The story is worth telling in some detail, for what it tells of the times.

Zhou Fuqing's temporary withdrawal from office came at a bad time for him. His appointment had not come easily, and to secure another one in his late fifties, when the mourning period ended, would be even more difficult, given the over-supply of candidates qualified for office at the time. On the other hand, he had not acquired great wealth from his previous service, and could not live out his old age in comfortable retirement in a pleasant haven. The home mansion in Shaoxing was anything but pleasing to him. Its fabric was deteriorating, and some of its rooms had had to be let to outsiders. In the clan itself there was no shortage of oddballs, decadents and fainéants, but very few people he could enjoy talking with. In that situation of frustrating idleness the opportunity to use his connections for gainful purposes must have been very tempting. Though he had the reputation of an honest official, he agreed to arrange a bribe for the high official who came down from the capital to superintend the triennial provincial examination in Hangzhou. This official had passed the Palace Examination at the same time as Zhou Fuqing, which made for a strong bond between them.

Five local Shaoxing families clubbed together to offer a bribe of 10,000 taels of silver to obtain preference for their sons who were to be examined. To the list of names Zhou Fuqing added that of his own son, Zhou Boyi: it was, after all, a golden opportunity for Boyi to break his string of failures. The operation was well planned, but ended in farce. In order to prevent bribery of the kind contemplated, the chief examiner was not allowed to receive guests on his journey from the capital, and once in his destination of Hangzhou would be totally secluded. Zhou Fuqing therefore arranged to intercept him in Suzhou. Since he could not pass over his letter containing the draft for the 10,000 taels in person, he sent his servant to deliver it to the chief examiner on his boat. Unfortunately, the chief examiner was closeted with his deputy at the time. After handing in his letter, the stupid servant got impatient, and loudly enquired why he had been kept waiting for a receipt for all that money. The chief examiner was thus forced to open the letter in front of his deputy, and the cat was out of the bag. That at least was the story passed down in the family.

The fact that the five eminently respectable families proposed the bribe, that the 'honest official' Zhou Fuqing agreed to transact the bribe, and further that the high official from the capital was expected to accept the bribe, indicates that subversion of the due processes of the examination system was by no means uncommon. Indeed, the literature of the time was full of tales of malpractices. There was even a regular scale of fees for stand-ins to take the place of nominal candidates. Such cheating was all right if it stayed undercover, but if exposed could not be condoned, as the statutory penalties were very severe. Zhou Fuqing was therefore very fearful when he learned that his servant had been arrested, and pulled strings to have the matter smoothed over, but again was unfortunate in that he had in the past offended some of the officials handling his case. They insisted on following the letter of the law. An even greater misfortune was that the reigning emperor, Guangxu, had come into his majority, and was set on reimposing discipline. When Zhou Fuqing's case came up to him he rejected the proposed verdict of banishment to the frontiers and decreed the penalty of beheading. Zhou Fuqing's was one of the three cases of corruption that the emperor made public throughout his realm in 1893 in order to act as a warning to others, thus adding to Zhou Fuqing's shame.

In the event, Zhou Fuqing was not beheaded. He was imprisoned, awaiting execution in the autumn of 1894, but he was reprieved at the last minute, though not released until a general amnesty was declared in 1901, after the Boxer Rebellion. Imprisonment came at a price. Apart from the bribes that were no doubt passed to soften the hearts of the prison authorities, a house had to be rented for his concubine and young son near to the prison in Hangzhou, so that they could keep him company. Whatever personal savings Zhou Fuqing had put by, they were obviously not adequate, because more family land had to be sold off, reducing the holdings to 20 *mu*, the bare minimum for sufficiency.

To return to that fateful day when yamen runners came to the family mansion in Shaoxing to demand the surrender to them of the criminal official Zhou Fuqing, it was his neglected second wife Jiang who took charge of things. She persuaded the runners to withdraw, and personally went by sedan chair to see the magistrate in his yamen to get his agreement not to pursue the matter actively. The runners did not reappear. Again, large sums of money were disbursed to secure those considerations. Yet there was still the danger of further repercussions, because for serious crimes the whole family of the guilty party could be held guilty. The male members of Zhou Fuqing's family therefore had to go into hiding. For Lu Xun and his brother Zhou Zuoren that meant taking refuge in their mother's native village. They stayed in the country with a succession of relatives for six months until the affair blew over, a to them not unpleasurable exile, though Lu Xun later emphasized the shame he felt. For their father Zhou Boyi, though, it was the end of the road. His degree of *xiucai* was stripped from him, and he was debarred from presenting himself ever again as a candidate. Thus the move that could (illicitly) have launched him on the career that decades of study had been directed towards resulted in that only avenue being closed. Not surprisingly, he fell into depression, took to drink, became ill, took to opium, fell ill again, took to his bed, and finally expired in 1896.

According to the third brother, Zhou Jianren, the disgrace of their father Zhou Boyi did not lead to him (the father) being ostracized by family and friends, or indeed any withdrawal of the courtesy shown him. Even less, therefore, would his innocent sons

have been cold-shouldered and treated with contempt. Nothing
in the multitudinous accounts of the three brothers' relations with
clan members, schoolfellows, teachers, or miscellaneous adults in
the following years points to any discrimination against them. The
malpractice grandfather Zhou Fuqing was guilty of was evidently
accepted as standard practice, so much so that some years later Lu
Xun's mother actually paid for someone to substitute for him when
it was his turn to take the local examination, despite what should
have been the awful warning of Zhou Fuqing's sentence. Nonetheless, Lu Xun felt the disgrace keenly. It left a permanent scar on
his psyche, an injury which was subsequently aggravated by the
humiliation of having to make repeated visits to the pawnshop to
hand over the family valuables in exchange for cash to pay his
father's doctor's bills. The pain of being reduced from the status
of 'young master', the scion of a gentry family deferred to by
neighbours and tradesmen, to that of a 'beggar' (to use his own
term), condescended to by clerks (as he thought), and the object
of snide gossip (real or imagined), must have cut deep, for he
recollected in his forties, after he had become a famous author, in
words that have been quoted time and again:

> Anyone who has fallen from comfortable circumstances onto hard
> times will on that road have seen the true features of his fellow
> men.

The implication of this is that his fellow men are a bad lot, who
are pleasant to those who are well off and unkind to those who
are badly off. Common experience tells us that this is true only of
the worst of humanity, those whose complaisant behaviour should
not be valued, and about whom one should be glad to be disabused.
The tone of Lu Xun's words is not, however, grateful. Yet ultimately
his later preeminence as an author and mordant social critic was

rooted in his unhappy experiences of that period. His *Battlecries (Nahan)* collection of short stories, almost all set against the grey-black background of the hometown of his youth, brought out into the light the demons that haunted him. If there is any doubt about it, his feeling for Shaoxing can be plainly seen in his wish expressed shortly before he left it in 1912 to see the whole town drowned in a flood. Likewise, his social critiques found an ugly face behind every grinning mask.

It is impossible to tell what would have become of Lu Xun had his family not been brought to its knees then. He might well have gone on to pursue classical studies and become one of the last *xiucai* of the Qing dynasty, or have entered one of the new schools with a modern curriculum, progressed from there to college, and fulfilled his father's last wish that he study in the West — in either case, ending up as a member of the contented bourgeoisie. As it was, lack of funds headed him to the Naval Academy in Nanking (Nanjing). The road from there led to Japan, where his character was formed and he was set against authority.

2

Education

On balance, Lu Xun was fortunate in the education he received in his youth, given that the end to which it was directed was, as it had to be for all boys of his class, success in the state examinations, which required writing highly formalistic essays using only the terms and concepts of Confucianism ('speaking in the person of the Sage'), and executing elaborate rhetorical exercises. His good fortune lay in having relatively free-thinking and tolerant mentors and teachers, who did not stick to a narrow syllabus or impose on him the most stultifying methods of learning.

Though the patriarch Zhou Fuqing was away in Peking during Lu Xun's childhood, he still decreed the broad lines of his grandson's education. It was he who decided when Lu Xun entered the clan primary school at the age of six (1887) that the first text he read should be an outline history of China, and who sensibly prescribed and graded the poets of Tang and Song for him at the age of nine. In his tenth year Lu Xun started on the core syllabus with the Confucian *Analects*, but more entertainingly had access to a book illustrating the plants and creatures referred to in the classical *Book of Songs*, another book of flower illustrations, and — his favourite — *The Classic of Mountains and Seas (Shanhai jing)*, which had pictures of bizarre creatures said to inhabit the lands beyond the Chinese frontiers. These created a lifelong interest in graphic art. He spent hours copying these illustrations with tracing paper, and then attempting to imitate them. In his teens he enlisted his younger brothers as assistants, under severe discipline, and bound his copies together in volumes. He got so good at copying that boys at school asked him to do some for them. Ming and Qing dynasty novels, which he found at home, yielded more illustrations. Though an absorbing interest to him, his hobby was regarded as frivolous and time wasting by his tutors, and he hid from his father the books he bought with his pocket money (though when discovered his father did not in fact reprimand him).

Lu Xun did not become an artist himself, but his brother Zhou Zuoren continued to send him books on oriental and occidental art when Lu Xun was working in Peking in his thirties, and he did design covers for his own and other publications. Lu Xun's most conspicuous association with art came in the 1930s, when he supported the woodcut movement, which graphically portrayed the life and lineaments of the poor and suffering. That he should have applied himself in boyhood and adolescence so single-mindedly to the illustrations in books while ignoring their content is, however, significant. It shows how limited his horizons were in the family mansion and in the town of Shaoxing. True, boys must be boys, and have their hobbies, but the world around him was being transformed under the invasion of Western arms and ideologies. In his environment there appears to have been no stimulus for him to consider the way things were and the way they might be. The assumption in his circles appeared to be unquestioning adherence to the culture they had followed for hundreds of years. Thinking was not part of it. Conformity was the key to a career in the bureaucracy, and in retirement time was passed in private pleasures like reading, collecting curios, chess and gardening. In a sense, Lu Xun was devoting himself to such a private pastime prematurely.

On the other hand, Lu Xun was not the youth he depicted in his later story "Hometown" (*Guxiang*), secluded behind the high walls of his family compound. In fact he regularly accompanied his mother on her annual visits to her paternal home in the country, and being a boy he was allowed to go onto the streets in town, besides taking family boat trips to see plays staged on the river banks, and such like. There was also a vacant plot of land opposite their mansion where visiting troupes and local artisans put on seasonal plays, rather like the miracle plays of medieval Europe. Naturally the Zhou boys joined the audience for those too. For all that, Lu Xun thought of himself in his youth as belonging to a class apart from the peasants and 'base mechanics' he had contact with, regarding them as part of the natural world like 'birds and flowers' (to use his words) — certainly not his equals.

Lu Xun's formal education began in 1892, when he entered the leading private school in Shaoxing, the Three-Flavour Studio (the three 'flavours' being classics, history and philosophy). This was presided over by Shou Jingwu (1849–1930), who embodied the philosophy of high thinking and plain living. Unlike many others who took up teaching for lack of an alternative, Shou Jingwu chose not to pursue office after passing the *xiucai* examination at the age of twenty, dedicating himself instead to teaching the young. He was one of the very few persons in Shaoxing who won and retained Lu Xun's respect. They kept in touch in later years.

Shou Jingwu taught his pupils by himself, with occasional help from his son. His schoolroom could accommodate only a dozen pupils, who each paid fees of eight yuan per year. The pupils provided their own desks and chairs. Being of different ages, their progress was monitored individually by their teacher. Traditionally the relationship between teacher and pupil was taken very seriously: it is reflected in the phrase still current in the language, 'reverence [someone] as teacher'. As such, the teacher had the authority of a master over his disciple or apprentice. He demanded unquestioning obedience, and could apply corporal punishment. Fortunately Shou Jingwu, though stern, was not cruel, and punished only lightly. In any case, Lu Xun presented no occasion for punishment, as he was very bright and had an unusually good memory. Many tales are told about him being commended by his teacher.

The faculty of memory was very important. Almost universally in China pupils were required to memorize the texts prescribed for them, and in Lu Xun's school it was no different. The boys (at that time girls normally received no schooling) had to get their texts by heart — which was no mean feat, as the language they were written in was archaic — and recite them correctly before their teacher explained what they were about, and that only roughly. As a result very few got to understand properly what they were reading at that stage, and none understand fully, as some passages of the classics they read defy understanding even by distinguished scholars. Yet the fact that the texts were memorized in boyhood was of course a great help when in a student's maturity they were required to yield up their secrets for the purposes of the state examinations. For Lu Xun personally the benefit of having trained his memory was made manifest in his eventual career as historian of Chinese fiction and more generally as a polemicist, where instant and accurate recall of people's past words was useful to him. The rhetorical skills he learned from classical literature also far surpassed those of his modern-educated adversaries.

In his six years of education under Shou Jingwu, corresponding to secondary school nowadays, Lu Xun conned the obligatory Four Books and Five Classics, and three other classical texts. In addition he was introduced to the prose literature of the Wei-Jin period (roughly the third to the fifth century A.D.), which he liked and which is said to have influenced his style. In his teenage years Lu Xun became something of a bibliophile, buying a large range of classical books, one category of which related to his hometown. Those he could not buy he borrowed, copied out in part or in full, and stitched together. The fact that he had enough pocket money to buy so many books, incidentally, shows that his family was not as destitute as is commonly made out, even after his grandfather was imprisoned. For lighter reading, like the old novels and pictorial volumes, he was able to draw on the collections of senior relatives. He had no particular interest in poetry, then or later, though he learned the techniques and rules of classical verse and in his maturity frequently composed poems in classical style to mark occasions.

Between 1912 and 1919, when Lu Xun led a bachelor existence in Peking, collecting books, collating texts and copying inscriptions became his sole enjoyment. In that, he took to an extreme hobbies he had developed in his boyhood, which represented a curatorial and antiquarian approach to the civilization in which he lived. Other men who rose to eminence in modern China have told of the grand ambitions they conceived in their youth to improve the world; right up to the time of leaving for the Naval Academy, Lu Xun preferred to ignore it. No doubt the disgrace of his grandfather and his sense of loss of social status had a dampening effect on potential youthful flamboyance.

The only trend in his mental make-up which might be deemed 'progressive' in his teenage was his distaste for the 'eight-legged essay' — the principal test at the state examinations. But his rigidly conservative teacher Shou Jingwu himself detested the eight-legged essay, and gave teaching in it over to his son. Lu Xun still half-heartedly persisted, and took part in the first round of the local three-part series after his first term at the Naval Academy, in December 1898. He was placed 137th out of 500 candidates. As for concern for contemporary events, the only sign of it was that in 1898 he did see copies of the *New Knowledge Paper* (*Zhixin bao*, published in Macau), because he wrote from Shaoxing to his brother Zhou Zuoren, then in Hangzhou, of a threat to their province of Zhejiang in the plan of the foreign powers to 'slice up' China, and of a rumour that three thousand mercenaries had invaded Hangzhou. But of broader issues there is no mention.

The impression should not be given, however, that Lu Xun was a bookworm and a milk-and-water child. On the contrary, he was given the nickname of 'lamb's tail' because of his liveliness, and got up to boyish pranks, like teasing his grandmother by pretending to fall over in front of her. And in his teens he indulged in quite elaborate escapades. Two famous ones were leading his schoolmates to wreck the classroom of another school where the teacher was said to beat his pupils cruelly, and to ambush an obnoxious military man who was known to cuff small boys who passed his door. On the latter occasion Lu Xun took along his grandfather's short sword. Luckily for all concerned, the military man did not show his face. The episode still provided the makings of a little play which Lu Xun and the other boys acted out at home. Playacting was in fact a regular diversion for them.

The chance to play the dashing hero for real came — briefly — when Lu Xun entered the Naval Academy in Nanking. This cadet training school, set up in 1890 to modernize the military as part of China's 'self-strengthening' movement, was not his first choice for further education. He would have preferred to go to a civilian college in Hangzhou, but the fees were too high. Yet it was not a totally novel choice in his family either. His uncle Fengsheng (that is, his grandfather's young son) was already studying at the academy, and a grand uncle had a supervisory post there. Incidentally, this grand uncle, who held the second degree of *juren* and was a staunch conservative, was responsible for Lu Xun changing his birth name of Zhou Zhangshou to Zhou Shuren on becoming a cadet, so as not to reflect dishonour on his clan by membership of the armed forces: the old adage that 'fine fellows do not become soldiers' was still widely believed. Predictably, Lu Xun was treated with disdain by some clan members when he returned to Shaoxing in uniform for vacations. Zhou Shuren remained Lu Xun's official name for the rest of his life. His younger brothers changed their names to match his: Zhou Zuoren and Zhou Jianren.

At the Naval Academy board, lodging and uniform were all provided free, and students received a small allowance. The preliminary stage of the course was language instruction: four days of English and two days of Chinese per week. Lu Xun found the teaching uninspiring. What irked him most, though, was the distinctions and privileges of rank observed even between students: he thought the place was run with the rigmarole of a prefect's yamen. Finally disappointed at being assigned to the Engine Room class (*guanlun ban*), which would destine him for a career below deck, he transferred to the new School of Mines and Railways, attached to the Nanking Army Academy.

While waiting for the new school to begin operation, Lu Xun returned to Shaoxing at the end of 1898, and took part in the first round of the state civil service examination, as we have said. Sadly, during his stay his youngest brother, born in 1893, fell ill and died, to general lamentation, as he was a much loved little boy.

Back in Nanking, Lu Xun found his new course, which started in February 1899, more to his liking. The foreign language used for it was German, which he did not like much better than English, but his Chinese essay topics were more interesting, and above all he was introduced to an entirely new field of knowledge: Western science. The technology of mining being the main component of his course, he studied textbooks on geology, mineralogy, hydraulics, mathematics and chemistry. The textbooks had been translated in previous decades by government translation bureaus. Because printed books were few, students made full copies for themselves in class. As copying texts had been Lu Xun's hobby, this came easily to him. Some examples of his bound copies are still extant.

At this stage Lu Xun seemed to take some pride in his martial status, first in attachment to the navy, then to the army. He had a seal carved with the sobriquet 'swordsman of the rasping blade' (*jiajian sheng*), referring to the sound made as the sword clears its sheath. That was an empty title, but another he gave himself, 'student on a charger' (*rongma shusheng*), had some substance to it. The latter is worthy of remark, because it does not at all tally with the image gained of Lu Xun in his mature years — slight, frail and deskbound. According to his own account, in his army days in Nanking he used to go horse riding every day after class, and even went as far as to compete in galloping with Manchu youths from their nearby cantonment, in response to their taunts. Less expert than they were, on one occasion he ended up bloody from a fall from his horse, but remounted and carried on. Another seal of his cut around the same time read 'book learning ruined me' (*wenzhang hai wo*). Taking the three seals together, we have the picture of a valiant youth ready to throw away his books and ride out to do battle. The vision was never physically realized, but did contribute to his later self-image as a 'warrior of the spirit'.

In other ways, too, the Nanking years were formative. 1898 was the year when things started moving fast at the centre of imperial government. After decades of urging by progressive intellectuals that internal changes were necessary to prevent the empire being dismembered by foreign powers, the Guangxu emperor promulgated a programme of sweeping reforms. They were soon rescinded by the Empress Dowager Cixi, who took power back into her own hands, and gave tacit encouragement to the anti-foreign Boxer movement. But after the Boxer siege of the foreign legations in Peking was broken by the Eight Nation expeditionary force, Cixi reversed her stand and enacted the Guangxu measures herself. These included abolishing the classics-based state examinations, supporting modern education (including female schooling), and sending students abroad — principally to Japan — for advanced study, so as to create an able cadre for the future management of the nation's business.

The upheavals in the north do not seem to have disturbed Lu Xun's life as a cadet in Nanking, but a new element began to work on his consciousness. He began to take notice not only of the sciences of the 'foreign devils', but also of their thought. He started to read magazines informed by Western ideas and others consisting of translated articles. These were introduced to his school by a new head in 1901. In the same year he read Yan Fu's translation of Thomas Huxley's *Evolution and Ethics*. Published as a book in 1898, Yan's free translation, which incorporated much commentary by himself relating to the Chinese situation, succeeded almost single-handedly in reversing the mindset of Chinese intellectuals, replacing their backward-looking or cyclical philosophy with a forward-looking Social Darwinist one, and sounding the alarm that their previously superior civilization (and race) was in danger of going under in the 'struggle for existence'. Lu Xun was immediately converted. Darwinism was to dominate his thought for decades to come.

Western literature also swam into his field of vision, mainly through the translations into classical Chinese of Lin Shu and his collaborators. Lin Shu broke through to a national readership with his translation of Dumas' *La dame aux camélias*. Lu Xun read this and the many novels that followed, by Dickens, Walter Scott, Rider Haggard, Conan Doyle, and others. Scott's *Ivanhoe* particularly impressed him, as the Saxon resistance to Norman rule there chronicled could easily transfer to the situation in China of the Han people being ruled by the Manchus. Somewhat later, in 1904, Lin's translation of Harriet Beecher Stowe's *Uncle Tom's Cabin* also made a deep impression on him. The translator explicitly pointed to the danger of the Chinese becoming slaves like the Negroes in America.

In 1901 Lu Xun was joined in Nanking by Zhou Zuoren, who enrolled in the Naval Academy, and was to stay the course there. The 'bonding' between the two brothers was very strong. They met at every opportunity, and continually exchanged reading matter — both classical Chinese literature and modern books and magazines. Zhou Zuoren was an omnivorous reader, and had ideas of his own, but always deferred to his elder brother. Given that Lu Xun was now head of the family, his own attitude towards his younger brothers was both protective-paternal and affectionate-fraternal.

Lu Xun graduated from the School of Mines and Railways in January 1902 with high grades and having collected a string of prizes along the way, but in the realization that he had not learned anything of practical use. His class had indeed gone down a mine, but the mine in question produced only enough coal to work its own water pumps. Lu Xun was therefore glad to be accepted for further study in Japan, whither he set sail on 21st March, across a to him uncharted sea.

3

Japan

I n Tokyo Lu Xun found himself one of thousands of Chinese
students, the majority on government grants, but some
privately funded. He was assigned to Kobun College, a
preparatory school whose main purpose was to teach the Japanese
language, but whose curriculum included general knowledge,
mathematics, and physical education classes. As a government
student, Lu Xun received a monthly allowance of three yuan.

Life for the Chinese students in Japan could not be very tranquil:
the potential for conflict was ever present. On the one hand they
were supervised by staff of the Chinese embassy, whose job was to
keep them in line as loyal servants of the Great Qing Empire. On
the other hand, Japan had become the refuge for Chinese dissidents
and radicals who were busy agitating for constitutional reform at
one end of the spectrum and bloody revolution at the other end.
They had their followers in the student body. The Zhejiang bunch
that Lu Xun was closest to were among the most extreme politically.
The students themselves, when their numbers allowed, also had
their own organs in magazines published along provincial lines.
Thus Lu Xun contributed articles to the magazine *Zhejiang Tide*
(*Zhejiang chao*) edited by his friend Xu Shouchang, from 1903
onwards.

In the wider setting of the host society, the Chinese students were not comfortable, either. The Japanese, having for centuries been culturally speaking a client state of China, now looked down on the Chinese. Militarily they were entitled to do so, having won a crushing victory over China in 1895. They were also a good generation ahead of the Chinese in mastering the natural and material sciences of the West, not to mention its intellectual culture. Little wonder, then, that Chinese students were jeered at in the streets. What particularly marked them out was their pigtails, or queues.

Since the seventeenth century all Chinese males, like their Manchu conquerors, were required to shave the front of their scalps and let the hair at the back grow long, to be knotted into a long braid. The Chinese students in Japan were faced with the choice between ridicule there if they kept their queues, and ridicule or worse if they returned to China without their queues. To add to the problem was the ideological factor: cutting off the queue would be regarded as rejection of allegiance to the Qing empire. Thus the 'question of hair' became a very important one.

Lu Xun took the step of cutting off his queue in 1903, about a year after he arrived in Japan. Partly this was indeed a gesture to mark the end of subservience, but at the same time it was for convenience. He had just joined a ju-jitsu class at college, where the queue got in the way. Lu Xun was not the first to cut off his queue: his friend and fellow ju-jitsu enthusiast Xu Shouchang had already done so. Yet the deed did take some resolution. 1903 was in fact the year of Lu Xun's greatest militancy in Japan. He equipped himself with a sword, possibly with the thought of joining the proposed Chinese Volunteer Corps that was ready to find death or glory in resisting the Russian threat to take over China's north-east provinces. The corps never got off the ground, but Lu Xun took up the reference to the example of ancient Sparta in its manifesto to publish a 'translation' entitled "The Soul of Sparta" (*Sibada zhi hun*) in *Zhejiang Tide* (June 1903). This piece lauded the Spartans' heroic defence of their homeland and posited taking up arms in a patriotic cause as the highest and overriding duty of every citizen. Its fiery spirit echoed that of Zou Rong's *Revolutionary Army (Geming jun)*, published in April of that year in Shanghai — for which Zou Rong was imprisoned.

Although Lu Xun's later actions were not lacking in moral courage, he never again expressed himself willing, even by implication, to literally take up the sword and lay his life on the line. Political assassinations were on the agenda of radical student groups in Japan, and some were actually carried out, but according to report, when Lu Xun was offered such an assignment he refused, asking who would support his mother if he were executed. And he hung back from joining revolutionary societies.

Leaving the heady atmosphere of Tokyo in August 1903, Lu Xun's first holiday at home brought him down to earth. Close-cropped hair was a badge of emancipation in Tokyo, to be shown to family and friends in photographs sent home, but in Shaoxing the lack of a queue was a pure embarrassment. His photograph had already scandalized members of the Zhou clan, and when he appeared in person wearing leather boots and a Japanese-style student's uniform, there was further wonder, shock and even outrage. The response of his grandfather, now out of prison, was a notable exception: he did not think it was anything to make a fuss about. Lu Xun had taken the precaution of buying a false queue on the way home, and he wore it on his first venture out onto the streets, complete with traditional long gown, but it was not very convincing, and it attracted catcalls from passers-by. The next day he resumed his foreign-style dress and abandoned the false queue, but the results were even worse: people shouted insults of 'false foreign devil' and worse. After that he gave up and stayed at home.

However, Lu Xun's reunion with his brothers was joyful. He proposed that Zhou Zuoren should follow him to Japan after he graduated from the Naval Academy, while his third brother Jianren should stay in Shaoxing to look after their mother. Jianren was not very happy about that, but Lu Xun promised that they would always stay united, and pool their future earnings — a promise that he repeated in 1906 when Zuoren did indeed go on to Japan with him. Already at this stage, Lu Xun evidently had a vision of a better future. Their house of the clan had gone into steep decline: his grandfather's crime proclaimed throughout the empire, his father dead at the age of thirty-five with nothing achieved, and their rents now barely sufficient for survival. The wider clan was in not much better condition: its mansions were decaying about it. But the gentry ideal of a large family living under the same roof in harmony and prosperity could be revived through the united efforts of the three able and intelligent brothers. The vision was eventually realized, not in Shaoxing but in Peking, at the end of 1919.

Back in Japan, Lu Xun embarked on his first major translation exercise: a full-length novel, Jules Verne's *De la terre à la lune* (*Journey to the Moon*). By this time the idea had caught on in China that novels were very powerful instruments for forming opinion and disseminating knowledge. They had the special advantage of reaching down and passing their message to the less well-educated strata of society. Just as the man in the street's conception of Chinese history was formed by popular historical novels, so they hoped that a more enlightened view of the world could be created through the writing and translation of modern novels. The first all-fiction magazine, called *New Fiction (Xin*

xiaoshuo), had been published in 1902 precisely for that purpose, and Lu Xun had bought that magazine. The first number happened to include the first instalment of a translation of Verne's *Vingt mille lieues sous les mers (Twenty Thousand Leagues under the Sea).* Not knowing French or English, Lu Xun translated Verne's other novel from an existing Japanese version. Though the novel had undergone some changes in the Japanese translation, and Lu Xun added more to accord with Chinese conventions, by and large enough of the content of the original survived to justify Lu Xun's claim in his preface that he was introducing modern science by the back door, in the guise of entertainment. At the same time, he was not averse to supplementing his income by the venture: he sold his manuscript for thirty yuan. In December of the same year he published the first two chapters of a third Verne novel, *Voyage au centre de la terre (Journey to the Centre of the Earth)* in *Zhejiang Tide.* That translation was not completed and issued in book form until 1906, in Nanking.

Clearly, 1903 was a busy year for Lu Xun. Apart from attending classes (not very diligently, it must be admitted), his keeping up with the magazines, buying and reading new books, working on translations, and mixing with radical elements kept him at full stretch. He read and wrote and smoked cigarettes late into the night; by morning his makeshift ashtray was filled with cigarette ends. Both the late nights and the smoking became lifelong habits, the latter much to the detriment of his health.

There are very few clues to Lu Xun's private thoughts in this, his first Tokyo period (1902–1904). About the only reliable account of his doings is from his schoolmate of the time, Xu Shouchang, and he is not very forthcoming. However, a brief memoir Xu published in 1944 does reveal something very significant. Xu writes that a constant topic of conversation between him and Lu Xun was the national character of the Chinese. They discussed three related questions:

> The first was, what is the ideal human character? The second was, what is most lacking in the Chinese race? The third was, what is the root of their ailment? ... As to our probing of the second question, we thought at that time that what our people lacked most was sincerity (*cheng*) and love (*ai*) — in other words, we were deeply infected with shameless pretence and mutual suspicion. No matter how fine-sounding our slogans, no matter how nice-looking our banners and manifestos, how grandiloquent and flowery our writing, the reality was entirely different.

This is not in fact what one would have expected them to talk about. One would have expected them to take their cue from the leading Chinese intellectuals of the day who were writing about political and educational reform, international affairs, and the 'new knowledge' of natural and social science, not about the Chinese moral character. Judging by his publications, Lu Xun's interests were centred on natural science: apart from translating Jules Verne, he wrote essays on the discovery of radium and on China's geology. His emotional expressions were patriotic, both in the Sparta piece and in the geology essay, where he issued an urgent appeal to protect China's mineral deposits against foreign exploitation. If Xu Shouchang's memory is accurate, the explanation for this digression to the Chinese character seems to be that they had discovered Arthur H. Smith's book, *Chinese Characteristics*.

This book, written by an American missionary after twenty years in China, appeared in Japanese translation in 1896. Lu Xun mentioned it respectfully more than once in later life, even recommending in his last illness that it be translated into Chinese. It is surely more than a coincidence that Smith had a chapter called "The Absence of Sincerity" and another called "The Absence of

Sympathy"; and to close the match with Xu Shouchang's wording, entitled a third chapter "Mutual Suspicion".

Smith's book, published in English in 1894, was confessedly an outsider's view of the common Chinese character. He is often either amused or bemused by the attitudes he discovers, though he has some very serious things to say, too; his impressions are by no means superficial or uninformed. Lu Xun, being on the inside, obviously understood some things better than Smith, but on the other hand Smith got around in China more than he did, and noticed more peculiarities. In that first period in Japan, Lu Xun made more pressing and factual matters his business, besides which neither his experience nor intellectual development were mature enough for him to comment very wisely on the Chinese character. But when he blossomed as an author in his late thirties, it was precisely the Chinese character that was his abiding preoccupation. In a sense it was his own ongoing task that he was talking about when he wrote in October 1936:

> I still hope that someone will translate Smith's *Chinese Charac-teristics*. Having read it, we can examine ourselves, analyse, realize what points he got right; then reform, struggle, get on with the job ourselves, without seeking for the pardon or praise of others. In that way we shall establish what the Chinese people are really like.

Here Lu Xun admits, by implication, that Smith did get some things right. That reassurance is not needed, though, as it is clear from the main body of Lu Xun's work that on several major points he shared Smith's view. To sum up our speculation, already at this point in his life Lu Xun was alerted by Smith's book to look beyond 'self-strengthening' measures to a 'deeper diagnosis' (Smith's words) of what needed to be done to make China a fit place to live in.

A small sign that Lu Xun's diagnosis would throw up more
obnoxious than admirable traits is given by a sentence he
interpolated in his 1903 translation of Verne's *Voyage au centre de
la terre* (via a Japanese version). When Professor Lidenbrock tests
his nephew Axel's courage by making him climb a church steeple,
and Axel balks, Lu Xun makes Lidenbrock rebuke him, "You
coward, you're like those misbegotten Chinese students who major
in bootlicking!" Needless to say, Jules Verne himself held no
opinions about Chinese students.

Lu Xun graduated from Kobun College in April 1904. By rights
he should have gone on to Tokyo Imperial University to study
mining and metallurgy, but the student quota was full. He accepted
the suggestion of a teacher at Kobun that he study medicine instead,
the teacher pointing out that medicine had led the breakthrough
of Western science in Japan, and could do the same in China. The
enthronement of Western science would be the basis for regenera-
tion of the nation. The personal consideration for Lu Xun was
that he blamed the death of his father on the superstitious medical
lore followed by doctors in his hometown, which direly needed
replacing.

Whereas other Chinese students elected to study medicine in
Tokyo, Lu Xun chose to go to Sendai University, a provincial
university which had never had a foreign student before. One
reason for this choice may have been Lu Xun's expressed distaste
for most of his compatriots in Tokyo. In the event he got more
than he bargained for in Sendai. The local newspaper heralded his
arrival, and he was given celebrity attention. No doubt abashed,
when introduced to his classmates he gave the impression of being
wooden and reserved. Relations did not get markedly warmer,
though at least some of his Japanese fellow students went out of
their way to show good will to him: he does not appear to have

made any close friends among them. One material advantage of
Sendai, however, was that the university waived tuition fees for
him, which left him with more spending money. His first purchase
with these pocketed fees was a fob watch.

The student regimen at Sendai was in stark contrast to the
leisurely routine at Kobun College. It did not suit Lu Xun at all.
Classes began at 7 a.m. and lasted until 2 p.m.. Afterwards students
had to write up the notes they had taken during their classes that
day, including making fair copies of the drawings and diagrams
they had taken down from the blackboard. These notes they bound
in volumes and used as textbooks for revision. The teaching was
all one-way, the teacher handing down prepared material, with
no provision for discussion. Having to struggle with the Japanese
language, unlike his classmates, Lu Xun found the regimen
especially strenuous, the pace too fast for him to really take anything
in. In a letter to a friend, dated October 1904, he complained that
he had no time to pursue his own interests: 'A sorry business!', he
exclaimed, twice. He feared that four years of that would make
him a brainless dummy.

Help was at hand, though. The anatomy teacher, Mr. Fujino,
took a personal interest in Lu Xun. Mr. Fujino regularly summoned
him to inspect his notes, and meticulously corrected them for him
in red ink, including his Japanese grammar. For Fujino's care and
concern Lu Xun was forever grateful. In later life he hung a
photograph of Fujino on the wall of his study, and wrote an
affectionate essay to commemorate him. Mr. Fujino's special
attentions had a negative consequence, however. When Lu Xun
passed the qualifying examination at the end of his first year of
study, being placed 68th out of 140 students, some of his classmates
suspected that Fujino had tipped him off about the examination
questions. Although other students came out to defend him, Lu

Xun deeply resented the implication that a Chinese student must be 'mentally deficient'.

Lu Xun's brooding over Japanese contempt for the Chinese came to a head following the victory of Japan over czarist Russia in 1905, as a result of which Japan wrested domination over Manchuria from Russia. He tells how in the second term of his second year at Sendai University (January 1906) he attended a course in bacteriology, in which a projector was used to show slides. In the intervals the teacher showed slides depicting the glorious victory, as encouraged by the Japanese government. One slide showed a captured Chinese spy about to be shot; a crowd of Chinese spectators looked on passively. While his Japanese classmates shouted 'Banzai!' in approval, Lu Xun felt humiliated. According to his explanation, he drew the conclusion that medicine could not cure what was wrong with the Chinese people: they suffered from a sickness of spirit. His course was now clear. He should take up his pen to cure this more fundamental ailment of his compatriots by arousing them from their mental lethargy and showing them the way to a healthy national future.

The incident of the slides and the conclusion that Lu Xun drew are much quoted as marking a crucial turning point in his life — like St Paul's revelation on the road to Damascus. Indeed it was a turning point, but the rationalization for his decision is inadequate. First, the question of humiliation. Personally Lu Xun was treated in the main with respect and consideration at Sendai. He went on outings with his classmates, and was given a send-off dinner by them when he left. Inevitably there were individuals prejudiced against him, but it is the nature of humanity anywhere that there should be such persons: it would be foolish to think otherwise. If on the other hand the sense of humiliation was vicarious, on behalf of his backward compatriots, he was already well aware of that backwardness: he did not need the slide to persuade him of it. Second, the question of the study of medicine. The original justification of scientific medicine playing a part in the elimination of superstition was still as valid as it ever was. The question Lu Xun asked his friend on his return to Tokyo, "Can medicine cure the Chinese blockhead, the Chinese blackguard?", could still be answered 'yes'. From the beginning the assumption had been that rational medical science would eventually have an effect on minds as well as bodies, and that expectation *was* being realized in China. But the role of the doctor would be anonymous; it would not be as dramatic and exposed as that of the writer, which Lu Xun had perhaps realized it was his true vocation to be. Factors left out of account in the explanation are, as noted, Lu Xun's dislike of the hard grind of the medical school, and his isolation in Sendai, which seemed not to suit him after all, as he repaired for all his vacations to Tokyo, where his Chinese friends were. For whatever reasons, Lu Xun withdrew from his medical studies in March 1906, and settled in Tokyo again.

Shortly afterwards, in July 1906, Lu Xun returned to Shaoxing and went through a marriage ceremony with one Zhu An, a bride chosen for him by his mother. The story of that marriage is a complex one, and will be reserved to a later chapter, when there is more history to consider. For now we only record the fact that Lu Xun stayed as briefly as he possibly could in Shaoxing before taking ship again to Japan.

The Chinese embassy in Tokyo displayed remarkable tolerance towards Lu Xun in supporting his withdrawal from Sendai and agreeing to his registration in June with the German Institute in Tokyo as a student of the German language. The German Institute did not require him to attend classes, and he obligingly put in few appearances. Lu Xun had already learned the basics of German in

Nanking, and German was again the principal foreign language in the Sendai medical school. Though he did make more progress by himself in his three more student years in Japan, he never gained more than a reading knowledge of the language; later on in China he needed an interpreter when he consulted a German doctor. In practice he was able to do just as he liked under his new registration — to read, write and translate, as a free agent, with his living expenses paid by the Qing government.

One use he put German to was as a means of access to the literature of the 'oppressed peoples' of the world (mostly Slavic), since affordable German translations, such as in the Reclam series, were available in Tokyo. Among native German writers, it enabled him to study one of vital importance to his intellectual development, namely Friedrich Nietzsche. Nietzsche drew upon theories now associated with Darwin to posit a progression from the 'worm' to the 'ape' and ultimately to a superior being whom he called the 'superman' — at least his readers associated the relevant passages of *Thus Spake Zarathustra* with Darwinism. Having a great contempt for his fellow Germans, Nietzsche saw about him too many 'worms' and 'apes'. In the guise of the prophet Zarathustra, he saw himself as a bridge to the 'superman'. Lu Xun could respond wholeheartedly to the idea of worms and apes: it was not difficult to him to envisage many of his fellow countrymen as stuck on the lower rungs of the evolutionary ladder. And while he could not go as far as to think himself a superman, he had already cherished the ambition to mount a charger and sally forth to slay dragons, as we have seen. It was but a short transition from there to the warrior with the pen, an awakened individual who could with his words inspire others (particularly young people) to break out of the prison of mental darkness. We shall have more to say about Nietzsche later.

True to his expressed intention, in 1907 Lu Xun attempted to launch a magazine in Tokyo, along with his brother Zhou Zuoren, his best friend Xu Shouchang, and one other. The title of *New Life (Xin sheng)* — actually 'Vita Nuova', from Dante — was chosen, and the cover designed, but the project foundered because some promised contributions were not delivered, and the promised funding did not materialize. Along with his collaborators Zhou Zuoren and Xu Shouchang, Lu Xun published his prepared essays in the new magazine *Henan* (the name of the province). They certainly could not be accused of being unambitious, as may be seen from the titles: "The History of Man" (*Ren zhi lishi*), "The Power of Mara Poetry" (*Maluo shili shuo*), "The Lessons of the History of Science" (*Kexueshi jiaopian*), and "The Lopsided Development of Civilization" (*Wenhua pianzhi lun*). Lu Xun's own knowledge was obviously not broad enough for him to comment authoritatively on all those subjects; he must have relied heavily on summaries and overviews written by Japanese and German thinkers. Still, he must be commended for trying. While his thoughts are not logically very well ordered, they do show some profundity.

Among these essays, Lu Xun's grasp of the subject matter was firmest in the case of "The History of Man". He had at his disposal Yan Fu's *On Evolution (Tianyan lun)* that we have referred to, a Japanese book on the same subject he bought in Nanking, and Ernst Haeckel's extension of Darwin's theories. The essay essentially summarized Haeckel's views — very competently, according to James Pusey. Yet Pusey points out that Lu Xun was not entirely subservient to Haeckel. For instance, he amended Haeckel's argument that some *races* were inferior, changing that to some human *types* were inferior — in his version, those of bestial nature, exemplified in greedy imperialists, of all stamps. As to why Lu Xun should have reviewed this fairly familiar topic at this point,

in all probability he was consolidating the 'scientific' foundation
for his own future ventures. He wanted to bring about change,
and the theory of evolution seemed not only to require change,
but predict that change would be for the better. Bestiality and
aggressiveness were relics of previous stages that would eventually
give way to a fully 'humane' humanity. To speed up the process,
superior individuals would bear the torch for a more civilized
future. In fact the realization of an ideal conceived in the human
brain was not something the science of evolution envisaged, but in
Lu Xun's more optimistic moods then and thereafter he was
sustained by such a belief. As he put it in his "The Diary of a
Madman" (*Kuangren riji*, 1918), 'true men' would (or should)
eliminate the sub-human throwbacks.

An idea of what the 'true men' might be like can be gained from
"The Power of Mara Poetry", together with a clue as to how Lu
Xun thought that literature could awaken a people. The 'Mara'
poets were rebellious poets of the nineteenth century condemned
by conservatives as 'Satanist' — Mara being the name of a demon
in Indian mythology similar to Satan. In line with his preoccupation
with peoples living under tyranny, Lu Xun chose as Mara poets
Pushkin and Lermontov from Russia; Mickiewicz, Slowacki and
Krasinski from Poland; and Petöfi from Hungary. Included too
were the English romantic poets Byron and Shelley. Byron in fact
took pride of place, largely because he matched words with deeds,
dying in the Greek struggle for emancipation from Turkish rule.
All these poets were depicted as fearless scourges not only of
physical tyranny, but also of the mental tyranny of outdated ideas
and stultifying morality. They were 'warriors in the spiritual realm'.
One is reminded of William Blake's lines, "... I shall not rest from
mental fight / Nor shall my sword sleep in my hand / Till we have
built Jerusalem / In England's green and pleasant land." We might

also note that Chinese poets are conspicuously absent from Lu Xun's list.

"The Lessons of the History of Science" dealt with the less flamboyant innovators and pathbreakers in the natural sciences, ranging from ancient Greece and Rome to nineteenth century Europe. Again Lu Xun accentuated progress through the rejection of accepted ideas. On the practical level his main point was that China had no future if she clung to the notion that she could match the foreigners simply by manufacture and armaments, without a change in the culture: fundamental scientific research, presently unheeded, was essential to her survival.

"The Lopsided Development of Civilization" can be read as a corrective to the current trend of following the West in its material and political culture. Lu Xun feared that an overthrow of the feudal order in China would only replace it with the domination of the bourgeois and merchant class, which would be even more oppressive. A democratic constitution could lead to the rule of the mindless masses, suppressing individuals. To set sights on material goods and comforts would also overwhelm the pursuit of spiritual values. The objective should be a nation composed of freethinking individuals. The youthful idealism of this piece is universal, but the particulars must have been beyond Lu Xun's ken. In fact he was recapitulating the views of Nietzsche and a Japanese thinker, Takayama Chokyu.

To sum up, a deep scepticism about the motives and breadth of mental horizons of those who were advocating and effecting reform in China is apparent in all these essays. This scepticism, verging on instinctive hostility, would persist in his attitude to all establishment figures in later life. On the positive side there is hope in the free-thinking, free-speaking 'true men' whose emergence the process of evolution should guarantee, but who for the present and immediate future would have an uphill struggle. That hope of a silver lining was necessary to sustain Lu Xun in his publishing endeavours. Naturally, Lu Xun had to think of himself as a 'true man' to be able to call forth more 'true men', though equally naturally he refrained from saying so.

As an unknown young man publishing in a student magazine in Japan, Lu Xun could not realistically expect his call to reach many of his fellow countrymen. He could not help that. Those few to whose eyes his essays came would have had to be highly educated to understand his message, as he not only wrote in classical Chinese, but also used abstruse archaic diction. That he could have helped, as the options of easy literary Chinese and the standard vernacular language (*baihua*) were open to him. That problem affected, too, a more ambitious publishing venture with a much wider potential market which followed in 1909. This was a two-volume collection of short stories in Chinese translation, entitled *Stories from Abroad (Yuwai xiaoshuo ji)*. Again its bias was towards Eastern Europe: seven stories from Russia, three from Poland, two from Czechoslovakia, one from Finland; England, France and America had only one each. Lu Xun masterminded the collection, but translated only three: two by Andreyev and one by Garshin, both Russians. The rest he edited, but they were translated by his brother, Zhou Zuoren. A fellow provincial, Jiang Yizhi, put up the capital of 150 yuan, and one thousand copies of Volume One were printed, five hundred copies of Volume Two. More volumes were planned, the cost to be met from the proceeds from the sales of the first two.

The books went on sale in Tokyo and Shanghai. Unfortunately, after six months the first volume sold only twenty copies, and the second one did no better. The reasons are multiple, but not hard to find. First, distribution: few local readers in Tokyo would want to read Chinese translations, and in Shanghai sales were made not from a bookshop but from Jiang Yizhi's silk goods shop. Second, possible lack of interest in the selection. Third, translation method: previous translations into classical Chinese of Western fiction had made concessions to Chinese conventions, while the Zhou brothers' translations were uncompromisingly literal. The highly prized euphony of the language was broken down, and the text read too choppily to be easily intelligible. Besides that, the brothers favoured archaic diction more positively than ever, having come under the influence of the eccentric philologist Zhang Taiyan. Some years later evidence as to that difficulty was unintentionally supplied by the celebrated scholar Cai Yuanpei, who wrote in reply to Lin Shu's charge that he had appointed ignoramuses to his staff at Peking University: "Mr. Zhou [Zhou Zuoren] used recondite diction in translating *Stories from Abroad*, such as to be beyond the comprehension of those of shallow learning." The collection, we may conclude, would probably have sold better had it been translated into the spoken language, for the benefit of 'those of shallow learning', but at that stage both Zhou brothers wrote confidently only in classical Chinese. Whatever the reasons, the venture was a total failure, and must have been extremely disheartening.

It was therefore as a disappointed young man that Lu Xun went back to China in August 1909. He was twenty-eight years old, but had completed no course of study in Japan, held no degree. His plan to go to Germany for further study had to be abandoned because the family income in Shaoxing had dwindled even further, and he needed to get a job to support his mother and brother: Zhou Zuoren had married a Japanese girl in the same year and was to stay in Japan for another two years. Lu Xun's literary enterprises had earned him some pocket money, but no reputation.

He had written about the mission of literature, but had produced no creative literature himself. He had mixed with Chinese radicals in Tokyo, some eminent, some to become eminent, but had remained on the periphery of revolutionary activity, essentially a bystander.

On the other hand, he had enormously broadened his knowledge in Japan. His eyes had been opened onto the wide world. He had acquired a very good competence in Japanese, which would not only continue to be useful to him as a conduit, but would also underpin very helpful relationships in Shanghai. His reading knowledge of German would be called on in his future translation work. What he had learned of the natural sciences, mostly at Sendai University, would enable him to teach school back in Zhejiang province. Last but far from least, the friends and acquaintances he made in Tokyo would form a mutual aid network that would support him in times of need and give him a way out of future predicaments.

4

Shaoxing and Peking

It was Lu Xun's faithful friend Xu Shouchang who found him a job on his return to China. Xu has been relegated in history to the shadow of Lu Xun, but in their careers Xu was usually one jump ahead of Lu Xun, and afforded him vital introductions. In principled behaviour he was also often more resolute. Xu had returned to China ahead of Lu Xun, and was installed as Dean of Studies at the new Zhejiang Normal College in Hangzhou, which prepared students for primary and secondary school teaching. In his job there Lu Xun taught chemistry to the lower stream and physiology to the upper stream.

At the college Lu Xun's colleagues found him rather cold and distant. When he occasionally relaxed, it was to entertain them by imitating the airs and graces of those set in authority above them. He only once visited the famed West Lake in Hangzhou in the year he spent there, and then he had to be dragged along by his friend Xu Shouchang. His teaching seemed to go reasonably well, leaving aside one occasion when he was the victim of a practical joke in a chemistry lesson. Yet trouble was never far away at that time. Conflict was in the air. The Qing government was clinging to power by its fingertips. In the preceding years rebellions had broken out in various parts of the empire. Provincial assemblies were belatedly set up in 1909 to give substance to plans for constitutional government, but they did nothing to dampen the fire of the revolutionaries. Obedience to authority was everywhere on the wane. In the December of 1909 the college at which Lu Xun taught was the scene of a not untypical conflict with authority.

A new hard line principal descended then on the college in full official regalia to demand worship of Confucius and the sweeping away of all modern heresies. The teaching staff, who had mostly been educated in Japan, did not take kindly to that. Xu Shouchang as dean led the resistance, and was dismissed. The other teachers supported the dean, and resigned *en masse*. After a couple of weeks the conflict ended with the resignation of the principal. In the photograph taken to celebrate the victory of the twenty-five reinstated teachers, Lu Xun is in the front row, but not in the centre, which correctly signifies his part in the struggle.

Lu Xun resigned his post in July 1910, apparently because he heard that a court official had been appointed as the new principal. He returned to Shaoxing and took up a post teaching natural sciences at Shaoxing Prefectural Middle School, at a big drop in salary. He was soon appointed Dean of Studies there. Conflict arose this time between the school head and the student body. Lu Xun was stuck uncomfortably in between. In November 1910 he wrote to Xu Shouchang that he would like to leave, but had nowhere else to go. His distractions were gathering plant specimens with his youngest brother Zhou Jianren (who on his advice had decided to become a botanist), and assembling scattered ancient scraps of fiction, as well as works relating to the history of Shaoxing. But he added in this same letter, "This is not scholarship, it is a substitute for 'wine and women'." That goes to show, incidentally, that he did not have sexual relations with the wife he had married fours years previously. Though he had to see her occasionally, as she lived in the clan mansion, he avoided her as much as possible.

In a further letter to Xu Shouchang written in January 1911, Lu Xun is even more despondent. He complains that getting things done in Shaoxing is more difficult than in Hangzhou. All those in power and office, from high to low, are despicable and evil-minded. It is there that he says he "would not mind if they all drowned in a flood". Meanwhile his own house's financial resources diminished further: the proceeds from selling more fields had been used up, and now the clan's communal land was being divided up for sale. Lu Xun took the painful decision of summoning Zhou Zuoren back home to relieve the burden. He personally went to Japan in May to deliver the message. The message was not well received, as Zhou Zuoren wanted to stay on and study French. "French," as Lu Xun commented in a letter, "does not fill stomachs." His favourite Tokyo bookshop was full of new books that he wanted to read, but he came away without buying a single one. He felt he had lost touch with the times, and his two years back home had turned him into a 'country bumpkin'.

By the summer of 1911 the vexing and time-consuming business of dean of studies got too much for Lu Xun and he resigned his post. He applied for a job with a Shanghai publisher, but was turned down. Therefore when the Xinhai [1911] Revolution broke out in October and his school was left without leadership, he and a former head resumed their posts. The provincial capital of Hangzhou declared for the revolution on 5th November. Lu Xun immediately organized his students into armed propaganda teams to reassure the citizenry that the revolution would bring them no harm. Fortunately they met with no resistance, as their arms consisted of Lu Xun's sword and the old Mauser rifles the students used for drill.

The real army arrived on the 9th of November, under the command of Wang Jinfa (1882–1915). Wang set up a provisional military government. Having known Lu Xun in Japan, Wang gave him the job of Principal of the Shaoxing Normal College (established in 1910). In his first address to his students, Lu Xun gave them permission to cut off their queues. The Manchu dynasty having fallen, there was no reason to retain them. For himself the disuse of the queue came as a great relief: he was no longer subject to insults in public for not having one. Indeed, he later recalled that that was the greatest benefit the revolution brought him.

However, as the Chinese saying goes, 'good times don't last'. Lu Xun agreed to his students publishing a newspaper, and contributed some articles to it himself. The newspaper got into trouble with Wang Jinfa because it criticized him and his entourage, including his concubines. Wang held Lu Xun partly responsible, and cut off funds for the college. His position having become scarcely tenable, Lu Xun was rescued again by his friend Xu Shouchang, who arranged for him to join the new Ministry of Education in Nanking, where Xu was already working. The ministry was headed by Cai Yuanpei, a native of Shaoxing, which no doubt helped in Lu Xun's appointment.

The case of Wang Jinfa was another lesson for Lu Xun, to be stored in his capacious memory as an example of the corruption of power. Wang had arrived in Shaoxing with full revolutionary credentials, but succumbed to the flattery and bribery of those seeking favours from him. Very soon he acted like an old-style imperial governor. The reason why Lu Xun could say that the greatest benefit the revolution brought him was relief from the pigtail nuisance was that otherwise the changes were superficial. One can understand this disappointment, which was generally felt. Yet realistically speaking nothing else could be expected. For widespread and fundamental change a whole new cadre, united in

ideology, would have to have been created, as happened later with
the communist take-over of China. As it was, the revolutionaries
of 1911 were united by nothing more than a desire to overthrow
the Manchus. Yet in time the content of a republic did come to fill
out the form of the republic. That story, though, would be long in
the telling.

Some time in that year of revolution Lu Xun wrote his first
work of fiction, a short story composed in the classical language
called "Holding to the Past" (*Huaijiu*). He left it behind when he
went to Nanking in February 1912, and Zhou Zuoren sent it to
the magazine *Fiction Monthly (Xiaoshuo yuebao)*, published in
Shanghai by the Commercial Press. It appeared in its issue of April
1913, under the penname Zhou Chuo. Zhou Chuo was actually
one of Zhou Zuoren's pennames, but the brothers often published
under each other's names. The story is rather modern in conception, in that the situation is seen through the eyes of a young lad,
and nothing very much happens. The theme is revolution, but only
anticipated revolution — in other words, the stir that rumours of
revolution cause, in a town very like Shaoxing. The strategy of the
gentry is to maintain their position whatever king may reign, while
the common people rake up the folklore of revolutions past. While
the characters are not obviously modelled on real individuals, their
voices were familiar in the Shaoxing setting. The editor of *Fiction
Monthly* thought highly of the story, but Lu Xun himself set little
store by it. He did not claim it as his own until 1934, when a
volume of his uncollected pieces was being put together. Yet it is
not an insignificant work. It showed that his reading and translation
of modern Russian fiction in particular had taught him how to put
a story together, and it foreshadowed his later stories in capturing
the mentality of the denizens of a backward society without being
overtly satirical or cynical, achieved here by the use of a boy

narrator — a device that he repeated in his famous story "Kong Yiji".

1st January 1912 was proclaimed the first day of The Chinese Republic by Sun Yatsen (1866–1925) in Nanking. Simultaneously Sun was installed as Provisional President. He immediately set up ministries to administer the republic. But up north in Peking the emperor did not abdicate till 12th February, and when he did he ceded authority not to Sun Yatsen but Yuan Shikai, leader of the New Army. Not being able to take on Yuan's army, Sun Yatsen gave way, and Yuan Shikai took over the presidency in March. He made Peking the capital.

The Ministry of Education having first been set up in Nanking, it was there that Lu Xun started work in February 1912. At that stage of the operation there was little the ministry could do effectively, resources were limited, and work was slack. Salaries were correspondingly low, only 30 yuan per month for Lu Xun. He spent a lot of time in libraries. With his new authority he was able to borrow rare books to continue his work on collating ancient literary texts. When after a couple of months the ministry relocated to Peking, Lu Xun followed it, arriving there in May. For a short time Cai Yuanpei continued as his minister. Cai (1868–1940) was to be an important figure in Lu Xun's life. He was universally respected as a scholar, both traditional and modern, and honoured on account of his political history, having been a founder-member of one of the revolutionary groups that overthrew the empire. Because of disagreements with Yuan Shikai, he resigned his post in July 1912 and spent some years in France before returning to head Peking University. In later years he took on the status of elder statesman. On more than one occasion he was to act as Lu Xun's patron.

Lu Xun installed himself in the Shaoxing Hostel, a rambling

compound to the south-west of the Forbidden City, where he rented rooms until 1919. One immediate benefit of the move to Peking was a steep increase in salary. As a Section Head he received 250 yuan a month; with promotion to Assistant Secretary in 1916 his salary rose to 300 a month. That compared to the 50 yuan a month that Zhou Zuoren was earning at the same time as a middle school teacher in Shaoxing. Lu Xun was thus able to make an ample allowance to his family in Shaoxing: initially 50 yuan a month, later rising to 100. He also remitted regular sums to his sister-in-law's family in Tokyo, Zhou Zuoren having married a girl from a poor family, and was able to be generous to young persons of his acquaintance: one student he subsidized to the total of 300 yuan over several years. Otherwise he spent money regularly only on books. Thanks to the detailed record he kept of his book purchases, we can see that he spent an average of 40 yuan a month on them in 1916. He did not gamble or frequent bawdy houses — he had seen the terrible effects of syphilis in cadavers dissected in anatomy classes at the Sendai Medical School. Neither did he go to the theatre: he saw the famed Peking opera only once, and wrote it off as 'chaotic'. His book purchases, correspondence, visits to and from friends, income and expenditure, and so on, are recorded in the diary he kept from 1912. Only rarely does the diary refer to ministry matters, and hardly at all to national events.

The atmosphere in Peking was not such as to encourage interest in politics. Civil servants like Lu Xun safeguarded themselves by taking no initiatives, and cultivating harmless hobbies, just as most officials did in the old days. If the hobbies could be pursued in the office, which they usually could because of lack of business, so much the better. The hobbies that Lu Xun pursued were those he had taken up as a teenager in Shaoxing and intermittently reverted to, namely the collecting, copying and restoring of ancient texts.

These newly included rubbings from monuments and steles: he spent much time painstakingly deciphering faded characters and methodically filling in blanks. Another new area of interest was Buddhist sutras, which he bought in some quantity in 1914. These he read, apparently, as an antidote to depression. In 1915 he contributed 60 yuan for printing copies of the *Hundred Parables Sutra (Baiyu jing)*, besides a personal order to mark his mother's sixtieth birthday. (The charitable printing and distribution of sutras was a way of earning good karma.) From his diary we see that his social life consisted of chatting of an evening with friends, almost all fellow provincials. One practical obstacle to his making friends more widely was that his Mandarin was of the southern variety, heavily marked by his Shaoxing dialect.

After Cai Yuanpei resigned in July 1912, the turnover among his successors as minister was very rapid. Between 1912 and 1926 thirty-four persons served as minister, some two or three times. Few or none had any interest in education, and Lu Xun regarded them with contempt. The enthusiasm in the ministry for aesthetics as a replacement for religion, proposed by Cai Yuanpei, evaporated as soon as it was heard that he was resigning: when Lu Xun went to talk on the subject as part of a series of summer lectures, nobody turned up to listen. Instead the worship of Confucius was revived on the orders of Yuan Shikai, and ministry officials were obliged to attend spring and autumn services to pay homage to the sage. Lu Xun described the ritual as a farce in his diary, but went along all the same.

While all these things were depressing, Lu Xun did do some positive things in his official capacity. The section he headed in the Social Education Division was responsible for libraries, museums and art galleries. He participated in some useful enterprises, the main one being the removal and expansion of the

Capital Library (Jingshi tushuguan), later renamed Peking Library. He was also involved in the setting up of the Museum of History and a Library of Popular Literature. Popular literature was an ongoing concern of the ministry. For a time Lu Xun chaired a committee charged with grading popular novels, with the object of commending some and banning others. In view of the trouble Lu Xun later had with government censors, it is ironic that at this stage he should have been a censor himself. However, the committee made little headway. The members could not agree on a standard: books that were proposed for banning by some members were thought worthy of a prize by other members. The matter of a National Phonetic Alphabet to standardize the pronunciation of Chinese characters also occasioned many meetings that Lu Xun attended, and he inspected a number of art exhibitions.

On his own behalf, Lu Xun prepared reconstituted editions and collections of ancient texts that remained unpublished, and completed his collection of factual and legendary material relating to the history of Shaoxing (*Kuaijijun gushu zaji*) which he did have printed in a hundred copies at his own expense (48 yuan) in 1915. He also published a translation from the German of some poems of Heinrich Heine in a magazine in 1914.

In the summer of 1913 Lu Xun took leave to go back to Shaoxing, where he was respectfully received, as befitted his status in the ministry, and he made another visit in December 1916, to celebrate his mother's sixtieth birthday.

In general in the years 1912 to 1918, when Lu Xun was in his thirties, the age of full physical and intellectual maturity, he was turned in on himself. It is not surprising that he kept his head down, as Peking was the scene of a continuous struggle for power. Yuan Shikai made himself emperor, but was soon forced to backtrack. The warlord Zhang Xun (nicknamed the Pigtail General)

even more briefly restored the Manchu emperor in 1917, and
presidents and first ministers came, went, and came back again. It
was hard not to give the new republic up as a bad job. When Lu
Xun had a fresh seal carved for himself in November 1916, the
characters had none of the flamboyance of his earlier seals. On the
contrary, they read 'Si Tang', which in its most melancholy
interpretation would mean 'waiting for death', or more neutrally
as 'waiting to see what will happen'. Either way, passivity.

As it happened, there was something worth waiting for. Change
was brewing. A key event, largely unnoticed at the time, was the
appointment of Cai Yuanpei as Chancellor of Peking University in
January 1917. In the two years that followed Cai created in the
university an atmosphere of independent thought and free debate,

and recruited many young intellectuals who had been educated
abroad. One key appointment was that of Chen Duxiu (1879–
1942), the firebrand editor of the magazine *New Youth (Xin
qingnian)*. The magazine was given a home too at Peking University.
It was to become the focal point of the new culture movement,
and Lu Xun was to step onto the national stage by publishing in it.

The intellectuals who rallied to the call in *New Youth* for a
cultural revolution took the same view as Lu Xun did of the
republic: that it had changed outer forms but left the inner core of
attitudes and practices as they were and had been for hundreds of
years. The difference was that, with the exception of Chen Duxiu,
they were younger than Lu Xun. Hu Shi, the most prestigious of
the activists, for instance, was ten years younger, and having just
got back from studying in the United States was at the same stage
of life as Lu Xun was when he returned from Japan. Even younger,
of course, was the phalanx of brilliant students who took to the
field in support of their teachers, and spread the movement with
their own magazines. They had neither suffered Lu Xun's personal

setbacks nor had gone through the deadening experience of bureaucratic servitude that he had. Whereas they enthusiastically took up the causes of 'closing down the shop of Confucius', launching a 'new literature', enthroning the vernacular language (*baihua*) in place of the literary language, establishing 'science and democracy', and so on, Lu Xun took a lot of persuading. Was not their programme (with the major exception of *baihua*) very similar to the one he had had for his *New Life* magazine in 1907? And what had happened to that?

When Qian Xuantong (1887–1939), who had known Lu Xun in Japan, came to see him in August 1917 to ask him to contribute to *New Youth*, Lu Xun expressed his scepticism. What was the point, he asked, of waking a few of those now slumbering in an airless 'iron house', when the only result would be that they then would be painfully conscious that they were being stifled to death? Lu Xun 'firmly believed' that would be the outcome, because those who held power would not change their ways. Yet he had to concede that he could not know the future, and therefore could not dismiss hope, because 'hope lay in the future'. So he agreed in principle, though he would not write his first contribution, a short story entitled "Diary of a Madman" (*Kuangren riji*), until April 1918.

A vital factor in Lu Xun's actual enlistment in the *New Youth* brigade was the presence in Peking of his brother Zhou Zuoren. On his arrival in Peking in April 1917, Cai Yuanpei found Zhou a job as compiler in the National History Institute attached to Peking University. In September of the same year he secured a joint appointment in the Arts Faculty as a lecturer, at a salary of 240 rising to 280 yuan per month. His assignment was to teach the histories of European literature and ancient Greek and Roman literature. Zhou was possibly unique among Chinese at the time in that he had studied Greek (in Japan), and he had written some

essays on early English literature. Though there were very large
gaps in his knowledge to be filled, by that time he could consult
English and Japanese secondary sources easily, and he managed to
produce a publishable book after one year, his *History of European
Literature (Ouzhou wenxue shi)*. Thus he gained respectability at
Peking University. Externally his first article to appear in *New
Youth*, a translation of an essay on Dostoevski's novels, was four
months ahead of Lu Xun's, and it was followed by other
contributions. Without doubt Zhou Zuoren's admission to the inner
circles was crucial to Lu Xun's being drawn in too. He was the
bridge to the university world where it was all happening; Lu Xun
was not admitted to that world until August 1920, when he was
appointed part-time lecturer at Peking University — on the
recommendation of Zhou Zuoren.

For the sake of completeness, we should also point out that one
important detail is missing from Lu Xun's account of Qian
Xuantong's visit to the Shaoxing Hostel, a visit made universally
known because it featured in his preface to *Battlecries*, and made
memorable by virtue of Lu Xun's production of the metaphor of
the 'iron house', subsequently quoted by all his chroniclers. Lu
Xun gives the impression that Qian, then a professor at Peking
University, came exclusively to talk to him. But not so. Zhou
Zuoren's diary entry for the same day makes it clear that Qian
intended to call on *both* of them. He intended to invite them both
to write for *New Youth*. The fact that Zhou Zuoren was the first
to respond may indicate that he, rather than Lu Xun, was Qian's
principal target. It has to be borne in mind when dealing with Lu
Xun's recollections that he was a writer, and the first call on a
writer is not accuracy but effectiveness. To bring Zhou Zuoren
into his story would not have enhanced its effectiveness.

When Lu Xun did publish his "Diary of a Madman", however,

it made a great impact. The campaign for a New Literature needed some good examples. Translations of foreign modern literature, into both classical and modern Chinese, had not been lacking, but Lu Xun's "Diary" has gone down in the history books as the first piece of original fiction in the vernacular language which has a distinctly modern feel to it. As Lu Xun said later, once he had started publishing in *New Youth*, there was no way of stopping.

The penname of 'Lu Xun' that he used for the first time to append to "The Diary of a Madman" soon became familiar to readers. For his short stories he used the penname 'Lu Xun'; for his 'impromptu pieces', i.e. short topical essays, which began in July 1918, he mostly used another penname, Tang Si. As those essays were precisely intended to 'awaken' people, which he had said the year before he was reluctant to do, it may be significant that this penname reversed the 'Si Tang' which meant 'waiting' (for death). Thereafter Lu Xun used a wide variety of pennames for the topical essays he published in newspapers and magazines, but as every few years he collected them in books that carried the name 'Lu Xun', his authorship was not concealed for very long. The 'Lu' in Lu Xun, incidentally, was his mother's maiden name, and 'Xun' probably means 'hasty', referring to the speed with which he wrote his compositions.

'Lu Xun' gradually supplanted Zhou Shuren's real name. He even used it to sign private letters. You could say his old self faded away, and a new man emerged. The smouldering fire that had built up in Zhou Shuren burst into flame when he became Lu Xun. The indignities and hurts Zhou Shuren had suffered, the resentment and indignation that Zhou Shuren had swallowed, were all expressed by Lu Xun — to people who were listening this time. It was the collective strategy of the New Men to attack the old order right across the board, from the high culture of the elite to the habits and values deeply rooted in Chinese society. In this chorus Lu Xun's voice was particularly distinctive and compelling because to him the old order was not an abstraction but a real blight on his life. In his fiction it appeared as a madhouse, in his essays as a charnel house.

"The Diary of a Madman" sketched out a ground-plan for the short stories that followed, later to be collected under the title *Battlecries (Nahan)*. The madman's 'delusion' on reading Chinese history was that behind the fine words Benevolence, Justice, Way and Virtue lay the reality of 'man eating man'. The later stories shed the pretence of 'delusion' and directly enacted scenes of heartlessness and cruelty and stupidity from Lu Xun's experience, the memory of which he 'could not shake off' [Preface to *Battle-cries*]. Yet if the stories were personal, they were at the same time typical, and it was their typicality that lent them such force and made them so widely read. Since life in China was essentially based on small towns and villages like those in which the stories were set, readers could easily associate with the characters and settings, and find a good deal to think about. Lu Xun's fictional creations became proverbial, in the sense that they could be used as shorthand to refer to personalities, plights and mind-sets that were all too common.

On May Fourth 1919 there took place in Tiananmen Square in Peking a demonstration of over three thousand students and teachers from various colleges against the Chinese accession to the Treaty of Versailles, which handed authority over the German Concession in Shandong province to Japan instead of back to China. The demonstration was forcibly suppressed, but fires of patriotism were lit around the nation. Such was the importance of the demonstration that the name 'May Fourth' was appropriated for the entire reform movement that was already under way. In the cultural sphere 'May Fourth' came to be applied narrowly to the new literature written between 1918 and 1921, and loosely extended to cover the whole period up to the Sino-Japanese War (1937).

Lu Xun did not take part in the May Fourth demonstration. He had no cause to do so, but in any case his feelings were negative: to him demonstrations were not only ineffective, but needlessly courted danger for the demonstrators. Zhou Zuoren, on the other hand, did have cause to participate, but happened to be in Japan at that time. He did attend a further demonstration in June, which had reverberations across the country in the form of student and worker strikes and merchants shutting their shops. So Lu Xun was proved right in that demonstrations were indeed dangerous — though on these occasions no one was killed — but wrong in that they were not ineffective. The energy they created certainly lent force to Lu Xun's pen, to say the least.

For the rest of the year of 1919 Lu Xun continued to write stories and topical essays and comments, but starting from February he had also been busy looking for a property that could accommodate his whole house — mother, wife, brothers with their wives and children. The six houses of the New Mansion in Shaoxing had contracted collectively to sell the mansion to a neighbour, and the completion date was the end of December. In November Lu Xun made the final payment on a large, rather rundown property in a backstreet called Badaowan. When renovation was complete he went to Shaoxing to supervise the removal.

Lu Xun's stay in Shaoxing in December is fairly faithfully reflected in the story "Hometown" (*Guxiang*), written in January 1921. That includes his re-encounter with the peasant who had been a boyhood playmate, now sadly reduced in fortune. But obviously a lot was left out too. One incident that was too personal

to receive mention in the story was the burning of his grandfather's
diaries. On his death in 1904 his grandfather had left piles of diaries,
written in a beautiful hand on fine paper. When Lu Xun ordered
that these were to be burned along with a mass of other papers,
his third brother, Zhou Jianren, demurred. This normally sub-
missive brother thought they must contain valuable records, like
those relating to their father's life and death, but Lu Xun dismissed
the diaries as being about "buying concubines, and the squabbles
among them", and went ahead with the burning. Clearly, Zhou
Jianren's view was right: historians of today would give their eye-
teeth to read those diaries, spanning so many years as they did. We
can only speculate as to Lu Xun's real reasons. It seems very odd
that someone who went to great lengths to resurrect ancient texts

that had nothing to do with him, and to collect and publish material
about Shaoxing which as a native did have something to do with
him, should want to destroy diaries which had everything to do
with his family's history. But that may have been the problem.
The page that his grandfather had written in the family history
had ultimately been a shaming one, and Lu Xun had had enough
of shame. He had grown up in a society which practised respect,
and he had been deeply hurt when respect was withdrawn from
him. In future he would show himself extremely sensitive to slurs
on his person in the debates he conducted. With that in mind, it is
not after all surprising that he should have wanted to wipe the
family slate clean.

   As we have said, the family Lu Xun gathered about him in Peking
at the end of 1919 included his wife, Zhu An. To tell the story of
their marriage, in some detail as behoves us, we have to backtrack,
and open a new chapter for the purpose.

5

Marriage with Zhu An

I n traditional China marriages were contracted for the younger
generation by the head of the family, in the interest of the
family. The wealth and standing of the family to be joined in
matrimony was the prime consideration. Apart from the opportunity to tap another source of funds if needed, marriage extended
the network of connections, connections that were useful in
prosperity and essential in adversity.

The health and character of the individuals to be joined in
matrimony was a secondary but still important consideration.
Obviously you didn't want new members of the family dying on
you or becoming thorns in your flesh. Reliable information on
that score was not easily obtainable, however. The young persons
being considered for marriage might have been seen only briefly,
if seen at all, by the prospective parents. The preferences of the
young persons themselves were not part of the process. They were
taken into account only if indulgent parents combined with strong-
willed children.

At the extreme, marriages could be agreed at birth between
good friends and allies. Otherwise it was sensible to wait and see if
a boy showed some promise of making a good living and a girl
was well domesticated. Still, the sooner marriages were settled the
better. For girls especially age was crucial: once the bloom of youth

had faded they were more or less unmarriageable, except to
widowers.

   In the eyes of gentry families, Lu Xun would not have seemed a
good catch as he approached maturity at the end of the 1890s. As
we recall, his grandfather's arrest in 1893 had made the family
reputation plummet, and his eight-year imprisonment had drained
the family coffers. His father's long illness and eventual death in
1896 was another big setback. Simply to raise the money for the
betrothal presents customary in Shaoxing (costing between one
and two hundred yuan) would have been difficult for his mother.
As for Lu Xun's personal prospects, there was nothing in his record
to give reassurance. In his six years of education in a private school

(1892–1898) he had conned the classics and latterly practised
examination essays and verses, but not been tested. In the May of
1898 he had secured a studentship at the Nanking Naval Academy,
but whether that was a good thing or bad thing was highly
debatable. In the provincial town of Shaoxing very few people
had the foresight to see that the new colleges were the only way to
the future; most, on the contrary, would have suspected that they
were only for those who could not afford a proper education — as
indeed Lu Xun could not. A military career, which Lu Xun seemed
embarked upon, would have raised further doubts, according to
the common prejudice expressed in the saying we have already
quoted in part, 'Good iron is not used to make nails, fine fellows
do not become soldiers'. Lu Xun's transfer in early 1899 to the
School of Mines and Railways would have been only a modest
improvement, as it came under the army. The reaction within his
own clan was negative enough to confirm these doubts.

   In spite of these adverse circumstances, or perhaps because of
them, Lu Xun's mother was anxious at the time of his departure
for Nanking in 1898 to have his marriage settled. Emotionally she

was no doubt looking forward to a happy event to offset the
depression caused by the family disasters, soon to be aggravated
by the sudden death of her fourth son at the age of five on 20th
November. As their remaining parent she had the right and duty
to arrange the marriage of her sons. As soon as Lu Xun left for
Nanking she accordingly made her first overture. If the proposal
she made then had worked out, Lu Xun's subsequent career would
have been profoundly different.

The match proposed seemed to be an ideal one, as the intended
partners were well acquainted, and well disposed to each other.
The most likely situation where that could have been the case was
that of family relationship. The girl concerned, Qingu by name,
was indeed Lu Xun's cousin, the eldest daughter of his mother's
brother. They had been together during the three or four months
that Lu Xun and Zhou Zuoren had spent in the country after the
arrest of Lu Xun's grandfather in 1893, along with a crowd of
other cousins. At the time Lu Xun was twelve and Qingu ten, too
tender an age for segregation of the sexes to have been strict. The
following year their acquaintance was renewed when Qingu's father
and mother took their four daughters with them to visit Lu Xun's
father and mother in Shaoxing. Thereafter Lu Xun accompanied
his mother every summer when she visited his grandmother at
Anqiaotou, a small village on the bank of the Qiantang River.
Qingu's family lived with her grandmother, so the children would
have stayed and eaten together in the same house.

Qingu was said to be well formed, well mannered, well tempered
and well educated — the latter because her father had no sons,
and had given all his daughters schooling. Though there is no
evidence of any calf love between Lu Xun and Qingu, he did later
describe those annual holidays in the country as 'paradise'. Lu
Xun's mother certainly got to know her niece well, and thoroughly

approved of her. The cousin relationship was no obstacle to their potential union: it would have been seen as 'making kinship closer'. The proposed marriage foundered, however, on superstition. It was discovered that Qingu was born in the year of the sheep, and it was believed that such women tended to bury their husbands. As Lu Xun's hold on life was supposed at his birth, again superstitiously, to be insecure, his mother decided not to take the risk, and the matter was dropped. Apparently her servant, Mother Chang, was voluble in dissuading her.

As far as is known, Lu Xun was never consulted on marriage with Qingu, or even suspected that was being contemplated. Therefore he had no occasion to express regret, but given Qingu's attractions and accomplishments it is most unlikely that he would have been dissatisfied with such a spouse. A contented marriage, as we will see from the opposite fact, would have led Lu Xun along different paths from those he took. In other words, his domestic circumstances crucially affected the course of his life.

Lu Xun's actual marriage had its origins in his mother Lu Rui's second initiative, which took place after he returned to Nanking in January 1899, having seen to the funeral of his little brother. The instigator of this match was a lively young relative who lived in the same New Mansion, the wife of a distant cousin of Lu Xun's father. She came up with a candidate, related to her by marriage, called Zhu An (born 1878). Zhu An's family was well-to-do, and although past the barrier when young women were unkindly classed as old maids, that is, over twenty, the fact that she was three years older than Lu Xun was not a hindrance, as the Shaoxing view was that a more mature girl was of more immediate help to her mother-in-law.

Zhu An, being a respectable young woman, would have rarely ventured abroad after puberty, and Lu Rui seems not to have encountered her at the time of the proposal. She would therefore have relied on the description of her that the intermediary supplied. Inevitably that would have been flattering, as she would have been under some pressure from the Zhu family (her mother-in-law's family) to push the marriage through once it was mooted. Though, as we have noted, Lu Xun was not the most eligible of bachelors, yet Zhu An at her age was not the most eligible of spinsters, either.

Written evidence of progress in the negotiations comes from the entry in Zhou Zuoren's diary for 16th March 1899: "Zhu family signifies consent. Uncle Hui to arrange dinner. Cost about five yuan (five tables)." The phrase 'signify consent' (*chukou*) refers to a written note from the female side in response to a written note from the male side, agreeing to the proposal in principle. Although this was soon followed by a joint boat trip to watch village opera which was clearly intended to get the families concerned better acquainted, the next step in the betrothal proceedings was a very long time in coming. Normally the male side would quickly follow up receiving the written consent by asking for the time of birth of the female, so as to have an astrologer check that the two parties' zodiac signs did not clash. But that step, called *qing geng*, did not happen until 13th April 1901, that is, two years later. The delay was caused by Lu Xun's own resistance to the proposal, which had been made without reference to him. It appears that his mother had to work on him to get him to agree, or at least not to refuse. The *qing geng* took place not long after Lu Xun returned to Nanking from spending the winter holiday at home. Very possibly Lu Xun's grandfather had a hand in resolving the matter, as he was released from prison on 9th April 1901. Whether the normal betrothal presents were foregone by the by that time desperate Zhu family is not known. If they were given as usual, then the raising of that money might have contributed to the delay.

Once the zodiac signs were declared satisfactory, the next step was formal betrothal (*wending*). There is no testimony to when that took place: the best guess is shortly before Lu Xun left for Japan in the spring of 1902.

The anxiety of the Zhu family was destined to be prolonged. Leaving advancing years aside, if the Zhou family proposal was withdrawn, the taint of rejection would cling to Zhu An, and her hopes of a decent marriage would be over. Anxious on her own behalf, Lu Xun's mother probably expected that her son's marriage could be concluded on his graduation from the Nanking Army Academy in January 1902. But a new factor intervened: Lu Xun was selected for further study at government expense in Japan. He was to proceed thither in March. What arguments were advanced for his not getting married before departing is not known; in any case he was still single when he left Shaoxing for Japan on the 21st of March.

From letters Lu Xun wrote to his mother from Japan it is clear that he was still resisting the proposed marriage. His suggestion that Zhu An marry someone else having been rejected by his mother, he then set two conditions: that she unbind her feet, and that she go to school. Lu Xun had never seen Zhu An, so we must assume that he had elicited the facts of her bound feet and illiteracy from questioning. Both conditions were impractical, and were ignored, but some explanation is called for. Middle and upper class Chinese females, that is, those who could employ servants to do the physical work of the house, had bound their feet for hundreds of years, though women of the Manchu race who had ruled China since the middle of the seventeenth century did not. The toes were bent under in childhood and tightly bound with long strips of cloth, to make a kind of small hoof, which was encased in pretty slippers. By the end of the nineteenth century, progressive

Chinese men (and women too) were vigorously campaigning against the practice, but to conventional families like Zhu An's the idea of 'natural feet' for respectable women was still thought scandalous. In any case, Zhu An was well into her twenties, and by then unbinding her feet would cause much pain but do nothing to restore them to their natural shape. As for education, again the conventional view was that daughters destined for domesticity and maternity had no business acquiring it. Their role would be to serve their husband and mother-in-law (on marriage they became part of the husband's family), and to have their own ideas, which is a danger attendant on education, was not what was wanted. At most they might learn to read by themselves, so that they could while away their leisure with light literature and deal with day-to-day business. True, times were changing. Missionary schools for girls existed, and secular, Chinese-run schools for girls had just been permitted, but a woman of Zhu An's age would have to have been very strong-minded to have attempted to get into a school. In fact she never did learn to read or write.

It is fairly obvious that Lu Xun, fired by new ideas and already planning to play his part in bringing China into the modern world, would not have wanted to be saddled with an old-fashioned wife like Zhu An. To him, foot binding and illiteracy in women were totems of feudalism. It is equally clear that Lu Xun's mother felt justified in pressing Zhu An on him, as Zhu An's shortcomings in Lu Xun's eyes were not shortcomings in hers, and on the positive side Zhu An possessed the qualities that she herself had been required to embody in her married life. Events were to prove that Zhu An would indeed be a dutiful and respectful daughter-in-law to her, and would serve her faithfully all her days. Externally Lu Xun's mother was under constant pressure from the Zhu family. The date set by the local adage, 'A daughter is not kept at home beyond the age of twenty-six', came and passed: by Chinese reckoning Zhu An was twenty-six in 1903.

Meanwhile, apart from one vacation in 1903, Lu Xun was out of reach of his family in Japan, where he could plead that his studies made such heavy demands on him that he could not take on a wife. Unfortunately there is no record of his state of mind at the time. He himself did not refer to it in later life, nor have the army of researchers published any solid information gleaned from third parties. His constant companion in Tokyo, Xu Shouchang, never mentioned the subject in his reminiscences. It is understandable that Lu Xun's intimates should have respected his privacy on personal matters, yet no such reticence is observed in regard to other persons at other times. The special feature here is that for fifty years Zhu An was allowed only the barest mention in Communist China, for the obvious reason that Lu Xun's soul mate for the last ten years of his life and the mother of his child was not his legal wife. Zhu An was left behind in Peking in 1926, and put out of mind.

About the only statement from Lu Xun bearing on his state of mind that survives from the years 1902–1906 is in the form of a poem inscribed on the back of a photograph of himself that he gave to Xu Shouchang in 1903. It was quite normal for young men on the threshold of their career to express their ambitions in verse. The wording of this poem is vague, and has given rise to various interpretations. It runs something like this:

> My heart has no wiles to escape the divine arrows
> Wind and rain mass darkly over the homeland
> I send my thoughts by the cold stars but the overlord ignores them
> I dedicate my blood to the survival of our race.

The most difficult trope here is the first one, about the divine arrows. Chinese mythology has no stories about arrows being aimed at hearts, but Greek mythology obviously has, in Cupid's business. By 1903 knowledge of Greek myths was common in those exposed to 'Western learning' — Lu Xun himself is known to have studied them in that very year — but that knowledge was often superficial. It is quite possible that Lu Xun borrowed the vehicle of the Cupid myth while ignoring the tenor, that is, that those struck by the arrows fall in love. To him Cupid may have been about effecting marriage unions, like the 'Old man under the Moon' in Chinese mythology who binds couples inescapably together. In this reading, the first three lines are about his impending marriage. He has tried unsuccessfully to avoid his engagement; enveloping gloom awaits him at home; his protests have been overruled by his mother (his 'overlord'). The fourth line breaks free to express his resolve: to put aside his own predicament and risk his life in the cause of patriotism. With revolution in the air at the time, and Chinese groups plotting to overthrow Manchu rule, besides the 'volunteer army' to fight Russia, the prospect of shedding blood was not an empty one. Perhaps Lu Xun felt he might not have long to live anyway.

That is at least one possible reading of the poem. Although speculative, it fits in with what can be reasonably surmised about Lu Xun's state of mind.

We return to reliability with the actual marriage, which took place in 1906. Lu Xun was then back in Tokyo, having withdrawn from his course in medicine at Sendai University. He received a telegram from Shaoxing, worded "Mother ill, return with all speed", and duly complied. In fact his mother was well. The telegram had been a trick to lure him to his own wedding, which had already been prepared. So on the auspicious day of the 6th of the 6th by the lunar calendar (6th of July by the solar calendar) 1906, Lu Xun obediently performed the traditional rituals, including dressing up in ancient costume and wearing a false queue. Correspondingly, the bride, dressed in red and black silk, was carried to the New Mansion in a sedan chair, borne by eight bearers and followed by a band of musicians. Lu Xun later recalled: "My family had heard that I had taken on the new fashions, and were worried that I might not worship my ancestors, and would oppose the old-style marriage ceremony. But I did what they told me, without saying a word." Such an attitude could not have contributed to the jollity of the proceedings, but bridegrooms were expected to be impassive in their behaviour. Where some expression of warm feelings would have been welcome was in the privacy of the wedding chamber after the ceremony, when the bride's veil was removed and the bridegroom got his first look at her face.

Alas, it was not to be. From the fact that Lu Xun moved after the first night to sleep in his mother's room and returned with indecent haste to Japan, it is evident that he did not like what he saw. Descriptions of Zhu An's appearance are uniformly unpleasant, to the point of grotesqueness in some commentators' hands. This, for instance, from Ma Tiji: "A nearly thirty year-old 'old maid', with sunken eyes, long face and big nose, dark complexioned; not only tiny in stature, but with shrunken breasts. All this, plus the 'three-inch' bound feet, gave the impression of stunted growth." These descriptions were all written after Lu Xun's elevation to sainthood, with the possibly unconscious desire to excuse or at least palliate Lu Xun's rejection of his bride. Unfortunately they invite the conclusion that he rejected her because she was ugly, and leave us to speculate that if on the contrary Zhu An had turned out to be a dazzling beauty, Lu Xun would have discarded his objections in principle and taken her to his bosom.

That Zhu An was small (or petite?) is beyond question, but she was not dwarfish. As Lu Xun was very short himself (5′3″), that should not have counted against her. Only two or three photographs of her have ever been published. One is a group photograph taken with her own family. She is seated alongside her mother; the two women are approximately of the same stature. Considering that Zhu An's mother had given birth to a son of considerable bulk (shown in the same photograph), her own smallness had obviously not affected her womanly functions. Zhu An's features are not distinct in that photograph. A portrait photograph taken later shows her features quite clearly, however. She has indeed deep-set eyes and a fairly large nose; her lips are full, her forehead high, and her hair drawn tightly back. The description of 'old maid' that we have seen used of her would certainly fit her. But there is no information as to what year the photograph was taken in. Most likely it was after she had moved to Peking, in which case she would have been over forty, and an 'old maid' was exactly what she was. She also looks more like a servant than a mistress, but again that is what she had become. In sum, this photograph of Zhu An confirms that she was not conventionally attractive, but on the other hand shows that she was not positively ugly. We may therefore dismiss the implication of Lu Xun's biographers that he discovered on his wedding night a stunted, repulsive creature who would have sent any normal male running for cover.

It nevertheless was the case that Lu Xun did his best to pretend that Zhu An did not exist. The common view is that their marriage was never consummated, this view being supported by the fact that they never shared the same bedroom after the first night. He was in Japan for three more years after their marriage, and after he returned to China in 1909 he took every opportunity his work gave him not to stay at home. When in 1912 he moved to Peking with the ministry he emphatically left his wife behind. In the seven years he was in Peking on his own he never once wrote to Zhu An, though he wrote frequently to everyone else. The one letter he received from her (penned of course by someone else), noted in his diary 26th November 1914, he did not reply to, dismissing it as 'quite ridiculous' (*po miu*); the speculation is that her letter suggested he take a concubine. Comments Lu Xun made about Zhu An in later life, like "She isn't my wife, she is my mother's", fairly reflect his behaviour towards her. He avoided talking to her, and when they perforce shared the same accommodation and she performed her domestic tasks, he used grunts or monosyllables to reply to her routine and necessary questions.

There can be no doubt that Lu Xun's neglect of Zhu An was hurtful to her. No one has ever suggested that Zhu An ever deliberately did anything hurtful to Lu Xun. Lu Xun must therefore be open to the charge of mental cruelty. He would not have seen it that way.

Lu Xun undoubtedly thought that it was he who was making the sacrifices. Materially he never faltered in his support of Zhu An, providing for her upkeep after they were finally separated in 1926. Emotionally he never acknowledged any debt to her. To her he applied the traditional yardstick (we may recall that his grandfather also left his wife at home when he went to Peking in 1878); it was only to his new partner (after 1925) that he applied the modern yardstick. Love did not enter into traditional expectations of marriage, and Lu Xun was armed against any accidental intrusion of love by the repulsion he felt towards the feudal mould in which Zhu An was cast. The most he owed her on a personal level was courtesy, which obligation he met to the extent of not openly criticizing her. As for sympathy, we see from a commentary he published in 1920 that he conceded that the female partner in a loveless traditional marriage was also a 'victim', but he never seems to have considered that two victims can work together to make a victory. To him, his own sacrifice and suffering were incomparably greater than Zhu An's, and she didn't have much to complain about. He had no regard for her intelligence, and thought the conversation she tried to make silly. An unintelligent woman should be satisfied if she were clothed and fed, could gossip with other women, and have her hookah to smoke (as Zhu An did). Traditionally a wife was not expected to share her husband's social life or understand his intellectual pursuits. In Zhu An's case, those were genuinely beyond her.

Essentially, then, Zhu An was not, and could not be, a companion. What she was when they lived together was, to put it bluntly, a servant, albeit a superior one. She served Lu Xun, but more of the time she served his mother, Lu Rui. How she felt about that we will consider when we get on to Lu Xun's new love, or first love, in the mid 1920s.

As a historical footnote, we should point out that Lu Xun was by no means the only modern intellectual to be entangled in the marriage web. To cite only one other example, Hu Shi was also engaged in his youth to marry an old-fashioned girl with bound feet, like Lu Xun. Hu Shi was born in 1891, and the marriage was due to take place in 1908, but he too resisted and departed for the United States, to study there for nine years. The mothers of both Hu Shi and Lu Xun were widowed, and both sons felt indebted to them. They regarded their consent to marriage as a sacrifice to the customs of their parent's generation. The difference was that after a long internal struggle Hu Shi eventually made the sacrifice willingly, produced children and remained married. Another difference was that after marriage Hu Shi's wife turned out to be a bit of a dragon, and was able to keep him from straying.

6

Happy Days

With Lu Xun settled in Peking, at the centre of his extended family, with young nephews and nieces to enliven the atmosphere, all signs were set fair in 1920. His continuing production of short stories, essays and translations had earned him public esteem, and academic recognition came in August 1920 with appointments to Peking University as part-time lecturer (to teach the history of Chinese fiction, and later literary theory also) and to Peking Normal University (likewise to teach the history of Chinese fiction). He retained his post at the Ministry of Education, but now the ministry was strapped for cash, and salaries were paid only partially and in arrears, so ministry work legitimately took a back seat.

Since Zhou Zuoren took a concurrent well-paid job at Yanjing University, his income in fact rose above that of Lu Xun, and his social standing as a full-time university professor was higher. Inevitably this must have caused a change in their relationship, as Zhou Zuoren had always been number two in the partnership, but at this time they continued to work together harmoniously.

In their new home, Lu Xun and Zhou Zuoren received distinguished visitors, including Cai Yuanpei and the leading lights of the May Fourth movement. The blind Russian poet Eroshenko stayed in their guestroom from 1922 to 1923 while he taught

Esperanto at Peking University. The Zhou brothers translated his works and lectures, and actively supported the teaching of Esperanto. A young man named Mao Zedong also called on 7th April 1920, to consult Zhou Zuoren on the New Village Movement in Japan, which sought to found communities where members combined the works of mind and hand.

In 1921 Zhou Zuoren expanded his activities, becoming a founding member of, and writing the manifesto for, the Society for Literary Research (Wenxue yanjiuhui), which published the leading literary journal in the 1920s, *Fiction Monthly (Xiaoshuo yuebao)*. For his part, Lu Xun began in the December of 1921 to publish in the supplement to the *Morning Paper (Chen bao)* his most acclaimed work, "The Authentic Biography of Ah Q" (*A Q zhengzhuan*). Publication continued serially up to February 1922, when the author killed the hero off. In Ah Q, a homeless odd-job man, Lu Xun invested the main character weaknesses of the Chinese male, and those left over he attributed to other characters in his story. 'Ah Q' traits, like rationalizing humiliation into victory, were summed up in a new word in the language, 'Ah Q-ism', which stood mainly for escaping reality by telling oneself comforting untruths. Lu Xun signed his contributions with a new penname, Ba Ren, because he at first meant to write them as skits, but as "Ah Q" was included in his *Battlecries* collection of 1923, again his authorship soon became publicly known.

Up to that point Lu Xun's academic work had been on byways rather than highways, antiquarian, and mostly unpublished. Given now the task of tackling a central topic in Chinese literary history for his university courses, he made a thorough job of it. While certain major works of fiction had already been researched in some depth, and scholars going back to the Ming dynasty had produced sophisticated analyses of the art and techniques of novel writing, there had previously been no study which traced the development of Chinese fiction from its origins in early tales and anecdotes through successive stages right up to the late Qing political and sentimental novels. Lu Xun had done the groundwork of digging out the old tales many years before, but now he had to evaluate that material and survey the more voluminous output of later ages. His lecture notes were worked up and published as a book, *A Brief History of Chinese Fiction (Zhongguo xiaoshuo shilue)*, which came out in two volumes (December 1923 and June 1924). Thus Lu Xun's credentials as a scholar were fully established. His work drew high praise from other scholars in the field, notably Hu Shi, and deservedly so: it combined the solid textual research of traditional Chinese scholarship with a broad overview of historical changes in conditions and ideology, besides an author's insight into composition, and is still a useful guide today. That does not mean it was proof against denigration. Chen Yuan, his adversary in a long dispute, alleged that Lu Xun had plagiarized the work of Shionoya Akushi on the history of Chinese literature. In fact a comparison between the two texts shows no more indebtedness than is normal in the transmission of scholarship; overall there is little in common between them.

In regard to literary theory, Lu Xun's other university course, again there was a harvest, this time in the way of influential books translated — his own contribution to literary theory was minimal. It may be fitting to remark at this point that Lu Xun's mind was very sharp — in fact none was sharper. But he was not good at dealing with a body of abstract thought. Later on he translated some key Marxist literary theory, but again produced nothing significant on his own behalf. In his wars of words with ideological opponents he conducted his arguments by reduction and caricature, not by countering squarely their reasoning. Of course he was out to win, not engage in gentlemanly debate, but still the absence of sustained cerebration in his work is undeniable. To return, however, to literary theory, in 1924 he translated Kuriyagawa Hakuson's *The Symbols of Anguish (Kumen de xiangzheng)* and in 1925 the same critic's *Out of the Ivory Tower (Chule xiangya zhi ta)*. The first drew upon the philosophy of *élan vital* (life force) of Bergson, which was conceived as an instinctive drive of all life forms to overcome obstacles in their path, and the psychology of Freud. In the author's own words, his main idea was that "the root of literature and art is the anguish and frustrations created by the repression of the life force, and the means of expression is symbolism, in the broad sense." The last words were meant to make clear that he was not referring specifically to the symbolist movement in late nineteenth century France. We must assume that Lu Xun would not have translated a book that he disagreed with. He would have seen in Kuriyagawa's argument confirmation of his own drive to express his discontent and dissent, and it would have been easy for him to assimilate Bergson's *élan vital* to his own belief in an evolutionary motion and force. As for symbolism specifically, Kuriyagawa's work may have encouraged him to embark on his overtly symbolic *Weeds (Yecao)*, which he did in September 1924.

The first crack in the family wall opened in October 1921, when Zhou Jianren left the commune to find work in Shanghai. He had not been able to get a foothold in Peking, and felt humiliated at living on his older brothers' charity. His relations with his Japanese wife had also reached breaking point. She was the younger sister of Zhou Zuoren's wife, and she resented the disparity in their fortunes. Initially the intention was that Jianren's wife and children would join him in Shanghai when he had established himself, but that never happened. Eventually Jianren met and married another woman in Shanghai.

On the other hand, the bond between the two elder brothers was temporarily strengthened by an attack of pleurisy that Zhou Zuoren suffered at the end of 1920. Hospitalization and convalescence in the Western Hills put him out of action for the better half of 1921. In this long illness Lu Xun saw to his needs with the greatest solicitude, and borrowed heavily to pay for his treatment. Zhou Zuoren could not have been unconscious of this further debt to Lu Xun. At the same time, Lu Xun's contact with Zhou Zuoren's wife must have been closer than ever before during her husband's absence. She was the keeper of the communal purse, and Lu Xun was for that time the sole purveyor of income. Furthermore, Lu Xun was fond of her children, and played with them a lot in normal times; while their father was away he would almost certainly have spent even more time with them. It is not unreasonable therefore to suspect that in that increased intimacy lay the origins of the eventual rupture between the two brothers, to which we will come shortly.

On Zhou Zuoren's restoration to health, things went well for a time: they continued to cooperate closely. In spite of the fact that his illness had caused him to revise his personal attitude to life, Zhou Zuoren remained loyal to the May Fourth mission of bringing enlightenment to the Chinese people. To him that meant upholding the doctrines of early twentieth century humanism and liberalism. To that end he recommended the views of Western sociologists, anthropologists and essayists, above all those of Havelock Ellis, whose civilized approach to sex and particularly his sympathetic understanding of female sexuality was a necessary antidote to the male-engendered prejudices of the Chinese. He and Lu Xun were the only ones of the original *New Youth* stalwarts who were still energetically carrying on the fight — the rest having gone into politics (Chen Duxiu became the General Secretary of the infant

Chinese Communist Party) or retreated into scholarship (like Hu Shi). Broadly speaking, the targets of Zhou Zuoren's and Lu Xun's essays were the same at this time. In manner they were complementary, Zhou Zuoren's being more mild and reasoned, Lu Xun's being sardonic, waspish, inventive and dramatic.

Sadly, the dream that Lu Xun had thought realized of a united family sheltered in their comfortable compound was suddenly shattered in 1923. That event was of such importance in Lu Xun's life that we devote a separate chapter to it.

7

The Break with Zhou Zuoren

To deal with this topic adequately we have to consider first the circumstances in which the Zhou brothers were brought together again after living apart from 1912 to 1917. On Zhou Zuoren's arrival in Peking, he joined Lu Xun in the Shaoxing Hostel, but that lodging could only be temporary. A dwelling large enough to accommodate their whole 'house' had to be found. We may recall that Lu Xun had vowed in 1903 and 1906 that the three brothers would live communally, pool their incomes, and go through thick and thin together. The time came in 1919 to realize that pledge.

The financial situation of the two brothers in Peking was sound. As a higher civil servant Lu Xun earned 300 yuan a month, and Zhou Zuoren's salary as a university lecturer was 280 yuan. Both salaries were well above the average for white-collar workers. A survey that Sidney Gamble conducted in Peking in 1926 ascertained that the top salary for schoolteachers was 80 yuan a month. Food was cheap, and the monthly wage for a live-in woman servant was only 2.5 to 3.5 yuan. Both Lu Xun and Zhou Zuoren also had additional income from their publications, and later on from part-time teaching.

The Badaowan house that Lu Xun eventually found was situated conveniently within the Xizhi Gate of the old city, to the northwest of the Imperial Palace. The plot was very large, but the buildings not well maintained. The accommodation consisted of three rows of rooms with courtyards in between. The selling price was 3,500 yuan, and the cost of repairs and renovation, plus various fees, added another one or two thousand yuan. Now how did Lu Xun raise that kind of money? The pat answer is from the proceeds of the sale of the New Mansion in Shaoxing, but it seems from entries in Lu Xun's diary that his share of the money was no more than 1,600 yuan (the New Mansion was sold for 12,000 yuan, and that sum was divided between six houses). The only note of borrowing in Lu Xun's diary at the time was of 500 yuan. Zhou Zuoren and Zhou Jianren had no savings to speak of. We can therefore reasonably conclude that the greater part of the cost of the house came from Lu Xun's savings, which in his bachelor years in Peking from 1912 to 1919 could have been considerable, even allowing for the payments he regularly made to his mother and other irregular support he gave his family, as he spent no money on luxuries (only books). In conformity with Lu Xun's role as head of the family (now that his father was dead) and as major investor, he, his mother Lu Rui and his wife Zhu An occupied the most space in the compound. Zhou Zuoren, his wife and three young children (born 1912, 1914 and 1915) occupied one end of the back row of rooms, and Zhou Jianren and his family, which grew to three children, occupied the middle of the back row. Lu Xun could well have had sole title to the property, but true to the pledge of 'one for all, all for one', it was registered in the name of all three brothers. Zhou Zuoren's wife was in charge of the family budget. Lu Xun handed over the bulk of his monthly salary to her, as of course did her husband.

So all seemed right with the world. The two elder bothers were in demand, highly respected, and comfortably off. Their mother

had her grandchildren to amuse her, and Zhu An, if anyone spared
a thought for her, could keep unobtrusive, at least.

The first split, as we have said, came in September 1921 when
Zhou Jianren went to Shanghai. The key relationship, however,
was between the two elder brothers, and that remained harmonious
until one day in July 1923. What it was that happened on that
fateful day is still a mystery. The only people who knew — Lu
Xun, Zhou Zuoren and his wife — never explained, and are all
long dead. Zhou Zuoren cut a key entry out of his diary for that
year when he sold it in his old age to the Lu Xun archives. Lu
Xun's diary records only this fact:

> From tonight changed to eat in my own room, and got my meal by
> myself. This is worth noting.   [dated 14th July 1923]

Previously Lu Xun had eaten in the rear quarters with Zhou
Zuoren, his wife, and Zhou Jianren's wife. Clearly, what had
happened caused him to cease to mix with those in the rear quarters,
and also to avoid eating with the other women who ate separately,
namely his mother Lu Rui, Zhu An and Xu Xianshu, a girl student
from Shaoxing, aged 22, who was staying with them and to whom
Lu Xun was legal guardian. It seems that Lu Xun assumed that
news of the incident would have spread to all the women in the
compound. The inference is that the incident itself placed him
under suspicion of impropriety.

At that time Zhou Zuoren was the only other man in the house.
Evidently he was kept in the dark for some days, because it was
not until the 19th of July that he delivered his now famous letter of
severance to Lu Xun. The letter survives in the Lu Xun archives. It
reads:

> Mr. Lu Xun, I found out only yesterday — but what is past is past.
> I am not a Christian, but fortunately I can still bear up, and I have

no wish to blame — we are all poor humans. My former rosy dreams
turn out to be illusory; what I see now is perhaps life in its true
colours. I intend to straighten out my thoughts and set out on a
new life. In future please do not come to the rear courtyard. That
is all I have to say. I wish you peace of mind, and that you will
behave with self-respect. 18ᵗʰ July, Zuoren

That Zhou Zuoren addresses Lu Xun by his penname instead
of fraternally in itself indicates the distance he puts between them.
It is also clear from his reference to Christianity that he believed
Lu Xun guilty of sinning against him ('we forgive those who trespass
against us'), not of any passing discourtesy or show of bad temper.
For Lu Xun's part, he evidently felt he could justify himself, for he
attempted then to explain his conduct to Zhou Zuoren, but the
latter would not listen. On the other hand, it was Lu Xun who
moved out of the family home, two weeks after the incident, taking
his wife Zhu An with him. Since he was head of the family and
principal investor in the property, that behaviour might indicate
tacit recognition that he was at fault. A more charitable explanation
would be that Lu Xun was again sacrificing his own interests for
the greater family good, because if separation was inevitable, the
alternative would have been to drive out the families of both his
brothers, given that Zhou Zuoren's wife and Zhou Jianren's wife
were sisters, and would stick together. It is also possible that he
saw the Badaowan house as a replacement for the New Mansion
in Shaoxing: communal property that might be disposed of only
as a last resort. In any case, the eventual outcome was to give the
Badaowan home wholly over to his juniors, as his mother Lu Rui
moved to live with Lu Xun once he found permanent accommodation elsewhere, in May 1924.

As no satisfactory explanation for the rift was given by the parties
directly involved, speculation has been given its head. Given that

the two brothers had been extremely close up to that point (in the years they lived apart, 1912–1917, Lu Xun wrote Zhou Zuoren 445 letters, and received 443 in reply), the cause of their falling out must have been very serious. Years later Lu Xun confided to his partner Xu Guangping that he had been 'driven out by a Japanese woman'; the guesswork all assumes that was the case, but divides over the origin.

Most of the testimony from friends and neighbours at the time agrees that Lu Xun was dissatisfied with Zhou Zuoren's wife's keeping of the household purse, but no dissension on that score could justify Zhou Zuoren's phrasing: the problem obviously went beyond financial squabbles. Hence speculation supposes at the minimum an improper act by Lu Xun, and at the maximum a long-standing improper relationship. The improper act, it is surmised, might have been spying on Zhou Zuoren's wife in a state of undress, or on her and her husband when they had sex. To account for the improper relationship we have to backtrack to Lu Xun's last year as a student in Tokyo.

In that last year (1908–1909), the two Zhou brothers, who lived together, rented lodgings where their food was served by a young woman called Habuto Nobuko (born 1888), the eldest of three sisters in a relatively humble family. One of the reasons why Lu Xun returned to China in 1909 was to earn money to support Zhou Zuoren and Nobuko, who had decided to marry. He did so support them until 1911, when Zhou Zuoren reluctantly returned to Shaoxing with his bride. It is thought that Lu Xun even sold off some of the precious little ancestral land to do that.

As head of the family Lu Xun could have been expected to support his brother while a student. The odd thing is the direct and exceptionally close relationship with Nobuko and the rest of the Habuto family that his diary reveals. He personally made regular payments to the Habutos in Tokyo for their upkeep, and for the schooling of the youngest sister, Fukuko (born 1900). The middle Habuto sister, Yushiko (born 1897), went to join Nobuko in Shaoxing when the latter gave birth to her first child, stayed on, and married Zhou Jianren, with Lu Xun's approval. Nobuko's brother, Shigehisa (born 1893), stayed for a time with the Zhous in the Badaowan house. So much for familiarity with the Habutos *in extenso*. An objective measurement of Lu Xun's familiarity with Nobuko in particular is the number of letters exchanged between them. In the seven years from 1912 to 1919 Nobuko wrote Lu Xun fifty-three letters, twenty-nine of which were enclosed with Zhou Zuoren's letters, twenty-four separate. He sent forty replies, thirty-seven enclosed with other letters, only three separate. None of these letters survive. Clearly their correspondence was not secret, but did betoken a personal relationship that went beyond that of simple in-laws. By conventional standards it would have suggested a suspect intimacy. Similarly, it would have been more acceptable for Lu Xun to channel his support for the Habuto family through their son-in-law, Zhou Zuoren. In fact Lu Xun was under no obligation whatever to support his sister-in-law's family: that should have been Zhou Zuoren's responsibility.

For all these reasons, some commentators in recent years (previously the subject was taboo) have theorized that Nobuko had been Lu Xun's lover in Japan before she became engaged to Zhou Zuoren, the latter simply inheriting her because Lu Xun was already married — a marriage much against his will, as we have seen. And this speculation leads back to that day in 1923, presuming that Lu Xun attempted to restore their former intimacy, but without finding Nobuko receptive. Speculation is all it is, however. There is no reliable indication of a sexual relationship between Lu Xun and Nobuko in Japan, and I find it hard to believe that Zhou Zuoren would have accepted the role of stand-in husband. It is more reasonable to assume that somehow Lu Xun very quickly came to be on friendly terms with the whole Habuto family. As the bossy sort, he might well have taken charge of all Zhou Zuoren's 'external relations', especially as Zhou Zuoren's spoken Japanese was at that stage rather poor.

Whatever the background to the 1923 incident was, it is almost certain that the offence was of a sexual nature. When a year later (11th June 1924) Lu Xun went back to the Badaowan house to fetch some of his books, Zhou Zuoren and his wife came out and 'abused and attacked' him, according to his diary. In front of witnesses, Nobuko made accusations against him, using 'filthy expressions' (*huiyu*). These 'filthy expressions' would have referred to lewd conduct on his part. Some of these accusations, Lu Xun commented in his diary, were 'fabricated', others 'inconsistent'. Since this diary entry was not for others' eyes (unless he could see into the future), we may surmise that Lu Xun genuinely felt traduced, and that he repudiated Nobuko's version of events, but on the other hand his wording implies that there may have been other 'parts' of the story that were factual (though no doubt in his eyes misinterpreted).

Another factor in Lu Xun's favour is the fact that there was not a united front against him on the part of the Habuto family. He privately visited Nobuko's sister Yushiko when she was in hospital in 1924, and she wrote to him several times subsequently. Nobuko's brother Shigehisa also called on Lu Xun a number of times in 1924 and 1925, and got some Japanese books for him. Clearly, they did not regard his behaviour as inexcusable. But in any case, appearances were against Lu Xun, and it was he who packed his bags.

If the incident brought to an end the 'rosy dreams' of Zhou

Zuoren, even more so was that true for Lu Xun. Dreams aside, he also had the trouble and expense of buying a new house, while living in cramped rooms with a wife he did not want — given the choice, Zhu An had decided to move out with him. Unsurprisingly, he was seriously ill for over a month, succumbing to an attack of tuberculosis, and was nursed back to health by that wife he did not want.

A last word with regard to Zhou Zuoren. His stubborn refusal even to listen to Lu Xun's side of the question seems to have derived from more than blind loyalty to his wife. Though he might not have wanted to admit it immediately to himself, I suspect he longed to free himself from Lu Xun's domination and tutelage. Certainly he had good cause to be grateful for the help and protection Lu Xun had given him all his life, but by 1923 he had proved his own worth and capability to make his own way; it was in fact to him rather than to Lu Xun that the current generation of university students looked as mentor. Yet Lu Xun still expected younger brother Zuoren to submit the drafts of his publications to him for correction. Though we cannot know the exact nature of their private relationship, it is probable that Lu Xun inherited to some degree the assumption of authority that Arthur Smith remarked on in his *Chinese Characteristics*:

> The influence of an elder brother over a younger ... is of the most direct and positive sort, and is entirely irreconcilable with what we mean by personal liberty. The younger brother is employed as a servant and would like to give up his place, but his elder brother will not let him do so.

The 1923 incident provided the occasion for Zhou Zuoren to give up his place. There is no record of the brothers ever meeting or directly communicating again after the ugly scene that took place in June 1924.

8

The Xi'an Interlude

Less than a month after the final, violent confrontation with Zhou Zuoren and his wife, Lu Xun set out on a five-week trip to Xi'an. Never before or after did he undertake such a lengthy excursion from the place where he lived and worked. He was included in a party of a dozen academics from Peking who were invited to teach a summer course at the newly founded Northwest University (Xibei daxue).

Xi'an, the capital of China in the Tang dynasty (A.D. 618–907), and then known as Chang'an, is geographically in the centre of China, in Shaanxi province. In those days travel to and from Peking was very difficult: it involved journeying by train, boat and road. On the outward journey Lu Xun left Peking on 7th July 1924 and arrived in Xi'an on the 14th; the return journey took from the 4th to the 12th of August. The boat passages along the Wei and Yellow rivers were somewhat hazardous, but reportedly did not unduly perturb him, seasoned boat traveller that he was.

Lu Xun appears to have had three reasons for accepting this invitation. The first would have been simply to get away from Peking for a while after the upset. The second would have been to earn a good fee for lecturing, given that he had taken on considerable debts to buy and extend a small house for himself, mother and wife. The third had to do with the story of Yang Guifei.

The love between the Tang emperor Xuanzong and his concubine Yang Guifei had been immortalized by the poet Bai Juyi in his "Song of Everlasting Regret" (*Changhen ge*). According to that poem, the emperor, driven from his capital in 756 by the rebellion of An Lushan, took with him this concubine, with whom he had been besotted for years, but was forced by his guards to consent to her being killed at Mawei Slope, to his 'everlasting regret'. Lu Xun had a different interpretation of the affair, and had been planning to write a novel or a play to embody this interpretation. At that time he had an interest in Freudian psychological theories. According to friends, his idea was that the emperor, possibly subconsciously, *wished* for the death of his concubine. The visit to Xi'an was an opportunity for him to get a feel for the place where the events happened.

As it turned out, Xi'an was a disappointment. The imagined splendours were nowhere apparent. The remaining monuments were neglected or unimpressive, or had been replaced by re-constructions. The city itself was dusty, tatty and rundown. Instead of giving Lu Xun inspiration, the visit killed his enthusiasm, and nothing ever got written. The Xi'an episode was not, however, a write-off for its biographical interest.

The academic visitors were given generous hospitality by the university, and accorded the honour of being dined by the civil and military governor of Shaanxi province, Liu Zhenhua. They were also invited to attend plays performed by the Social Reform Company (Yisushe). This company, founded in 1912, preserved the outer garb and singing technique of the traditional Qin (Shaanxi) Opera, but wrote its own scripts on socially progressive themes. Lu Xun had heard of its achievements as a ministry functionary, and warmed to it even more when he discovered that its director, Lü Nanzhong, was a fellow native of Shaoxing. He attended five performances, and inscribed a motto on a placard presented to the troupe, which read *gudiao dutan* (ancient tunes uniquely played). At the end of the trip he donated 50 yuan to the company.

To fulfil his contract, Lu Xun gave twelve lectures to students and staff on the to him familiar subject of "The historical development of Chinese fiction". They were not a success: Lu Xun found his audience wooden and unresponsive. The reasons may have been that his audience had not sufficient educational background to know the materials he referred to, and that they could not understand much of what he said, as neither the local pronunciation nor Lu Xun's pronunciation was standard for Mandarin. The provincial governor requested Lu Xun to give a supplementary lecture to his army training school on a more general topic, but Lu Xun persisted in talking briefly about Chinese fiction. As we know, he was quite capable of delivering a talk of current interest, but he deliberately avoided controversy out of wariness for his own safety: after all, Shaanxi had a history of military despotism.

One way Shaanxi made its own rules was in allowing the production and smoking of opium; hence the local people were familiar with signs of addiction. They thought they detected them in Lu Xun, on account of his gauntness and his teeth being yellow and his gums black. They were assured that his addiction was to cigarettes. Yet Lu Xun did indeed try smoking opium on this visit, together with his young friend Sun Fuyuan. Unlike Sun, Lu Xun was able to master the technique of using the opium pipe, doubtless because of having observed his father and uncles suck at the thing, but he reported that all he experienced was a bitter taste.

A more constant diversion for Lu Xun was hunting the antique shops for rubbings and curios like terracotta figurines. One item that he particularly sought after was the bronze trigger mechanism used on old crossbows. This gave rise to an amusing misunderstanding. This mechanism, properly called *nuji* was pronounced *luji* by him. Lu Xun's guide could not understand why he was going from one antique shop to another asking for 'salted chicken', which is what *luji* means. However, Lu Xun eventually succeeded in buying some genuine articles for his collection. For two good crossbow triggers he paid 14 yuan, which may not sound a big sum, but it amounted to half his regular household expenditure at that time.

This raises again the matter of Lu Xun's spending habits and attitude to money. According to the entries in his diary, he spent around 50 yuan on curios and presents on this trip, which would have been unremarkable were it not that he had recently borrowed 800 yuan from two friends. His biographers picture him fretting under this burden and humiliation, anxious to be quit of his debt at the earliest opportunity. Yet we can see from the pattern of his spending in Xi'an that he was in no great hurry to repay what he owed. It seems that he subscribed to the habit common among his countrymen of living on borrowed money. It was not that there was an intention to renege on debts, only that the debtor repaid his loan in his own good time. It was in fact very bad form for a creditor to mention repayment; in the meantime the borrower did not go out of his way to economize. In Lu Xun's case, he would have been correct if he assumed that his financial difficulties were only temporary: in the following year he was able to repay 500 yuan of debt, and as well as clearing the books entirely in 1926, make substantial loans in his own turn. As for Lu Xun's donation of 50 yuan to the drama troupe, that would have been a social obligation. Given his standing as a famous writer, he would have been expected to be generous to a troupe whose performances he attended regularly, especially as its director was a fellow townsman. *Noblesse oblige.*

9

Embattled and In Love

To return to the normality of Peking, and Lu Xun's career
there, the effects of the blow he had suffered from his
rupture with his brother were evident in the work he
produced. Immediately following his recovery from the illness that
ensued he wrote few outward-looking essays. His creative energies
were channelled into new short stories that were to make up his
second collection *Wavering (Panghuang)* — begun in February 1924
— and the symbolic prose-poems that were to make up the
collection *Weeds* — begun in September 1924. In contrast to his
first collection of fiction, which though undated is set in what we
might call the old society, the new stories are more contemporary
and more urban, are more about intellectuals than village folk, but
if anything are more gloomy. Common themes are frustrated
ambitions and failure. We read in his stories of characters rendered
inert by hopelessness. We read in his prose-poems of figures
stranded in the no-man's land between darkness and light, of a
man driven to travel on, knowing only that he cannot retrace his
steps, and refusing all kindness, welcoming suffering. The most
vivid of his characters is the woman in "A Devastating Tremor"
(Tuibaixian de chandong) who sells her body in order to raise
her little daughter, and then is spurned by her when she grows
up. One is irresistibly reminded of Lu Xun's statement to Xu

Guangping that he had shed his blood for others, only to be laughed at. In one piece he even resorted to the image of Christ on the cross. In his final agony the Saviour is intoxicated by waves of pity and hatred that flow both from him to the crowd and from the crowd to him. The implication is that Lu Xun himself had decided that if he was to be crucified, he would perversely find exhilaration in it.

   The picture is bleak, yet authors have multiple personalities. Beyond the identity that the author assumes as narrator of the stories, as the prose-poet, as the essayist, there is also the private letter writer, and finally the future reminiscer. None of them is to be wholly trusted, but each tells a fraction of the truth of what it was like to be Lu Xun in those days. Undoubtedly he was despondent, and had every reason to be. The isolation he had escaped from by gathering the clan about him had returned with a vengeance. He did also despair, as he wrote in his letters, at the lack of impact on national life that the work of himself and other reformers had had: not only did the holders of power completely ignore them, within their own camp there had also been much backsliding. Financially he was hardpressed, too. Yet the effect of this gloom was not to paralyse his will, but to galvanize him into activity. In the middle of writing those dark stories he took up the cudgels again. Conflict gave him the will to live. He saw himself doomed to defeat, but he would go down fighting, and his enemies would not go unbloodied.

   So it was that when in November 1924 a new magazine was launched, he responded energetically. Given this platform, and the magazine's promise of no holds barred, he perfected over the next two years the technique of the polemical essay, the so-called *zawen*. Thereafter *zawen* was his principal means of expression, and he was recognized as undisputed master of the form.

The magazine in question was a weekly called *Threads of Talk (Yusi)*. It was founded at Peking University by the 'Zhejiang Mafia', headed by Zhou Zuoren, who was effectively the chief editor. That created a rather odd situation, because Lu Xun did not correspond directly with him, but it proved no barrier to the publication of his articles. Lu Xun's *Weeds* pieces were published in it, as well as his *zawen*. If we have to explain this continuing collaboration, we can first of all assume that the two brothers did not wish to incite curiosity by advertising the rift between them. Secondly, Lu Xun was as well established a 'mafia' member as Zhou Zuoren was. Thirdly, their social policies were still in agreement. Fourthly, Lu Xun's contributions were important to the success of the magazine.

Threads of Talk expanded rapidly from its small beginnings in the university. From March 1925 it was published by the Beixin Bookshop, and had national distribution. It was closed down in Peking in October 1927 by the warlord government, whereupon it moved to Shanghai. From the end of 1927 Lu Xun edited it there for over a year. It finally closed in March 1930, after 265 issues, which was a very long run for magazines of that kind.

By 1924 resistance to the 'new culture' and 'new literature' had more or less collapsed, and the new men ruled the publishing roost. The victory gained, the new men divided. *Threads of Talk* became the main voice for the Japanese-educated Zhejiang group, *Modern Critic (Xiandai pinglun)* the same for the 'Anglo-American' group, while in the south the Creation Society (Chuangzao she), which stood first for romanticism then for revolution, had its own publications. Needless to say, those groups were not watertight, nor did their magazines monopolize the arena. There were many other minor and more short-lived magazines, including one founded and edited by Lu Xun himself, called *The Outback*

(*Mangyuan*), which was issued as a supplement to a leading newspaper. Some of those magazines were happy to coexist, but between others there was hostility. *Threads of Talk* and *Modern Critic* were soon at each other's throats.

One might wonder how Lu Xun found the time to write for every issue of *Threads of Talk*, besides editing on his own behalf, producing a stream of translations and teaching at several universities, when he still held the post of Section Head at the Ministry of Education. The answer is to be found in a letter he wrote on 26th February 1924 in answer to a student. He said he was at the ministry from 3 to 6 p.m. on three days a week, at which time he could still receive visitors (!).

The biggest row with the *Modern Critic* group was over the Women's Normal College issue. Both Lu Xun and Zhou Zuoren were part-time lecturers at the college. They took the side of the students in their dispute with the woman principal, Yang Yinyu. British-educated Chen Yuan (Chen Xiying) of the *Modern Critic* took the side of the principal. Increasingly acrimonious articles were exchanged. In this campaign the normally pacific Zhou Zuoren got no less worked up than Lu Xun, but was not as cutting. They also joined forces to take on Zhang Shizhao, the current Minister of Education and the principal's backer, in a war of words that got the support of the university community. Eventually Yang Yinyu and Zhang Shizhao both resigned, so the Zhou brothers could chalk up a victory.

That summary, however, passes over an event which finally lifted Lu Xun's depression, and in fact changed the course of his life. In allying with the students of the Women's Normal College against their principal, he became friendly with a young woman who was to be his one and only love, and would share the last ten years of his life. We now have to retell that episode in some detail.

In July 1923 Lu Xun had been appointed lecturer at the Women's Normal College (later renamed Women's Normal University) to lecture for one hour per week on the history of Chinese fiction, at a salary of 13.5 yuan a month. The principal of the college was Lu Xun's old friend Xu Shouchang, doing his bit to help as usual. Sitting in front of his class when he began teaching in October was a second-year student from Canton (Guangdong) province called Xu Guangping (born 1898), who took a great interest in him. At the time, however, she was in love with a fellow student, Li Xiaohui. Li died in February 1924 from scarlet fever, which he had caught from Xu Guangping — she recovered, he didn't. After she regained her health she was occupied with protests against the new woman principal, Yang Yinyu (appointed 28th February 1924). She wrote her first letter to Lu Xun on the 11th of March 1925.

We have to imagine the kind of figure Lu Xun cut in student eyes as he stood on the podium in the lecture room. He was already a celebrity, clothed in the mantle of a leading proponent of the new thought, a maker of public opinion, and a founder of the new literature. In appearance too he was quite striking. No wonder, then, that he attracted an admiring audience, whom he rewarded with entertaining lectures. And going on from there, no wonder that he gradually gathered round him a coterie of student followers from the colleges where he lectured, including a band of female students from the Normal College. The closest to him were from his home province of Zhejiang and other parts of the south. They were on visiting terms.

Xu Guangping was a student activist, a big and bold young woman. In her very first letter to Lu Xun she came on very strong, exhibiting all the vibrancy and impetuosity of youth. Her immediate aim seemed to be to enlist Lu Xun in the struggle against her principal, but she addressed him (repeatedly) as 'teacher', not in the narrow sense, but in the sense of mentor, philosopher and friend, whom she looked to to lead her through the labyrinth of life and 'save her soul'. She openly placed her life in Lu Xun's hands.

Lu Xun replied to this letter immediately. Obviously he knew who she was, as she not only sat in the front row, but always raised her hand to ask questions. He took her by surprise by addressing her as 'Brother Guangping' (*Guangping xiong*) to indicate that he was treating her not as a student, not even as a female, but as an equal. On the simplest level, he found someone to share his private thoughts with, and so relieve his isolation: right from the beginning he expressed himself surprisingly frankly, as if glad to have someone to talk to. Once started, their letters flew fast and furiously. Very soon, amid earnest discussion of how to cope with life, a note of playfulness, allied to flirtation, crept in.

In less than a month Lu Xun was referring to her as 'little imp', which Xu Guangping then took as the name by which she signed her letters. Shortly thereafter, on the 12th of April, Xu Guangping paid her first visit to Lu Xun's small house on West Third Lane, where he lived with his wife and mother. (This house survives on the site of the Lu Xun Museum in Peking.) She took along a student friend, but it seems the visit was no common social call: she wanted to spy out the land, and get an idea of Lu Xun's relations with his wife. In her next letter, indeed, she described her visit as "exploring his secret nest". She would have been satisfied that Lu Xun and Zhu An shared nothing but the roof over their heads.

Their relationship moved into another dimension in the next month, May 1925. Ignoring Lu Xun's advice to proceed prudently, Xu Guangping as a committee member of the Student Autonomy Group took part in shutting the principal Yang Yinyu out of the university, and in retaliation found herself expelled, along with five others. Lu Xun then took up the matter in the press, and as a lecturer at the university organized a letter of protest, signed by himself and five other teachers, including Zhou Zuoren. A protracted polemic then followed between those who supported the student rebels and those who supported the disciplinarian principal. Lu Xun and Zhou Zuoren were the doughtiest champions of the students. In this polemic Lu Xun did not of course disclose his special relationship with Xu Guangping, but behind the scenes they had become comrades in arms. For the first time since the clash between teachers and principal in Hangzhou in 1910, Lu Xun had been drawn from the sidelines into the middle of the battlefield, where people's careers were at stake; in fact his own job was put at jeopardy. After more ructions in the following months, Lu Xun was indeed sacked by Zhang Shizhao, the Minister of Education, on the 14th of August, whereupon several of his ministry colleagues sent in their resignations in sympathy with him.

On 22nd August the authorities, backed by military police, broke into the Women's Normal University to occupy the premises and expel dissidents. Xu Guangping and Xu Xianshu sought asylum for several days in Lu Xun's house. A 'Revolutionary Women's Normal University' was set up in opposition. In December Zhang Shizhao resigned office, and the rebels were welcomed back into the fold. A new principal was appointed in January 1926, and peace smiled on the community. Lu Xun personally was also fortunate, in that his job at the Ministry was restored by court order on 16th January, he having sued for wrongful dismissal.

While all this was going on, Lu Xun and Xu Guangping maintained their correspondence. Their letters of July 1925 contained less and less discussion of thought and society, and more and more teasing, in the tone of lovers. After Lu Xun's death, Xu Guangping told the actress who portrayed her in the film *The Life of Lu Xun* that they 'pledged their love' (*dingqing*) in October 1925. The fact that they ceased to exchange letters after July is however evidence that their closeness of contact enabled them to dispense with writing before that date. And going further back, on 26th June, the day of the Dragon Boat Festival, Lu Xun had laid his hand on Xu Guangping. He invited her and four other girls to lunch at his house. They ganged up to get him drunk. Indeed, he did become inebriated. He playfully pretended to chastise the girls by gently slapping the hand of the two younger girls, and pressing down on Xu Guangping's head. In those days physical contact between a male teacher and a female student was strictly taboo. There is little doubt that Lu Xun took the opportunity when the barriers were temporarily down to do something he had been longing to do. Xu Guangping certainly got the message, for in their following letters she not only teased him unmercifully, but dared to reverse their roles, casting him as errant younger brother and herself as his chiding senior. In the matter of courtship she truly was the one with experience, and Lu Xun the ingénue.

Between December 1925 and February 1926 Xu Guangping published three compositions in magazines that reflected their commitment — she used a penname, of course. In the one called "Fengzi is My Love" (*Fengzi shi wode ai*), she openly talked of 'vanquishing' and 'making captive'. Fengzi (the Wind God) concedes to the 'me' of this prose poem, "You have conquered". The prose poem's conclusion is a plain confession:

> Even though Fengzi has his greatness, has his position, since he has stooped to clasp my humble self ardently by the hand, then what matter if I overreach myself! What matter if we are not equal! What matter if we are alike or not alike! What matter if it is legal or illegal! That is all irrelevant to us, neither here nor there. The main thing is, Fengzi is my love ... Ah! Fengzi.

This was published in a newspaper supplement that Lu Xun edited. We may be sure therefore that Lu Xun endorsed Xu Guangping's sentiments.

That Lu Xun should have been 'conquered', should have been made 'captive', is quite understandable. The love he felt towards mother and brother belonged to the traditional side of his life. Sexual love was something the modern side of him prized and desired, but what his traditional marriage denied to him. The alternative of asceticism, the suppression of desire, he rejected and ridiculed, because as a modern intellectual he espoused the philosophy of healthy biology; yet asceticism is what he had practised for twenty years. As an obscure civil servant, and a married one at that, he had had no point of contact with the female sex. The outlet of sex with prostitutes he seems to have spurned, unlike some of his colleagues in the ministry and the universities. But after he took up lecturing at various colleges in the early 1920s he found girl students seeking his company, as we have said. He only needed to overcome his inhibitions to fall in love with one of them. In his own words, he finally 'dared to love', but he would not have made that breakthrough without Xu Guangping's aid and encouragement. One other student, Xu Xianshu, who was on the scene before Xu Guangping, appears to have waited in the wings, but too patiently and meekly to make anything happen.

If meeting Xu Guangping was the most momentous event in Lu Xun's private life, a happening in March 1926 was of similar scale in his public life. On March 18th students and citizens held a rally in Tiananmen Square to protest against caving in to Japanese intimidation. As they prepared to march on the residence of the then head of state, soldiers opened fire on them, killing or wounding over 200 people. Horror at this infamous incident united the capital's intellectuals, including Lu Xun and his brother. They both had their own students among the dead, and both were driven to publish articles condemning the slaughter. Typically, Lu Xun's command of rhetoric gave his more power, but Zhou Zuoren's were more forthright, as he named names, demanding punishment of the political leaders Duan Qirui and Zhang Shizhao, and too the military commanders. Lu Xun thought the danger of retribution from the government real enough to go into hiding: he sought refuge in a Japanese, German and French hospital in succession. Up till then he had only conducted verbal duels with fellow intellectuals, or attacked targets that posed no physical threat to him. Now for the first time he had put his life at hazard through what he wrote. This added a new heroic dimension to his reputation, and radicalized his own thinking.

The situation in Peking deteriorated rapidly. Duan Qirui's garrison troops were driven out of Peking by an alliance of two other warlords, Zhang Zuolin and Wu Peifu. If the liberals thought Duan Qirui was bad, they found that the new military rulers were worse. They went out to 'get the Reds'. Suspected 'Reds' were arrested and executed. Consequently liberal-left writers and academics deserted Peking in droves. Lu Xun and Zhou Zuoren were both on the blacklist. Zhou Zuoren stayed on. If the worse came to the worst he could run up a Japanese flag over his house for protection, his wife being Japanese. Eventually he retreated from the front line to the middle ground of cultural commentary and talk of books. He and Lu Xun were never to meet again, nor join in any common cause. Lu Xun, for his part, could see attractions in leaving Peking, and making a new start.

At that point he could look back with satisfaction on the three years since the rupture with his brother. In fact it had been the most productive period of his life, despite his frequent illnesses and emotional distress, which visibly aged him. He had completed a book of short stories, a book of prose-poems, and numerous translations. The *zawen* he wrote were not only very many, but included some of his best. Two collections of his *zawen* were edited and published in this period. In addition to which he edited a number of magazines and taught at several universities and schools (eight in all in 1925). His letter writing continued unabated. He had stood up to be counted in the Women's Normal College strife, which took him 'out of the ivory tower' (the title of a book he translated then), and had acquired a thirst for battle, as may be seen from a letter he wrote to a friend on 17th June 1926:

> Since last year I have made many enemies because I took pleasure in expressing my views in the press regardless of the consequences ... I shall perhaps go somewhere else this autumn, probably the south, although the place hasn't been decided ... I still want to go somewhere where the action is, and carry on stirring up trouble.

His activity had evidently been a tonic to him, for he added, "My thinking recently has actually been more optimistic than before, not very despondent at all."

The unmentioned factor that buoyed him up most of all was the prospect of sharing his future with his sweetheart Xu Guang-ping. Here he had to consult practicality as well as his emotions. In his essays and stories Lu Xun had stressed that romantic unions and emancipation for women had to have a viable economic basis. That condition could be met. By the mid-twenties his fame as a scholar and intellectual assured him of a well-paid university post anywhere in the country; moreover, he had a considerable income from his writing and editing. He would be able to both continue to support Zhu An and his mother in Peking and set up a comfortable home for his new partner elsewhere. The offer of such a university post came from Xiamen (Amoy) in July 1926, but at first he did not have to provide for his partner: coincidentally

Xu Guangping graduated from university and was offered a job at
a school in Guangzhou (Canton City), the capital of her native
province. A temporary separation suited them both. All these
private considerations conspired with political danger to put Lu
Xun on a train leaving Peking for the south on 26th August 1926.
The train was bound for Shanghai, and Xu Guangping was on it
too. In Shanghai he stayed in hotels, she with relatives. On 2nd
September Lu Xun went on to Xiamen, while Xu Guangping left
for Guangzhou, on different boats.

Their departure together from Peking by no means marked an
open avowal of their relationship. Having suffered enough slights
in his youth, Lu Xun was very protective of his reputation and
respectability, and was almost pathologically sensitive to criticism.

At the same time he was aware that as a commentator on moral
and ethical matters, his credibility would be on the line if it was
put about that he had abandoned his wife of twenty years and run
off with a student eighteen years his junior. Nor did he want Xu
Guangping, for her part, to 'sacrifice' her good name because of
him, or be viewed as his concubine. So whether they secretly
enjoyed sexual relations or not — and it is quite likely they did not
— Lu Xun took care that they should not be seen to be cohabiting,
even when later in Guangzhou and initially in Shanghai they lived
and worked in the closest proximity. That did not of course forestall
all gossip and speculation about them, but it did prevent their
affair becoming common knowledge until it was so old that it was
no longer a good talking point.

With Lu Xun being in Xiamen and Xu Guangping in Guangzhou, they resumed their correspondence. In these letters Lu Xun
was the indecisive and care-ridden one, Xu Guangping the sensible
and resolute one. Though he did not directly express them, he no
doubt had worries over his adequacy as a mate for the big and

healthy Xu Guangping, being himself well past his prime, in frail health, and without his front teeth (they had been knocked out when he fell from a rickshaw in spring 1923), as well as being new to the game of love. Nevertheless, he was by now emotionally dependent on Xu Guangping, and on arrival in Xiamen immediately regretted their agreement to stay apart for two years and accumulate savings to buttress them against adverse winds in the future. In fact he did leave Xiamen after only six months. Xu Guangping's letters had persuaded him that his concern for 'position' (*diwei*) and traditional proprieties and obligations was stifling him, and that he should cast off his 'serfdom': in a word, he really 'could love'.

To avoid getting too far ahead of ourselves we have to leave the romance there, and return to Lu Xun in Xiamen.

10

Lu Xun in Transit:
Xiamen and Guangzhou

To Lu Xun his departure from Peking was a great release, and a new beginning. He had cast off the strictures, and the disrepute, of being a civil servant, and left behind the cold comfort of his home. The death wish that had lately driven his restless activity had been overcome, and he could look forward to the love and support of an educated young woman. That prospect of a good new life considerably modified his boast of 'disregard of the consequences' in regard to his future utterances, as he now had a lot to lose. While continuing to be combative, not to say pugnacious, he was cautious in choosing his targets, and framed his opinions on current affairs ambiguously. He was in fact in a difficult position, for he left Peking with the reputation of a firebrand, thanks to his prominent part in the victory over the authorities in the Women's Normal University matter, and the powerful essays he had written after the March Eighteenth massacre — in particular the piece called "In Memory of Miss Liu Hezhen" (*Jinian Liu Hezhen jun*), which was read nationwide. So the radical students at the universities in Xiamen and Guangzhou he was heading for had great expectations of him. Lu Xun, for his part, did not wish to put his own life in danger again, or encourage young people to endanger themselves either. The latter consideration had always weighed heavily with him, and the shedding of young blood in Peking had reinforced that caution. So he had to walk a tightrope. On the one hand he could not keep quiet; on the other hand any expression of strong indignation might incite the impressionable to potentially dangerous action. In fact he could not always keep his balance. Contrary to his inhibition he did on occasion call on students to stand up and speak out in Xiamen and Guangzhou.

Meanwhile the balance of power in China was changing. The Guomindang (Nationalist Party) of Sun Yatsen (who died in March 1925) had regrouped under the military leadership of Chiang Kaishek, and launched the Northern Expedition from Guangzhou to unify the country. In September to October 1926, around the time that Lu Xun left Peking, the Guomindang forces took the key city of Wuhan on the Yangtze River. That was good news for people like Lu Xun, as the Guomindang ideology was quasi socialist, and the ousting of the warlords was very much to be desired. He wrote in a letter to Xu Guangping, dated 14th September 1926, "We get a great deal of news here of the success of the Northern Expedition. It is immensely uplifting." In the long-term, however, best hopes were not realized. Some warlords came to an accommodation with the Guomindang and remained in control of large parts of the country, especially the north, including Peking, and Manchuria. Politically, too, rivalry with their Communist Party ally, leading to open warfare, drove the Guomindang towards conservatism — or reaction, as their critics would have it. Yet for the time being the developments in the south offered the first hope for a very long time of a real improvement in the government of China.

Less dramatic than the military victories but equally as far-reaching in their consequences were the political reforms that had taken place within the Guomindang. The decisive move was made in 1923, when Sun Yatsen turned to the Soviet Union for counsel and support. Soviet envoys came to advise him politically, Soviet generals to advise militarily. Lenin replaced Napoleon as the source of Sun's inspiration. A new national anthem was adopted in 1924, pledging loyalty to the Guomindang, and the Guomindang emblem of a white star against a dark blue background was incorporated in the new national flag. In prospect, therefore, was a one-party state that would share many characteristics with the Soviet Union. The chief difference was that power was not to be exercised in the name of one class — the proletariat — but in the name of the united people. In that way China was to conform more closely to the models of 'national socialism' that were soon to emerge in Germany and Italy. As in the Soviet Union, however, the people were as yet 'unawakened', so they had to be led and represented by the conscious vanguard of the Party in the first (rather lengthy) stage of revolution, which Sun Yatsen called 'tutelage'.

We can see now how momentous these developments were. But up north in Peking Lu Xun did not remark on them. If they did take his passing notice, no doubt he thought that it was the usual shenanigans, just another group jockeying for power, like the military overlords who came and went in Peking. In fact what was forming was a system that would get him and all those who took to a public platform in its grip, in his lifetime under Guomindang rule, and later, much more closely and comprehensively, under Communist rule. Interestingly, the person who put in place the mechanisms of ideological control while he was effective head of the Guomindang Propaganda Bureau from October 1925 to March 1926 was a young man called Mao Zedong, on loan at the time from the Communist Party.

No premonition of those things to come clouded Lu Xun's horizon when he arrived at Xiamen University, as it was called then, but neither did the sun shine for very long. He soon found himself a fish out of water. The university was a private one, founded by a Malayan Chinese businessman, and headed academically by a Chinese of British nationality named Lim Boon Keng (Lin Wenqing in Mandarin). Lim was a Confucianist who required his students to write their compositions in literary Chinese. Socially his staff affected British manners, Lim having graduated from Edinburgh University, which did not go down too well with Lu Xun, either. Lu Xun had gone to Xiamen University on the invitation of Lin Yutang, the newly appointed Dean of Humanities. Lin was formerly a colleague at Peking University, a fellow contributor to the *Threads of Talk* magazine, on the same blacklist as he had been, and a personal friend into the bargain. Lu Xun's appointment was as professor in the Department of Chinese and research professor in the Institute of National Studies. The head of the Institute was an even older friend, Shen Jianshi, also recruited from Peking University, and also on the government blacklist.

Lu Xun's terms of employment at Amoy University were very good. His salary of 400 yuan a month was high, and he taught only two courses, History of Literature and his old standby History of Fiction. They were both well attended, and his students were keen, if not very brilliant. The university high-ups treated him with deference. Behind the smiles, however, Lu Xun suspected daggers: sniping behind his back. Just six weeks after his arrival in Xiamen he wrote to Zhang Tingqian:

> If Peking is a big ditch, then Xiamen is a little ditch. If the big ditch is foul, can the little ditch stay clean? It is hard to get anything done here. The attacks and ostracism are no less than in Peking.

We can see from this that he had gained a low opinion of most of his colleagues. From his other correspondence we learn that he thought them dull, superficial and scheming. One in particular was a thorn in his flesh. This was Gu Jiegang (1893–1980), an up-and-coming scholar also recruited from Peking University, who was later to be acknowledged as one of China's most eminent historians. Like Lu Xun, he held a post in the Institute of National Studies. Their relationship is worth going into in some detail, for what it tells of how Lu Xun got on with colleagues, or rather, did not get on with colleagues.

The two first became acquainted in Peking, where Gu Jiegang was employed as a researcher in the field of National Studies at Peking University. Gu visited Lu Xun in his home, along with others, in 1924 and 1926. They exchanged a couple of letters, and Lu Xun designed the cover for a magazine that Gu was involved with, *The National Studies Quarterly* (*Guoxue jikan*). In June and August 1926 Gu sent Lu Xun books to which he had contributed. He may have learned by then that they were both bound for Xiamen University, and wanted to win Lu Xun's good opinion. Soon after their arrival in Xiamen, Gu presented Lu Xun with another book of his. Evidently Gu still saw in Lu Xun a potential ally.

On closer acquaintance, Lu Xun was not favourably impressed. On 20th September he wrote to Xu Guangping: "Gu Jiegang is a disciple of Hu Shi, and there are two or three others, apparently recommended by Gu, who are of the same sort, only even more superficial... They put on a good outward show, but their talk is tasteless." Hu Shi was in truth Gu's mentor: he had set in motion the professional reordering of the historical tradition that Gu Jiegang was engaged on. Hu Shi and Lu Xun had been allies in the May Fourth movement, and they respected each other's work on early Chinese fiction, but Lu Xun had been alienated by Hu Shi's call for students to stick to their books, as opposed to being active in social reform. Therefore being a disciple of Hu Shi was a black mark. On the other hand, Gu Jiegang's superior formerly in the research institute at Peking University and now at Xiamen University was not Hu Shi, but Shen Jianshi, Lu Xun's old friend, and it was he who had brought Gu to Xiamen. So Gu's immediate patron was Shen.

Ten days later in another letter to Xu Guangping, Lu Xun expressed greater hostility. Gu was now "of the Chen Yuan ilk". Lu Xun had not openly clashed with Hu Shi, but had been at daggers drawn with Chen Yuan in the Women's Normal University fracas. The bracketing with Chen Yuan put Gu quite beyond the pale. Specifically Lu Xun complained that Gu had referred to him as *mingshipai* (cranky scholar), and that Gu had in fact managed to infiltrate as many as seven of his henchmen into Xiamen University. In the matter of name-calling, Gu might have been incensed too if he had known that Lu Xun called him 'Nose' (because his nose was red), and made jokes about his stutter. As for the planting of 'henchmen', that was by no means uncommon, then or now. Lu Xun himself both benefited from that kind of generosity, and was an active patron in turn. At Xiamen University he had with him his own disciples, Sun Fuyuan and Zhang Tingjian, and he had tried, unsuccessfully, to get a job for Xu Shouchang. But it is human nature to think of all the favours one receives and confers as well deserved, and those of others as favouritism and cronyism. To make a final point, Gu Jiegang had no authority to make appointments: his recommendations had to be supported by Lin Yutang and Shen Jianshi, Lu Xun's friends. Lu Xun complained to Xu Guangping of their stupidity.

In further letters, Lu Xun added another name, "the *Modern Critic* clique", to those petty people by whom he was surrounded, and said he had given up hope for anything good coming out of the research institute, but apart from an instance of underhand spying had no further misdeeds of theirs to report.

Besides the tittle-tattle of name-calling, it seems from all this that in the main Gu Jiegang was found guilty by association, first with Hu Shi, then with Chen Yuan, then with the *Modern Critic* group. Antagonism on this level reflected the degree to which the new intellectual elite was now divided and factionalized along political lines and according to cultural allegiances, despite a large measure of common purpose. Actually, Gu Jiegang had no known connection with Chen Yuan or with the *Modern Critic*; Lu Xun must simply have regarded him as a bird of the same feather. The odd thing is that taking Gu as an individual, his endeavours were of a kind that Lu Xun might have been expected to sympathize with. As a historian he sought to replace the history of emperors and ministers with that of broad social and intellectual trends, and give the common people their rightful place. As a sociologist he was interested in popular culture and a keen collector of folk songs. And as a Chinese patriot he had composed anti-imperialist songs at the time of the May Thirtieth incident (1925), when British-officered police fired on demonstrating workers in Shanghai. On this evidence, one is tempted to conclude that Lu Xun's hostility to him was motivated by sheer rivalry, compounded by insecurity. There was after all some truth in the jibe that he was a 'cranky scholar', in that he had had no formal academic training in his chosen field.

Yet personal relations are founded on subtle things that go unrecorded and elude reconstruction. Gu Jiegang may well have been an unpleasant character, and Lu Xun's dislike of him may have been justified. Support for Lu Xun's side of the argument comes from an unexpected source, namely his alienated brother, Zhou Zuoren. Quite innocently of any reference to Lu Xun, Zhou pronounced verdict on Gu in a letter to a friend written in March 1929. Remarking that Gu had had another bust-up with his superior

at Sun Yatsen University in Guangzhou, Zhou wrote: "The news is
that he is coming to Beiping [Peking]. This gent is perfectly capable
of conducting research and putting our history in better order, but
he so likes to take things in hand that he ends up making a mess
of things. It is a great pity." With this judgement in mind, Gu's
manoeuvrings in Xiamen fall into better perspective. It seems that
Zhou would not have got on any better with Gu as a colleague
than Lu Xun did — but there is a significant difference in the
reasons they gave. Zhou found fault with Gu's character, Lu Xun
identified him as a member of a hostile faction. While Zhou was
content to consider Gu on his personal merits, Lu Xun was already
accustomed to think in terms of social forces.

Leaving university politics aside, this was Lu Xun's first experience of life as a full-time academic, and one senses that it left him
unfulfilled. In his relations with the student body, he did dutifully
assist with editing two student magazines, but without assuming
the role of mentor. He also did continue to write, but chiefly reminiscences, later to be collected under the title of *Morning Flowers
Gathered at Eventide (Zhaohua xishi)*, which were consonant with
the serenity proper to academic life. The few *zawen* he wrote only
responded to attacks on him deriving from his doings in Peking.
He was forced to assess his suitability for the academic profession
rather sooner than he expected, for he received an approach in
the October from Sun Yatsen University in Guangzhou. He confided
his reflections on the subject to Xu Guangping in a letter dated 1st
November 1926. He wrote:

> I am very undecided about my future course. The question is, should
> I write, or should I teach? Because those two things are incompatible.
> To write you need passion; to teach you need detachment. If you
> combine the two, and are not serious about it, then you become
> glib and shallow in both respects. If you do take both seriously,

then your blood will be boiling at this moment, and you will have to be cool and mild the next moment, which will sap your energies and still result in the worst of both worlds.... As I see it, if I write perhaps it will do some good for China, and not to write would be a pity. On the other hand, if I were to research a topic concerning Chinese literature, I could probably come up with something new to people, and there again it would be a pity to give that up. I think perhaps it would be best to write some things that would be of benefit, and as for research, do that in my leisure time.

If the polarities postulated in this letter seem too extreme, it is because Lu Xun viewed 'beneficial' writing as the kind he had been refining over the years — the challenging and contentious *zawen*. It was in writing them that he felt fully alive, that his 'blood boiled'. In that sense he was quite right, it was hard to reconcile that sort of writing with the dispassion required of an academic. He already felt frustrated at confining the expression of his disgust with Amoy University to private letters, but he could hardly bite the hand that fed him. It was not until after he sent in his resignation on 31st December 1926 that he did publish a piece critical of the place.

Another source of dissatisfaction in Xiamen was sheer boredom. What distinguished that coastal town then as today was its status as a port for international trade, where a foreign concession had been set up on the tiny offshore island of Gulangyu. Under British administration, the island was a safe haven for investment, and overseas Chinese from all over south-east Asia built mansions there. These mansions, together with the foreign consulates, made an impressive display of architecture, but they did not interest Lu Xun. Collecting seashells on the shore that bordered the university soon lost its appeal, too. Otherwise the problem was not too little company, but too much: he complained of a constant stream of local people calling on him in the evening, people who had no

conversation to make. Presumably they visited him simply as a
celebrity come to town. Underlying all his frustration and discontent
in Xiamen, though, was the gap left in his life by the absence of
Xu Guangping. The avid and impatient correspondence they
conducted could only partially make up for that.

Ironically, it was not Lu Xun's presence but the news that he
was resigning that sent waves through the university. The principal
Lim Boon Keng as well as the students tried to persuade him to
stay, and as he wrote to Xu Guangping, "the movement to keep
[Lu Xun] has changed to a movement to reform the school." It
was too late, his resignation was not to be withdrawn. However,
he was not yet ready to take the decisive step of doing away with
all paymasters, and leaving himself entirely free to write as he
pleased. He had accepted the offer from Sun Yatsen University.

The prospect of leaving Xiamen gave Lu Xun a fillip. He was
obviously in good fettle when he attended a farewell meal at the
local middle school, also named after Sun Yatsen. In his speech he
urged the pupils to follow Sun Yatsen's example, and work for the
revolution: "You should take the principles of Mr. Sun Yatsen,
and the knowledge derived from other progressive books, forge
them into a weapon for revolution, and blast away at all old
customs, all old thought, and all old cannibalist systems!" Those
anyway were his words as reported afterwards. If acted upon, they
would have produced a new generation of Lu Xuns.

Lu Xun had every reason to expect the atmosphere in Guangzhou to be quite different from that in Xiamen. It was after all the
base of the Northern Expedition, whose success had pleased him
so much. And the university itself was host to left Guomindang
and communist academics, including Guo Moruo, who as head of
the School of Literature was one of those who recommended Lu
Xun. Guo was also a leader of the Creation Society, a radical literary

group which by then had converted from romanticism to revolution, and Lu Xun hoped to join forces with them. (That hope was
not fulfilled, as the group had dispersed by the time he got to
Guangzhou.) With Xu Guangping's help Lu Xun overcame his
reservations about doing administrative work — the post being
head of the Literature Department and Dean — and being isolated
as an 'outsider' through not knowing the local language of
Cantonese. He arrived in Guangzhou on 18th January 1927.

Lu Xun's main private aim was met. He was reunited with Xu
Guangping, and soon after his arrival she was hired as his personal
assistant, interpreted for his public lectures, and after a few months
moved in to share lodgings with him and his old friend Xu
Shouchang, whom he had invited to teach at the university. (They
each occupied a separate room.) Lu Xun was certainly kept busy
with university affairs and coping with visitors, but he had a good
salary to compensate: 500 yuan a month.

Guangzhou was a precarious place politically. Although the
Guomindang-Chinese Communist Party alliance was still in force,
affiliation with the Communist Party was a dangerous one. Before
Lu Xun arrived, for instance, Xu Guangping played a part in
expelling two 'rightist' students from the Girls Normal School
where she taught, and was accused of being a 'Communist Party
running dog' in consequence. At the university Lu Xun himself
was to be caught in a bind. Radical students criticized him for
'keeping his head down', and Guomindang supporters suspected
him of being pro-communist. One can see his dilemma from the
first speech he gave to the Students Union (25th January). He
attempted to damp down excessive hopes by declaring at the outset
that he was not a 'fighter' or 'revolutionary' — if he was, he would
not be behind the revolutionary lines in Guangzhou, but up at the
front. Nevertheless he found Guangzhou 'too quiet'. The students

should speak out: what was to be feared was passivity. Those whose thinking was new ought to speak out, and those whose thinking was old also should speak out — though the latter only because they would thereby reveal that they were bound for extinction. Evidently Lu Xun's view of free debate at university was not the same as Cai Yuanpei's at Peking University: Cai simply claimed to hold the ring, without prejudice.

Lu Xun took a similar line when he took a trip to Hong Kong to address students at Hong Kong University on 18th February. His speech was later published under the title of "Silent China" (*Wusheng zhi Zhongguo*). There he was on surer ground, as to him the only force that held sway in Hong Kong was the conservatism imposed by the colonial government. He was able not only to urge the students to find their voice, but also to propose that Confucius and company should be dropped from their syllabus, and the literary language be banished from their classrooms.

Back at Sun Yatsen University there were more speeches to be made. In that setting it was practically a duty to uphold the idea of continuing revolution, as the statesman whose name the university bore had written in his will, "The revolution has not yet succeeded. Comrades must still strive to achieve it." Both Sun Yatsen's Guomindang and the Chinese Communist Party were therefore in favour of revolution, though their conceptions of it were not the same. In the course of his stay in Guangzhou Lu Xun did address the major issue of revolution in speeches and newspaper articles, but he could keep to common ground. His 'revolution' had no identifying Marxist elements, like class struggle, in it. When for example he addressed his students at the beginning of term (1st March 1927), he propounded the view that "At ground level everything is still old, people's thinking is still old", and that young people should attack feudal thought. That was standard talk, and quite innocuous.

The real Lu Xun appeared in other speeches he gave and articles he wrote, which while still cautious and veiled, warned against 'false' revolutionaries, 'fair weather' revolutionaries, who watch to see the way the wind blows. In a major speech delivered at Huangpu (Whompoa) Military Academy on 8th April, entitled "Literature in a Revolutionary Age" (*Geming shidai de wenxue*), he warned against confusing 'revolutionary literature' with real revolution. The educated people who write revolutionary literature are not those who take up arms to carry revolution forward: the latter are the only effective ones. The scepticism inherent in this view reflects Lu Xun's experience both of the 1911 revolution and of the May Fourth reformers who fell by the wayside. At the same time it expresses his scorn for the somewhat fanciful scenarios being invented by young writers on the left.

The break in the Guomindang-Chinese Communist Party alliance came in April 1927. On the 10th April came the news that Nanking and Shanghai had fallen to the Northern Expedition. The victory gave the Guomindang the confidence to conduct a purge of communists. First on 12th April in Shanghai, then on 15th April in Guangzhou widespread arrests and executions of communists took place, much of course to Lu Xun's horror. He had already threatened to resign from the university if Gu Jiegang, his old bugbear at Amoy University, was appointed, and his opposition had been ignored. The purge determined the issue. As dean he tried but failed to get university support for securing the release of detained students. He resigned all his posts on 21st April, and despite appeals to reconsider, held to his resolve. His resignation was accepted by the university on the 6th of June. He stayed in Guangzhou writing and giving speeches until 27th September, when he set off for Shanghai, via Hong Kong. He was not best pleased when he was held up at the Hong Kong customs by an inspector who suspected him of smuggling opium because of his gaunt appearance. It seems the signs of opium addiction were as familiar in Hong Kong as they were in Xi'an.

The Guomindang purge caused Lu Xun to radically revise his philosophy of life. He recalled later that the fact that students informed on other students and assisted in their arrest, so sending them to their death, destroyed his evolutionary faith that the younger generation would be an improvement on the older. In fact he had already expressed outrage at junior protégés turning against him, but no doubt the scale and horror of the Guangzhou incident was critical. Politically, his hope in the Northern Expedition was disappointed. The Guomindang revolution that had promised progress he now came to see as the latest in a long series of Chinese bloodletting. The cyclical view of history seemed

more valid than the linear one. We can take his word that the guttering flame of his faith in evolutionary theory went out at this point. It wasn't much, but it was something. It left a vacuum that demanded to be filled.

Actually it was a confusion to think that social progress (which is what he wanted) had any connection with evolution, or even with Social Darwinism — that is, the 'survival of the fittest' in the human world. And even assuming there was a connection, evolution would make progress only with the passing of several generations. We have seen that Lu Xun expected immediate results from his critiques, and was downcast when he did not get them. It is quite possible that to Lu Xun evolutionary progress was akin to the Way (Tao, or Dao) in Chinese philosophy, which once propounded would strike a responsive chord in everyone's heart. Every Chinese schoolboy knew that the great writer Han Yu of the Tang dynasty had 'lifted the empire from its stupor' by preaching the Way. Incidentally, if Lu Xun bears comparison with any figure in Chinese history, it is with Han Yu. They had in common a brilliant mind, verbal mastery, ferocious disputatiousness and literary inventiveness, and both could be witty and playful at times. The fact that Lu Xun did not like Han Yu tends to confirm rather than invalidate the claim of resemblance.

In his remaining months in Guangzhou Lu Xun wrote some solid scholarly articles, and made speeches critical of conformity and dictatorship, but without directly attacking dangerous targets. He also resumed contributing to *Threads of Talk* and other magazines *zawen* that were critical of political reversals and betrayals. But he was not yet won over to believing in the masses. He wrote in "In response to Mr. Youheng" (*Da Youheng xiansheng*) in September 1927 that his previous attacks on society had been pointless, because society did not know it was being attacked. If it had, he would have been done for. Luckily the majority of the 400 million population could not read. "The vindictiveness of the multitude is by no means less than that of scholars and warlords." Such a dim view of the Chinese masses was repeated elsewhere, and was nothing new. In Shanghai Lu Xun was to be gradually educated out of it.

11

Settling in Shanghai

Lu Xun and Xu Guangping reached Shanghai on 3rd October 1927. By the time of their arrival, Shanghai had become the centre of the literary world in China, publishing the major magazines and housing the majority of leading writers, including some classed as right-wing, but preponderantly liberal and left-wing. They all could enjoy the protection of the International Settlement, where Chinese laws did not run. Lu Xun was warmly received by the leading lights of the liberal-left. Most of the established writers he had met before. They included Yu Dafu, Mao Dun, Ye Shengtao, Zhu Ziqing, and Xia Mianzun. Lin Yutang had left Xiamen and was also in Shanghai; Lu Xun's relations with him were still very cordial. Some of the *Modern Critic* group had gravitated to Shanghai, too; Lu Xun's relations with them remained the reverse of cordial, but he didn't have to meet them.

Lu Xun was very pleased with his reception. He wrote on 14th October, "I have been here ten days now, and to my surprise see many familiar faces. Social calls have kept me very busy. Quite a number of places have made proposals of jobs to me, too, but I want to shut my door and concentrate on translating and writing." Indeed, after his experiences in Xiamen and Guangzhou he had had enough of university teaching (and university politics), and

was prepared to earn his living as a freelance writer, translator
and editor. His confidence was well founded. He was in fact able
to earn a substantial income from his pen over the remaining nine
years of his life. His average monthly earnings in Shanghai have
been calculated to have averaged over 500 yuan per month. Even
given his continuing maintenance payments of 100 yuan a month
to his mother and Zhu An in Peking, his financial situation was
very good, if not permanently assured. For his first four years his
income was supplemented by an allowance from a very unlikely
source. In December 1927 he was invited by a body called the
Higher Education Yuan (Daxue yuan) to accept the position of
Specially Appointed Writer, on a stipend of 300 yuan a month,
with no specified duties. Only two other distinguished scholars
were so appointed. The stipend was paid from January 1928 to
December 1931. The odd thing was that the paymaster was the
Guomindang government, to which Lu Xun was hardly sympathetic. It is plain that he was not eager to advertise the connection,
as he had the cheques 'laundered' by Zhou Jianren's wife. So how
come he was so lucky? The answer is simple: the head of the Higher
Education Yuan was Cai Yuanpei, his old patron.

    In Shanghai 'Lu Xun' was a name to conjure with. He was sought
after by the press, and invited to give guest lectures at universities.
His writing attracted the highest rates of pay from publishers. His
earlier works had been included in school courses all over China
as outstanding examples of the New Literature. His books went
into many reprints, and were widely pirated. Translations were
made into foreign languages. He had nothing to do with government or business circles, but he mixed with the most prominent
persons on the left of centre. One rather amusing sidelight on his
fame was provided by a little incident that took place in Hangzhou.
A female student from Shanghai on a visit to the West Lake was

approached by a man who said he was Lu Xun. He offered to take her under his wing as her mentor. Overwhelmed by the honour, the girl was taken in by the impersonation, and later wrote to this 'mentor'. The letter found its way to the real Lu Xun, who of course denied making any overture to her. She needed to come and see him in person to be convinced she had been deceived.

In order to avoid getting into a tangle, we shall divide our account of Lu Xun in Shanghai between his private and professional life. First his private life.

In Shanghai Lu Xun was reunited with his third brother, Zhou Jianren, who had by then remarried. Zhou Jianren had a job with the Commercial Press. He and his wife were of great help to Lu Xun and Xu Guangping initially in helping them to find lodgings, and generally showing them the ropes. Thereafter they all saw a lot of each other, and Lu Xun often included Zhou Jianren in dinner parties. He also gave him generous financial support.

The most intimate relationship was of course with Xu Guang-ping. Lu Xun was emboldened to finally take the step of sharing a room with her on the 8th October, five days after their arrival in Shanghai. We have his own story of his progress. In a letter to Wei Suyuan dated 22nd March 1929 he recalled:

> There was a lot of gossip in Peking and Shanghai about me taking Miss Xu to live with me in Amoy. That made me very angry, but I let it go. Actually I do love the opposite sex, but I never dared [make advances] because I was aware of all kinds of faults that I feared would demean the other person. But when I did fall in love, did get up courage, then I didn't care about anything. Afterwards I went to Guangzhou, and explained myself to Miss Xu, and invited her to live in the same house — but naturally there were other people there too. When I moved to Shanghai the year before last I urged her to come with me. She is now living in Shanghai, helping me to do work like editing. You see how it is: the people who were so

busy spreading rumours are all in Shanghai now, but oddly enough they stay dumb.

For a letter of a great writer, this one is scarcely very coherent. It reflects Lu Xun's continuing ambivalence. His confessed caution about not living alone in Guangzhou with Xu Guangping belies his pretension that he had decided to throw caution to the winds, and the focus on her working with him in Shanghai again avoids direct mention of cohabitation, in spite of the overall purport of the passage being to say that love had triumphed. As he rightly observes, his relationship with Xu Guangping was an accepted fact in Shanghai, and no longer the subject of hot gossip, yet when he and Xu Guangping went on their long promised, long delayed 'honeymoon' to Hangzhou (12th to 17th July 1928), he actually insisted that the friend who invited them (Xu Qinwen) sleep in the same hotel room with them, in the middle of the three beds! It was not until Xu Guangping was visibly pregnant in 1929 that they made their 'marriage' (they were never legally married) known to their families.

As far as their working relationship was concerned, Xu Guangping remained Lu Xun's 'helper' to the end of her days. In fact she had independently published a number of articles as a student, and several more under Lu Xun's supervision in Guangzhou. At first she planned to make a career of her own in Shanghai, and got to the point of launching a women's magazine called *Revolutionary Women (Geming de funü)* with some college friends, but Lu Xun complained that if she went on like that he would be back in the state of having to 'fend for himself'. Xu Guangping relented, and reverted to her sole role of helpmeet and amanuensis.

Lu Xun was notoriously averse to pleasure seeking. Apart from the one to Hangzhou, he never made excursions, and even on that occasion he fretted about the work he was missing. Though he complained that his "unhappy lot was bending over a desk all day", in fact that was what he liked best. More exactly, he liked reading and writing well into the night when all was quiet — a habit he acquired in his student days — with his cigarettes his only company. He was said to have smoked fifty cigarettes a day.

When Lu Xun left the house to attend functions and meals, go to bookshops, and so on, he normally went alone. For pure relaxation he took Xu Guangping to the cinema, very frequently in his last years. He never missed a Charlie Chan movie, and was fond of Laurel and Hardy too. Going to the pictures was a permitted luxury: they always went by car and sat in the best seats, like swells. They had live-in servants to do the heavy household work, and when their son came along a nurse to look after him. According to an oft-repeated story, Lu Xun showed his affection for his wife by lying down beside her after she had retired to bed, and, lighting a cigarette, would speak to her of the affairs of the day. Before he had finished his cigarette, she was often asleep. For a period of five months, starting at the end of October 1928 he devoted more time to her, teaching her to read Japanese. He used as a textbook a "Marxist Reader" that had been translated into Japanese. Extraordinarily unsuitable pedagogically though the book was — Xu Guangping later admitted that the technical terms and involved syntax made it very difficult — the exercise no doubt raised her political awareness, and was also useful to Lu Xun, who was then trying to get a hold of Marxism.

Xu Guangping gave birth to Lu Xun's son in late September 1929. In the May of that year, when Lu Xun was in Peking visiting his mother, he wrote to his pregnant wife his tenderest letter, one that Xu Guangping read and reread. It was written on stationery decorated on one sheet with a painting of red loquat fruits, two big and one small, and on the other sheet with a painting of two lotus pods filled with seeds, one tall and one short. Lu Xun's words were simple, but full of solicitude:

> I wonder whether my good girl has gone to bed or not. I don't think she could be asleep yet ... I just wish for my good girl to be well behaved and take good care of herself. I myself should be calm and even tempered all the while you are expecting, so as not to cause my little hedgehog to worry.

'Little hedgehog' was one of the several private terms of endearment invented in their first exchange of letters. In her reply Xu Guangping coined a new one for him, 'little lotus pod', referring to the painting, as Lu Xun was shorter than her. Lu Xun then corrected her interpretation, explaining that it was the seeds in the pod he was thinking of. He probably did not want to be reminded of his small stature.

The actual birth of Haiying, their son, was a difficult one, and in the end had to be achieved with the aid of forceps. He was delivered safely, but was frequently ill in infancy: Lu Xun was continually running for the doctor. Some of the child's troubles were caused by the inexperience of his parents. Lu Xun had strange ideas about how the baby ought to be bathed, for instance, which made him get a serious chill. Not bathing him, conversely, made him get a rash. In the end his parents gave up, and employed a nurse to look after him.

The first nurse was a young woman from Shaoxing who had run away from her husband who ill-treated her. Her husband tracked her down, and threatened to take her back by force. Lu Xun paid 150 yuan to redeem her, a considerable sum. She was a willing worker, but hardly more experienced in the care of children than Lu Xun and his wife, so was succeeded by a woman of about fifty, who stayed with the family until Lu Xun died.

As a little boy Haiying was quite wilful and naughty, like a lot of little boys. And like all fathers, Lu Xun treated him at times with indulgent approval, and was driven at other times to extreme exasperation. Although Lu Xun had not intended to have children (Haiying's birth, as he said in a private letter, was due to his 'incaution'), and later complained (letter dated 6th December 1934) that it was 'very tiresome' having a kid around all the time, the child brought a happiness into his life that he could not have found otherwise.

In her domestic economy Xu Guangping was said to have skimped and scraped. The houses they rented were very plainly furnished. She made their own clothes, and indulged in no personal luxuries. She also had to put up with Lu Xun's black moods and bleak silences. In one famous manifestation of bad temper he spent the night on the balcony. But these rifts were transitory, and probably no worse than most couples go through. To the last Xu Guangping respected Lu Xun as her teacher and superior, and he knew the debt he owed her. Their financial independence alone owed a great deal to her help in copying and checking the manuscripts that he produced and sold for a living. But if their married relationship was more reciprocal than merely that of master and pupil, Xu Guangping still lived in Lu Xun's shadow, and had given up her career for him. My guess is that it was to acknowledge this debt that Lu Xun published a collection of their private letters in 1933, an act that Zhou Zuoren called 'irrational' when he heard of it. The collection was called *Letters from Two Places (Liang di shu)*.

On the face of it, Lu Xun's decision to publish the batches of letters that he and Xu Guangping exchanged while they were in Peking, when he was in Xiamen, and when he revisited Peking in 1929, *was* puzzling. Granted that some well-known writers of the romantic school had published their love letters and intimate diaries in the preceding decade, and that letters to friends (occasionally to wives too) had always been considered a publishable form of literature in China, yet Lu Xun was far from belonging to the romantic school, and had all along been protective of his private life. The most plausible explanation is that Lu Xun wished to have Xu Guangping's part in his life recognized, and affirm her status as his true partner and soul mate. At the same time, we cannot ignore the fact that the financial gains from publication were not inconsiderable: in 1933 the book sold 4,000 copies and earned 1,000 yuan in royalties; naturally it continued to sell thereafter.

In his preface to *Letters from Two Places* Lu Xun stressed that the letters were not the usual lovers' twitterings but instead had substantial content, in the form of discussion about general ideas and contemporary events. They do show Xu Guangping in a good light: after her first flush of girlish enthusiasm and desire to impress, she develops a maturity in style and thought that is genuinely estimable. As we have remarked, she could assess situations more sensibly than Lu Xun. We know from comparison with the original letters that were preserved that some emotional excesses were suppressed in the published versions, along with actionable remarks about living persons; nonetheless a number of slushy exchanges survive. I suppose they were retained because they expressed the affection between them. While there may have been some snickering in private about Lu Xun in particular being revealed as adolescent, in the event the letters attracted little or no public derision, so one can say that their aim was broadly achieved, and Xu Guangping took her place in history alongside Lu Xun.

Meanwhile, what of the for long unmentionable Zhu An? She kept her mother-in-law company in Peking. Zhu An was not supposed to know anything, but the news of Lu Xun's union with Xu Guangping came as no surprise to her, she having expected it ever since they left Peking together in 1926. She was pleased to hear of the birth of their son, Haiying, in September 1929, because the family line was continued, and also because in the traditional view Xu Guangping's son was her son too, as she was Lu Xun's senior wife. As she fondly believed, Haiying would make sacrifices to her spirit in the afterlife. Unfortunately, her fear of being a lonely ghost would have been realized, because Haiying never did make the sacrifices she hoped for after her death in 1947, four years after her mother-in-law passed away. As Zhu An was illiterate, only a few spoken words of hers survive (as reported by a young family friend), but they are such that she will never be forgotten. After she learned that Lu Xun and Xu Guangping were 'married', she said:

> In the past Mr. Zhou [i.e. Lu Xun] wasn't very good to me. My idea was, if I served him well, and did whatever he wished, in the end he would be nice to me. I was like a snail, crawling up from the foot of the wall bit by bit. Surely one day, I thought, I would get to the top. But now there is no way I can do that. I have run out of strength to climb. No matter how good I am to him, it is of no use. It looks as if in this lifetime I shall have to serve the old lady alone.

No one could write a more fitting epitaph for Zhu An. Lu Xun saw her as integral to the 'serfdom' — the feudal obligations and observances — that he wished to escape from, but we can see from these words that Zhu An was not content with serfdom either, if that meant being treated merely as an appendage, and not as a human being.

To turn now to Lu Xun's public and professional life, one thread ran more or less constantly through all his remaining years, and that was his preoccupation with the question of revolutionary literature. In a way it was forced on him, because his business was literature, in particular socially relevant literature, and revolution was going on all the time. Having broken with the Guomindang, the Chinese Communist Party under the leadership of Qu Qiubai launched a series of armed insurrections in the latter part of 1927, on the urging of Moscow. They were desperate and doomed to failure. Afterwards this 'left deviationist' line was repudiated, and communist bases were set up in remote mountain districts, the chief one being the Jiangxi Soviet base camp. It was then the task of the Guomindang forces to destroy these bases. The first offensives were repulsed by the Red Army, but the Guomindang's superiority in numbers and weapons finally told, and the Jiangxi base was evacuated in October 1934. There followed the epic Long March of the Red Army across to the west of China, then north to Yan'an, where it came to a halt one year later, the ranks greatly reduced as a result of battles and sickness along the way. In all those years the communists were hard pressed militarily, but ideologically the tide turned in their favour. The visible persecution of labour activists and cultural workers in the cities naturally generated sympathy for the victims among students and liberals, and in the 1930s the Guomindang insistence on giving priority to putting down the communists over resisting Japanese aggression lost it a lot of support among the general population.

As part of its cultural offensive the Chinese Communist Party targeted prominent intellectuals who it seemed could be won over. Lu Xun had been contacted while in Guangzhou and again soon after his arrival in Shanghai, but he was not ready to commit himself. The first views on the role of literature that he expressed, in lectures like that given at Fudan University in November 1927, held to the middle ground of the socially progressive but artistically independent writer. The theoretical basis of his thinking was supplied by Kuriyagawa, namely that literature arises from dissidence and discontent: writers will always be at odds with those in power. On top of that, the current hot topic was the relationship between the writer, the natural ally of revolution, and armed uprising itself. In this struggle, Lu Xun argues, the writer is irrelevant, out of the picture. Revolution will destroy the poet's ideals and illusions. He will go down like certain visionary poets did in the Bolshevik revolution in Russia. So the writer has not much to look forward to. As a sensitive artist he feels and expresses the suffering of the common people, but not in any society will he be welcome. The best entertainment he can put on is his own execution, either by the sword or by the firing squad. So it was a gloomy view that he offered, darkened no doubt by his feeling of futility in Guangzhou.

This view was at odds with a specifically revolutionary doctrine for literature that cohered in the mid-twenties among intellectuals who were Communist Party members or communist sympathizers. The leaders of the May Fourth Movement, Lu Xun among them, had taken their values from pre-World War One Western civilization, whereas this younger generation matured in a world transformed by the Bolshevik revolution in Russia. The former could sympathize with the poor and downtrodden out of a sense of justice and common humanity; the latter accepted the Marxist faith that the working class were the spearhead of social progress. The new men had a firm agenda for society, based on class struggle. For literature and the arts to be relevant to the progress of mankind, they would have to serve that agenda. It was not enough to expose darkness and evil: the writer had to have the right ideology to identify, endorse and give prominence to the strong new growths that would move society forward to a socialist future. The working class were therefore not to be portrayed as passive victims, but as positive, defiant, hardy characters. Thus the literary programme was to dovetail with the political programme.

Though these young theorists were to Lu Xun's mind out of touch with reality, there was common ground between them. Most importantly they agreed on overturning the old society, and like him attacked contemporary conservative writers and thinkers. So Lu Xun revived the notion he had had on moving to Guangzhou of joining hands with the radicals of the Creation Society. He got as far as signing a manifesto with them on 1st January 1928 for the relaunch of the *Creation Weekly (Chuangzao zhoubao)*, but the magazine never came out. The leftist magazines that did appear the next month all turned to attack Lu Xun instead.

What had happened was that a bunch of young hotheads recently returned from Japan had joined the old guard of the Creation Society in launching a campaign for the more narrow and prescriptive 'proletarian literature'. This involved the negating of the previous May Fourth literature (just as the May Fourth people had negated their immediate predecessors). Lu Xun was probably the leading light of the May Fourth literature movement, so he became a prime target. His critics conceded that Lu Xun had uttered 'a few protests', but all along he had been 'wavering' (the title of his second collection of short stories), and not found a way out. He could not stay on the sidelines, they said: he had to commit himself to one class interest or another.

It is tempting to see in this attack on Lu Xun a deep-laid plot. We have noted that the Chinese Communist Party had already put out feelers to him, without any positive response. Was its strategy now to soften up the target by attacking him before calling off the attack and welcoming him with open arms? It is possible, but unlikely, because the Party did not exercise close control at that time over the activities of its adherents in the cultural sphere. The attack was more probably motivated by competition among factions to be out in front in the display of revolutionary zeal.

To arm himself against such attacks, Lu Xun began in February 1928 to buy a large number of Marxist-Leninist works in Japanese translation (communism had quite a strong following in Japan). The insults against him became more and more offensive. Besides being bracketed with the rest of his generation of writers as 'living in inebriation and dying in a dream', it was alleged specifically that Lu Xun's works 'represented the leisured bourgeoisie or the benighted petit-bourgeoisie', and reflected only 'the sadness of the faller-by-the-wayside in a period of social change'. Lu Xun's first counter-attack was published in March in *Threads of Talk*. It was fairly easy for him to undermine his opponents' position by pointing out that, having no literature of their own to speak of, they were paper tigers — all roars, but no claws.

A much more substantial critique of Lu Xun came out in the same month of March, when A Ying (Qian Xingcun) published an essay entitled "The Age of Ah Q is Dead and Gone" (*Siqule de A Q shidai*). His main point was certainly an arguable one. He maintained that to the older generation Ah Q (Lu Xun's most famous satirical creation) may once have been recognizable as the Chinese Everyman, but his day was past, and Ah Q meant nothing to the present generation of young people who were today's keen readers and activists. In A Ying's view, Lu Xun still lived in the past along with Ah Q: he still chuntered on about Chinese weaknesses, still saw ghosts from the past all around him, still saw as his enemies hypocritical 'proper men', who were actually small fry. The present age could not be grasped by 'cunning and venomous literature' or by 'clever and facetious writers'. This criticism contained enough truth to cut close to the bone.

Lu Xun was under certain constraints in making his reply. The

source of the idea of 'proletarian literature' was of course the Soviet
Union, and it was of course backed in China by the Chinese
Communist Party. Now Lu Xun had great respect for the USSR,
and had been translating Russian literature for years. The Chinese
Communist Party had also showed itself friendly to him. Hence
he could not attack his critics' position root and branch. But he
could hold his own in any slanging-match, and a slanging-match is
what he resorted to, returning opprobrious phrases with interest.
Strangely enough, however, he did not reply directly to the most
unbridled vituperation, which was contained in an article published
in the *Creation Monthly* in August 1928. This called him 'feudal
dreg', 'double-dyed counter-revolutionary' and 'disappointed
fascist'. The article was by Guo Moruo, the most senior member
of the Creation Society, albeit under a pseudonym that was not
publicly acknowledged to be Guo's until after his death in 1978.
After Liberation, Guo was treated as a grand old man of letters,
second only to Lu Xun in the pantheon. If Lu Xun knew who the
author was, perhaps he did not counter-attack because he did not
want to take Guo on personally, having had hopes of joining forces
with him. If he did not know who the author was, he may have
thought the article was beneath him because of its childishness.
That Guo should have been moved to write the article at all is also
a bit of a puzzle. It certainly was not based on a deep understanding
of Lu Xun's works, as Guo later confessed to only having skimmed
a few. It may have been written on directions from the Party, but
as Guo was in Japan that would be difficult to ascertain. Guo could
have been influenced there by the Japanese communist sect known
as Fukomotoism, which had its own strategy of 'first split, then
unite'. But equally likely, it may have stemmed from pure and
simple rivalry.

What is certain is that the attack on Lu Xun from the extreme left was eventually called off on the orders of the Central Committee of the Chinese Communist Party, and the erstwhile adversaries ended up — on the surface — all good pals.

In retrospect Lu Xun did not regret this polemic, not all for the best of reasons. He was grateful to the hotheads for getting him to seriously study the matters of proletarian literature, Marxist aesthetics, and Marxist social theory, which is a good enough reason. More questionable was his satisfaction, expressed in a letter, that: "For the past six months everyone has been talking about Lu Xun. No matter how much they abuse me, it may be seen that if there were no Lu Xun, China would be a rather tamer place." In mitigation of this too cocky tone, it may be pleaded that Lu Xun needed this reassurance that he was no longer marginalized, as he had been in Xiamen and Guangzhou.

Ultimately Lu Xun was won over because he was ready to be won over. He was constantly bemoaning the lack of signs that his writing had any effect. Once he had decided that evolutionary theory could not further sustain him, he was empty, out on his own. He was taking sides only *against*, not *for* anything. How welcome, therefore, was the prospect of belonging to a camp — a camp, moreover, that had adopted evolution for its own purpose of constructing a new social order, an inevitable future for human kind, the necessary goal of the march of history. And how very nice, too, if he were to be offered a position of leadership in that camp, which is indeed what happened.

But let us return to chronology. The attacks on Lu Xun from the far left began to peter out about the end of 1928. Possibly coincidentally, possibly as a scout sent by the Central Committee, a young Party member from Lu Xun's home province of Zhejiang named Feng Xuefeng called on Lu Xun in December, to seek his guidance over translating Marxist literary theory from the Japanese.

He took up residence opposite Lu Xun's lodgings and called on him frequently thereafter, winning his confidence.

Lu Xun was not aware that peace was being prepared. He continued to make slighting remarks about his detractors, but when he came to state his own position in May 1929 his performance was disappointing. This was on his visit to Peking to see his mother, and announce that Xu Guangping was pregnant. He gave a speech to Yanjing University students on the subject of "An Overview of Today's New Literature". By then he had finished translating *The Theory of Art* by Lunacharsky, the Russian authority on Marxist aesthetics, and a string of articles in Japanese on Soviet literature, as well as some examples. Perhaps for that reason, in his speech he denigrates apparently all of modern Chinese literature and recommends only foreign literature — it was that which set the standard. His main point is that "Politics leads the way, literature changes in its wake." He goes on, "The notion that literature can change the environment is idealist verbiage; the real outcome is not as the writers foresee." His presumption now is that the only literature worth talking about is 'revolutionary literature', but before the old society disintegrates there is no possibility of revolutionary literature. Writers only curse, hit out, bellyache, seek excitement, dream utopian dreams, or jump on bandwagons. They are all doomed to disappointment.

It is plain that Lu Xun's reading has narrowed his horizons considerably. The implication of his remarks is that the literature of the present stage is not worth the paper it is written on. His own writings must be included somewhere in his list of shabby and uncommendable products. And the inspiration that set him on a literary career in 1906 — that it was the way to cure men's minds — is now well and truly buried. On the other hand his confidence in his personal standing at that moment in history must have been reinforced by the enthusiastic welcome he received from students at the various universities and colleges in Peking where he gave lectures. He attracted an audience of 'over a thousand' at Peking University, and was petitioned to go back and teach there. His very popularity should have told him that literature was actually a very potent force in society. Though in contrast he perceived more hostility than welcome among the established intellectuals, some of them former friends, that also should have gone to show that his words were not going unnoticed.

In September 1929, the same month his son was born, the Chinese Communist Party decided the time was ripe to actively recruit Lu Xun. The Party had set up a cultural branch in Shanghai that year headed by Pan Hannian. Besides being illegal, openly communist bodies had only limited appeal and effectiveness, so the policy was to set up 'united front' bodies, ostensibly headed by respected persons of good will, but in fact directed by an inner cell of Party members. It was such a broad front organization that Party representatives proposed to Lu Xun (not telling him of course about Party control). And the person chosen to make the first approach was Lu Xun's young friend and neighbour, Feng Xuefeng. Lu Xun was immediately receptive to the idea, and, given the choice of naming the body as a token of respect, agreed to the proposed title of The Chinese League of Left-wing Writers (Zhongguo zuoyi zuojia lianmeng). Lu Xun was duly appointed to the planning committee. If he knew that all the other members belonged to the Chinese Communist Party, he did not let that deter him.

The inner programme of the League was to promote and publish 'revolutionary literature', as the Creation Society and Sun Society (Taiyang she) had been doing. Though Lu Xun was now ready to endorse revolutionary literature in principle, he was still dismissive of the home product. The members of the Central Committee of the Chinese Communist Party were, however, entirely different from the brash youths who had been making a noise in Shanghai. They were the real revolutionaries, whom he had been at pains to distinguish from the writers who imagined themselves revolutionaries. If it was the will of the real revolutionaries that there should be a campaign to promote left-wing literature of that kind, then that call had to be hearkened to, even if it meant cooperating with those he had denigrated.

After he had thrown in his lot with the League, Lu Xun was constantly at odds with himself. On the one hand he had to repay the trust of the mighty Communist Party, which, as he thought, had created a new and better social order in the USSR, and in China was fighting bravely, against heavy odds, to eliminate the relics of feudalism and overturn the political regime of the Guomindang, with which he was now disenchanted. On the other hand he could not respect most of the communist theorists and writers he now had to work with. Compliance with the party line contended with self-assertion for the rest of his life. The fact that he could only bend so far put a great strain on him, but added greatly to the respect in which he was held then and afterwards.

Before proceeding to the business of the League of Left-wing Writers we shall look at some other matters Lu Xun concerned himself with. In 1929 he had written little noteworthy on his own account. In 1930 he resumed his sniping at fellow writers, some provoked, some unprovoked. That kind of article was quite short — just a page long in book form. He really got the bit between his teeth again when he was criticized by Liang Shiqiu over his 'stiff translation' of Marxist treatises. His article in response ran to eighteen printed pages. It was composed on 24th January 1930.

Since Lu Xun sweated blood over translating Marxist art theory, it was a major issue for him, but to explain this controversy in detail would take us too far into technicalities of language. Suffice it to say that in closely following the sentence structure of the 'original' text, Lu Xun thought that he was not only achieving exactness but also doing a service to the Chinese language in making the expression of thought better connected logically. He was not alone in thinking that native Chinese writing was too loose, relying on association rather than clear and coherent sequence. But his opponent in the debate argued that Lu Xun had gone too far in imitating the foreign model, making his translations not merely strange but often unintelligible. Lu Xun in turn admitted that his method made some of his sentences difficult to understand now, but held that in time the alien constructions would become naturalized, and readers would then have no troubling in following.

One has to say that Lu Xun was wrong: the texts in question read no more easily today than they did then. The truth is that he was led astray by his trust in Japanese translation. Not knowing Russian, he retranslated from Japanese versions, and contrary to what he believed, Japanese 'translationese' has never been naturalized. The Japanese versions only made texts that were already difficult to understand in the original even more impenetrable. Unfortunately, Lu Xun thought he was serving a noble cause and persisted in his ideas. The story is an object lesson in how obstinacy in a very intelligent man can lead to obtuseness.

The other big issue Lu Xun engaged with Liang Shiqiu on was a continuation of the debate on the class nature of literature. It is clear that Lu Xun was defending the cause of 'proletarian literature', but because he devoted most of his words to picking holes and chopping logic, very little of a constructive nature emerged. We do learn, however, that he thought that the proletarian literature of the future would take over the whole show, and not be content with the one seat at the table that Liang was willing to offer it. But the first fruits of proletarian literature had set only in the Soviet Union. He still did not allow that the so-called proletarian literature in China was the genuine article, and he continued to pour scorn on the Chinese theorists, naming particularly Cheng Fangwu and A Ying. A collateral clue to his thinking may be gained from a note (dated 8th February 1930) that he appended to his translation of Fadeyev's *The Rout* (*Huimie*). The minimum qualification for understanding this novel of revolutionary war was, he said, to study 'materialist literary history and aesthetic theory'. By 'materialist' he meant Marxist. Obviously he thought he himself now understood Marxist theory, and could apply it.

12

Uneasy Leadership

Lu Xun's first physical step into the communist camp came on 15th February 1930, when he attended a secret meeting of a front organization called The General Assembly of the Chinese Freedom Movement, signed its manifesto, and was elected to its executive committee. The manifesto was signed by fifty-one persons, mostly leftist writers. It protested against press censorship and all other forms of suppression of freedom of speech and assembly — it being conveniently forgotten that the communists had been in favour of those things when they had a hand on the levers of power previously. The first approach to Lu Xun to get him to join was made by his young friend Feng Xuefeng, and that was followed up by several visits by the senior cadre Pan Hannian. Lu Xun was rather reluctant, but he yielded to persuasion. As he predicted, the movement was soon outlawed by the authorities, and it faded away.

On 16th February Lu Xun attended another secret meeting, that of the preparatory committee of what was to be the big show, the League of Left-wing Writers, held in a coffee house. At the meeting Lu Xun was elected to the three-man presidential council (the others were Xia Yan and A Ying) and also to the steering committee, along with six others. The resolutions passed at the meeting were reported in the *New Shoots Monthly (Mengya yuekan)* on 1st March.

Obviously intended to reconcile past differences, they rejected
factionalism and individual strife, as well as unscientific criticism,
mistaking the real enemy (i.e. the forces of reaction), and thinking
that literature could be separated from the political struggle. More
positively, the meeting resolved to expedite the birth of a new
society by propagating its ideals, and to construct a new literary
theory. Quite a bit of the content of these resolutions reflected
criticisms that Lu Xun had made of the errors of his juniors.

On 24th February Feng Naichao visited Lu Xun to seek his
approval of the draft manifesto of the League, which had been
drawn up on the model of similar Soviet groups. Feng was one of
the wolf-cubs who had attacked the old lion, but he emerged from
the lion's den unscathed, indeed with his approval for the slogan
of 'proletarian revolutionary literature'. Yet just one day before
the inaugural meeting of the League on 2nd March, Lu Xun wrote
a piece entitled "Non-revolutionary Ardour for Revolution"
(*Feigeming de jijin geming lunzhe*), in which he again derided the
'revolutionary writer' (the inverted commas are Lu Xun's) Cheng
Fangwu, Feng Naichao's senior in the Creation Society, for "hiding
away in Tokyo, then making off to Paris" as soon as he ran into a
little opposition and had gained some 'clout'.

If Lu Xun could not resist this last sally, surely his address to
the inaugural meeting of the League would be encouraging, rallying
the troops for the struggle to come? No, it was not. He did allow
that an effective united front could be forged if all involved put
aside their differences and made the interests of the worker and
peasant masses their common concern, but otherwise his tone was
admonitory and reproving. He warned against many political
weaknesses and dangers, citing the precedent of the 'salon socialists'
in the West who were totally dismayed by the 'filth and blood' of
real revolution when they encountered it, and of poets like the

Russian Yesenin who committed suicide when his dreams were shattered. If the poets and writers who trumpeted revolution expected to be rewarded with admiration and privileges by the victorious proletariat, they had another think coming. So much he had learned from his reading about revolution in Europe.

Turning to the situation in China, Lu Xun warned that they must carry on a relentless and uncompromising struggle against the old society, which had always subverted the new forces that challenged it. By tolerating the existence of revolutionary literature in the last one or two years, the old society had rendered it harmless: the workman's crude rice bowl was placed in the dining room along with the antique china, to look merely 'cute' there. Yet the revolutionary writers thought they had been successful, and congratulated themselves. But the fact was, revolutionary literature was a wing of the revolutionary struggle, and could only grow in step with the strength of proletarian society. Given that the actual social position of the proletariat was low, if the standing of proletarian literature was high, that only showed that the writers had divorced themselves from the proletariat and retreated into the arms of the old society.

He went on to point out the need to expand and strengthen the left-wing ranks. They were already publishing a lot of magazines and books, but only the same few were writing. Those people spread themselves too thin, and commanded no real expertise. Giving the knife a final twist, he recalled the attacks on him by the Creation and Sun societies, confessing that he soon got bored by them, because they were too feeble and repetitious. He had been disappointed at not being 'sniped at' by anyone with a grasp of Marxist criticism.

The printed version of this speech was 'amplified' when published, so it may not have been so offensive when delivered,

but considering that Lu Xun was addressing the self-same members
of the Creation and Sun societies (they made up the core membership of the League) to their face, it could not have gone down very
well. Rather than the grand exercise in conciliation that the
organizers were no doubt hoping for, it resembled more a head-
master remonstrating with delinquent pupils. He himself yielded
no ground, all his points having been made before and here repeated
basically unchanged. Evidently he believed that the invitation to
be a leader of the League meant that his own stand had been
vindicated. If he also thought that his erstwhile opponents would
repent their errors and accept his leadership, he was to be deceived,
as we shall see.

Meanwhile, the Guomindang authorities did not close their eyes
to Lu Xun's activities. Because his name figured prominently among
the members of the Chinese Freedom Movement and he had given
some lectures under its auspices, in March 1930 the Zhejiang
Provincial Branch of the Guomindang applied to the central
government for a warrant to be issued for his arrest. Though Lu
Xun thought this was only a warning shot, he took the danger
seriously enough to seek refuge for a month in a room over the
Uchiyama Bookshop, whose Japanese owner was his good friend.
The move to arrest him hardened Lu Xun's attitude towards the
Guomindang. Up till then he had not shown out-and-out hostility
to the Guomindang; he was after all receiving a generous stipend
from government coffers, and he knew a number of senior members
of the party. Cai Yuanpei, his patron, was still a member, as were
others whose position was very left of centre. Lu Xun said that all
along his targets had been the forces of darkness in China that
dated back hundreds, nay thousands, of years. But now he saw
clearly that the Guomindang was protecting and defending those
forces of darkness, so was itself fair game. In point of fact, his

association with the Chinese Communist Party ensured that sooner or later he would attack the Guomindang by name.

In the event, the authorities neither then nor ever attempted to arrest Lu Xun. He took measures to forestall arrest (or assassination) by keeping his address secret, renting accommodation in the name of Japanese friends, meeting strangers only in public places, and actually going into hiding at times, but it is hard to believe that Guomindang special agents could not have picked him up any time they wanted. The authorities did proscribe the front organizations he joined, did close down magazines he published in, and did prohibit publication of his works, but they left his person untouched, despite the provocation he gave them. Lesser figures on the left wing were not as fortunate, but Lu Xun was protected first of all by his fame, and secondly by his Japanese connections. Besides which, he never joined the banned Chinese Communist Party, which was the prime reason for arrest and execution. He was aware of the danger of getting directly involved in politics. In May 1930 Li Lisan, currently head of the Propaganda Department of the Central Committee, while in Shanghai for a secret meeting of delegates from the Chinese Soviets, arranged to meet Lu Xun, hoping to persuade him to back his line. Lu Xun thought it more prudent to protect his independence.

If Lu Xun's speech at the Left League meeting showed no respect for his junior colleagues, his private thoughts were even less complimentary. They were revealed in a letter he wrote to Zhang Tingqian, his former lieutenant in Peking, on 27th March. As Lu Xun had had all his remaining lower teeth removed three days before, no doubt he was in a particularly bad mood, but the suspicions he expressed were by no means unusual for him. He had claimed credit in his speech for bringing on a batch of 'young fighters' while he was in Peking through the literary societies he had founded and funded, but in his letter he speaks of the danger in cultivating disciples of them using him as a 'ladder':

> I was well aware that if these gentlemen of the coming generation could climb higher by that means, they would not scruple to tread on my shoulders. Actually there are very few people in China apart from myself who can be a ladder. Hence, in helping over the last ten years the Unnamed Society (Weiming she), the Hurricane Society (Kuangbiao she), the Morning Blossoms Society (Zhaohua she), I have met with either failure or deception. Nevertheless, my desire to see bright new talent emerge in China has not died, so this time I acceded to the invitation of young people to join first the Freedom Movement, then the League of Left-wing Writers. In the meeting hall were assembled all the revolutionary writers in Shanghai, but in my eyes they are all pallid and anaemic, which means I have to run the danger again of becoming a ladder — though I fear they are unlikely to have the ability to climb the ladder.

He amplifies on his disillusionment with his protégés in Peking in this way:

> Those who were previously called fighters are now bent on deviousness, or else have quite run out of steam, to the degree that their words and deeds are laughably trite and commonplace. To consort with them would be embarrassing, to fight alongside them would be impossible. In a nutshell, they have bogged me down in the mud.

Lu Xun's sentiments reflect as badly on himself as those he runs down. He could hardly in justice blame his protégés in Peking for losing their edge, as Peking was no longer the place for fighters to be. Had he himself not left Peking partly because it ceased to be possible to speak his mind there? It seems from his lifelong record that Lu Xun was extremely generous of his time and money in assisting young writers and translators when they deferred to him as pupils to master, and submitted their work to him for correction, but felt betrayed when they went their own way. Though he would have been horrified at the thought, this was one element of 'feudalism' that he hadn't shaken off.

As for the young revolutionary writers in Shanghai, Lu Xun completely misread the situation. Had he not said that they had already achieved success in their own eyes? If that success had been achieved in part at least by attacking Lu Xun, he had already served his purpose. Those people would certainly not be coming to Lu Xun in future for him to improve their scripts. They were now honouring him purely on the orders of their political leadership.

That is not to say that Lu Xun did not acquire new disciples from among his juniors in the League. Feng Xuefeng had already come under his wing, and Qu Qiubai and Hu Feng were soon to become his intimates. In that they genuinely got close to him in spirit, it did not do them any good in the long run. Qu Qiubai died in a Guomindang prison after expressing his disillusionment with political life, Hu Feng was declared a traitor and imprisoned in 1955, and Feng Xuefeng was labelled a 'rightist' in 1957. Xiao Jun, one of Lu Xun's later adherents, was one of the first to get into trouble over Mao Zedong's policy for literature and the arts in Yan'an. The Lu Xun 'ladder' led to a fall, not to the stars.

In a sense, though, all members of the League did benefit from Lu Xun joining them, in that he waged powerful war against the factions opposed to the League, and so ensured its prominence in the literary arena. That does not mean that the League in any way dominated the actual output of creative literature in the six years of its existence (it was dissolved at the end of 1935), as most creative writers stood aside from the contests and followed their own lights. The 1930s in fact produced the best fruits of the new literature inaugurated by the May Fourth Movement, and a great variety of them too.

Lu Xun confessed in a letter written towards the end of February 1930 that he was spoiling for another fight, as after laying low all his enemies of the last two years he was feeling rather bored. He thought he would chastise some "fellows who have put the bite on me for no reason". His first opportunity came in April, when his old adversary Liang Shiqiu offered himself as a target.

Very ill-advisedly, Liang had responded to a taunt in one of the League magazines that he was a 'capitalist running dog' by attempting to turn the metaphor of the running dog against his accuser, protesting that, unlike detractors of his ilk, he obeyed no master. This allowed the debate to be personalized, thus playing into the hands of a master of denigration like Lu Xun, who weighed in at that point. He was able to conclude at the end of his comment that Liang was not only a 'capitalist running dog', but was 'disowned' and 'deadbeat' to boot.

No doubt thinking that anything after that would be an anticlimax, Lu Xun ended the exchange there, though Liang Shiqiu published a reply. The actual content of Lu Xun's diatribe was quite unjustified. Liang Shiqiu and his fellows were not, as Lu Xun made out, trying to curry favour with the Guomindang regime. They were honest liberals attempting to uphold what they conceived to be civilized values and criticizing what they thought of as simple cant. If anyone danced to the tune of political masters, it was those in the Left League. But the time had passed to acknowledge honesty in men, on whichever side they were.

On the national scene, the tide of war ebbed and flowed. The Red Army suffered heavy losses in Hunan province, where the Changsha Soviet set up by the Party on 27th July 1930 lasted only nine days before being overcome. On the other hand, Guomindang attempts to drive the Red Army from its base in Jiangxi were unsuccessful. Three encirclement offensives in the same year of

1932 were repulsed. The Guomindang sought to eliminate communism in civil society, too. On 10th September 1930 the Central Committee of the Guomindang issued orders for left-wing organizations to be banned and their members arrested. On 3rd January 1931 it passed an emergency law allowing life imprisonment and the death penalty to be imposed for the crimes of 'endangering the Republic' and 'disturbing public order'. Censorship was stepped up, bookshops were raided, stock confiscated, and sometimes the booksellers arrested. The Guomindang police and security agencies could not, however, act independently in the foreign concessions. Unless the foreign powers collaborated, which they rarely did, the dissidents were relatively safe there, as we have said.

The Guomindang also took measures to counter the Left League on its own turf, the literary arena. In June 1930 the Nationalist Literature Movement (*Minzuzhuyi wenyi yundong*) was launched, with generous funding. The word 'nationalist' here means the doctrine of the nation or race, not of the Nationalist Party. The movement was of course opposed to Soviet-style communism, but also to Chinese feudalism. Its declared aim was to tap the virile and healthy roots of Chinese culture. Nonetheless, that prescription was difficult to fulfil to order, and no satisfying works of that kind were published in the lifetime of the movement's magazines, the chief of which, *Vanguard Weekly (Qianfeng zhoubao)* ceased publication on February 1931, after twenty-six issues. Needless to say, what was published drew the fire of the Left League.

Following the foundation of the Left League, Lu Xun devoted most of his written words to translation, either translating Soviet works himself or editing the translations of others and adding colophons in his own name — for instance, an "Afterword" to a translation of Sholokov's novel *Quietly Flows the Don* in September

1930. At the same time he lent his support to the promotion of socialist pictorial art. For example, he contributed posters, military paintings, satirical drawings, woodcuts and prints from his own collection to an exhibition of Soviet revolutionary works of art held in a bookshop in July 1930. Long before, as a civil servant in Peking in the 1910s, Lu Xun had started to buy books of paintings from abroad (fine art being one of his ministerial responsibilities). His more recent research into Marxism directed his purchases towards socialist art. For some of these volumes he paid fabulous sums. A consignment of four years' issues of the German pictorial series *Die Schaffenden* cost him 527 yuan, and for a single volume of *Der Maler Daumier* (Honoré Daumier, the 19th century French satirical cartoonist) he paid 66.5 yuan. His average monthly expenditure on books in 1930 was 200 yuan. In 1931 he paid 120 yuan for twelve prints of Käthe Kollwitz, who had been recommended to him by Agnes Smedley, an American journalist who was backing the left-wing cause in China. He could afford all these because he received arrears of royalties from the Beixin Bookshop of over 8,000 yuan at the end of 1929 (though that did not stop him pleading poverty to his correspondents at the time).

Perhaps the most enjoyable event for Lu Xun in 1930 was the fiftieth birthday party (by Chinese reckoning) held for him on 17th September at a Dutch restaurant called Surabaya. 'Over one hundred' guests, all left-wing, attended it. In his speech of thanks Lu Xun reiterated that young intellectuals could not produce proletarian literature, but did offer the constructive advice that they should get material for their work by sharing the lives of workers and peasants. The literary forms they could get from Western literature. For his part, he would continue to supply (through translation) the best of Western works to them.

The fact that Lu Xun raised again on what should have been a

carefree occasion the question of proletarian literature showed
how much it bothered him. It was in truth a thorny, not to say
intractable, issue. We shall have to digress from our narrative to
offer an explanation. The difficulty that the Left League, like the
Creation and Sun societies before it, had to face was that the case
for proletarian literature and/or revolutionary literature was paper-
thin. At that time in Chinese history the proletariat was unlettered.
The working class, or common people, had their oral entertain-
ments, some verbally quite sophisticated ones, such as tales and
ballads, but they were traditional arts with no modern political
freight. Equally the active revolutionaries were too busily engaged
in revolution to be writing literature. In actuality, all the League
could offer was literature that incited revolution by engendering
class hatred, or that sympathized with the hapless lot of workers
and peasants. In either case it would be vicarious, that is to say,
written *on behalf of* revolutionaries and proletarians, and therefore
not the genuine article. Moreover, if the literature was carried in
the magazines and books published by the League, it would reach
only the educated, by class bourgeois or petit bourgeois, certainly
not the working class.

There would be nothing wrong with that outcome if the aim
was only to enlist recruits for the political struggle against the
Guomindang. After all, the leaders of the Chinese Communist Party
were all from the bourgeoisie or petit bourgeoisie themselves (if
we extend those terms to rural society). The problem was that
Marxist ideology reposed wisdom and goodness in the working
class, and the Communist Party claimed to operate a 'dictatorship
of the proletariat', so theoretically the working class had to be the
ultimate touchstone and arbiters. As a self-respecting intellectual,
Lu Xun could not pretend that the working class in China had had
a look in so far. He could believe, through an act of faith, that

they played a part in the Soviet Union. Therefore he was able to
recommend Soviet literature, but not able to recommend Chinese
literature. His prescription, as in his birthday speech, was for the
literate authors to bridge the gap between themselves and their
material by 'going among the people'. If they did, they would
certainly write with more understanding, but then what? Accurate
and truthful description of the condition of life of the labouring
masses was not the purpose of proletarian literature. The masses
(or their leaders at least) had to be endowed with political
consciousness, and ultimately had to 'stand up' against their class
oppressors. That was the defining element of 'socialist realism' in
proletarian literature, which differentiated it from the simply
'realist' literature of non-socialist authors.

Considering that Lu Xun had gone against his conscience in
adding some bright spots in his *Battlecries* stories, and ridiculed
the optimistic endings of Creation Society stories, he would have
had to go into reverse to approve of such literature. As recently as
July 1929 he had written in praise of truthfulness in fiction,
mocking the frauds who "hung lots of grand signboards up on the
literary stalls", and that echoed what Lu Xun had said in April
1927 in his speech at the Huangpu Military Academy: "Good works
cannot be written to order. They flow naturally from a man's heart
with no regard for their possible effect." Lu Xun afterwards simply
avoided facing the fact that both revolutionary literature and
proletarian literature incorporated an element of make-believe.
That probably explains why despite all the mental effort he put in
to acquire a grasp of Marxist literary theory, he made very little
contribution of his own to it.

13

Commitment

I f something was needed to strengthen Lu Xun's commitment to the communist cause, it came along on 17th January 1931. On that day Lu Xun's young friend and helper Rou Shi was arrested along with other communists attending a Party cell meeting. Further arrests were made in the following days. Twenty-four of those arrested were shot in the Longhua Prison in Shanghai on 7th February. Of them, five belonged to the League of Left-wing Writers. They became known as the 'Five Martyrs'. Those and other arrests elsewhere were made possible by internal betrayal: it is now generally accepted that the tip-offs were given by an opposing faction within the Party. That of course was not known at the time, therefore the Five Martyrs were thought martyred only by the Guomindang.

Rou Shi (born 1902) had gone to Shanghai in 1928 from his birthplace of Ninghai in Zhejiang province, where he had been involved in peasant disturbances while teaching school. He had taken over the editorship of *Threads of Talk* from Lu Xun in December 1928. Subsequently he joined the Freedom Movement and the Left League, where he was a member of the steering committee. He joined the Chinese Communist Party in 1930. He helped to organize Lu Xun's fiftieth birthday party in September 1930. Rou Shi lived near Lu Xun and frequently called on him, in fact he practically became one of the family, being included in dinners Lu Xun gave for other people, and going along on family outings to the cinema and the like. Although Rou Shi was independently the author of some works of fiction, he always went along with Lu Xun's wishes. He took responsibility for the Morning Blossoms (Zhaohua) magazines, which introduced Northern and Eastern European literature and prints, and a series of pictorial art volumes, all of which were close to Lu Xun's heart. When the news of the arrest of this close disciple filtered through to Lu Xun he was both shocked and alarmed. On 20th January he went into hiding in a Japanese owned hotel with his wife and child and the child's nurse, sleeping all together in one small room. He did not leave until 28th February.

We recall that Lu Xun's final commitment to wage war against the authorities in Peking in 1926 arose from the shooting of some of his students. The declaration that Lu Xun published following the execution of his disciple Rou Shi in Shanghai in 1931 similarly committed him irrevocably to war against the Guomindang.

Because of the general clampdown on publishing houses that accompanied the wave of arrests, it was not until April 1931 that the Left League was able to respond to the execution of the Five Martyrs, by publishing a special issue of *Forward Patrol (Qianshao)* that they secretly printed themselves. In that issue Lu Xun published a "Short Biography of Rou Shi" (*Rou Shi xiaozhuan*) and a pivotal essay entitled "Chinese Proletarian Revolutionary Literature and the Blood of Its Pioneers" (*Zhongguo wuchanjieji geming wenxue he qianqu de xie*). The gloves were off, and the thunderous rhetoric rolled. As this kind of rhetoric hardly survives nowadays, it will be instructive to quote at some length:

> China's proletarian revolutionary literature comes into being at the junction of today and tomorrow. Engendered in vilification and

oppression, finally in this darkness its first chapter has been written with the fresh blood of our comrades.

Our downtrodden masses have historically suffered the most vicious subjugation. They have even been denied the boon of learning to read and write, and have had to endure this persecution in silence. The complex Chinese pictographs prevent them from educating themselves. When our young intellectuals realized their mission to be pioneers, they stepped in with the first war cries. These war cries, together with the shouts of revolt of the downtrodden masses themselves, struck terror in the rulers. The running-dog literati rallied to the attack, or spread rumours, or acted as spies, but it was all done under cover, using pseudonyms, which only went to show that they were themselves creatures of darkness.

The rulers were aware that the running-dog literati could not repel the thrust of proletarian revolutionary literature, so they proscribed books and journals, closed bookshops, passed evil publication laws, and blacklisted authors. At the same time they resorted to the most extreme measures, arresting, imprisoning and secretly executing left-wing writers — they still have not admitted the deed. All this proves that they are indeed creatures of darkness, and also proves the strength of the Chinese proletarian revolutionary literature camp, for as their biographies set out, the youth, the courage and above all the achievements of the day-to-day works of our fallen comrades are enough to make the whole pack of running dogs too scared to bark.

Nevertheless, these comrades have been assassinated, and this is something of a loss to proletarian revolutionary literature, and causes great grief to us. But proletarian revolutionary literature continues to grow, because it belongs to the revolutionary broad downtrodden masses. For every day the masses exist they grow stronger, and proletarian revolutionary literature grows with them. The blood of our comrades has demonstrated that proletarian revolutionary literature has in common with the revolutionary downtrodden masses the subjection to oppression and slaughter, and shares with them the same struggle and the same fate, and is indeed the literature of the revolutionary downtrodden masses....

> We now commemorate our comrades fallen in battle with great sadness and total recall, that is, we will well remember that the first page in the history of Chinese proletarian revolutionary literature has been recorded with the fresh blood of our comrades. It will forever display the vileness and violence of our enemies and give the lead to our ceaseless struggle.

It is difficult to separate the logic from the emotion of this piece. Previously Lu Xun had been unwilling to concede that the work of left-wing writers in China qualified as proletarian revolutionary literature. Now he seemed to be saying that the slaughter of the Five Martyrs retrospectively transformed what had been 'war cries' of young intellectuals into authentic revolutionary literature, because the bloody suppression of the writers sealed their unity with the revolutionary masses who were similarly bloodily suppressed. Lu Xun's position was in logic very shaky and in fact quite incorrect, because the Five Martyrs were not arrested as members of the Left League but as members of the Chinese Communist Party attending a political meeting along with other Chinese Communist Party members (who unaccountably were not given the same status of martyrs when shot). The significance of the piece for Lu Xun's biography is emotional: it marks his total commitment to the cause of proletarian revolutionary literature, and, through its unreserved embrace of leftist political rhetoric, to the broad political struggle too.

Lu Xun wrote another article under the same impulsion that he entrusted to Agnes Smedley, who was to get it published in an American monthly called *New Masses*, but there is some doubt that it ever appeared there. In its original Chinese version it was entitled "The Present State of Literature in Darkest China" (*Heian Zhongguo de wenyijie de xianzhuang*). This article made the same claim that the writers arrayed against the Left League were feeble

and unproductive, and in the end proletarian revolutionary
literature would prevail over such 'hoodlums, spies, running dogs
and executioners'; in fact proletarian revolutionary literature was
the *only* literary movement in China at that time. However, Lu
Xun admitted, "unfortunately there are as yet in the left-wing ranks
no writers of worker or peasant origin." The reason given was the
same as before, that the Chinese writing system took ten years of
education to master.

There may have been some truth in the claim that the proletarian
revolutionary literature movement was the only strong *movement*
in China at that time, but although some promising fiction had
started to come out of the left-wing stable, it was still stronger on
talk than on works. As we have noted, the quality literature was
being written outside of 'movements'.

In 1931 Lu Xun continued to devote some of his energy and
resources to supporting the graphic arts, in particular the woodcut.
So he arranged for the Japanese engraver, Uchiyama Kakichi, to
give classes to young Chinese artists, and in May gave an opening
speech for an exhibition of the work of the Artists of the 1929
Association (Yi-ba yishe), in which he praised them as 'new, young,
progressive'. In February, pursuing his long-term interest in book
illustrations, he produced at his own expense a deluxe edition of
the illustrations of the German artist Meffert to go with the Chinese
translation of Gladkow's Soviet novel *Cement*.

In July 1931 the old Lu Xun reasserted himself. Having been
pushed over the edge into uncritical endorsement of Chinese
revolutionary literature by the execution of Rou Shi, he regained
his balance. In a speech entitled "A Glance at Shanghai Literature"
(*Shanghai wenyi zhi yipie*), given to the Academy of Social Sciences,
he sketched in caricature fashion the literary trends in Shanghai
from the end of the Qing dynasty to the present day, along the

lines of an alliance between 'dandies and gangsters'. After paying off some old scores on the way, he came to the nub of his matter, the situation of 'revolutionary literature'. Here he got down to some serious analysis. He bluntly attributed the rise of revolutionary literature to the social situation:

> When the Northern Expedition was launched from Guangdong, the active contingent of young people went off to do practical work; at that time there was no manifest movement for revolutionary literature. No vigorous activity in favour of revolutionary literature took place in Shanghai until there was an abrupt change in the political environment, whereby the revolution suffered a reversal, class divisions opened up, the Guomindang in the name of 'cleansing the party' slaughtered large numbers of communists and revolutionary masses, and the surviving youths found themselves oppressed once more. So the rise of revolutionary literature was superficially different from other countries in that it was not owing to the rising tide of revolution, but to the setback to revolution.

This is a sober and detached assessment of the situation. Lu Xun goes on to say that given the real social basis for the movement, it did attract some perfectly sound adherents, but there were faults in the strategy of that earlier phase:

> For one thing, without making any detailed analysis of Chinese society, they mechanically applied methods suited only for Soviet areas. For another thing, they — especially Mr. Cheng Fangwu — gave people to understand that revolution was an extremely frightening thing by putting on a fearsome ultra-left expression, as if to say that come the revolution, all non-revolutionaries would come to a sticky end. As a result, people looked upon the revolution with terror. Actually, revolution makes people live, not die. This letting people know that 'revolution has a sting in its tail' was only them shouting off their mouths; it showed that they were also infected with the poison of 'dandy plus gangster'.

That also is fair comment. From there Lu Xun moves on to

criticize opportunist 'petit bourgeois' writers who joined the leftist camp when the wind was fair, but turned against their comrades when the weather changed. Two of those cases he expands on, naming names. Returning to general questions, he asks whether the present cadre of left-wing writers can produce good proletarian literature. His answer is, only with great difficulty. Granted that a writer does not have to be a thief to describe a thief, that feat is only possible because writer and thief belong to the same society (the old society). As writers have no contact with the proletariat, they belong to two different worlds, and it is hard to avoid distortion. Hence he approves the new slogan of the Left League, 'the proletarianization of the writer', meaning that the writer should live among the revolutionary masses and share their experiences.

The end of the speech is devoted to disposing of the new holders of power, who were worse than the old, and the rival kinds of literature that were then on offer, which were all quite valueless in his opinion.

The tone of this speech is magisterial. It does not give the slightest indication that he was a spokesman for the Left League, or betray any protectiveness towards its members. Though it is implicit that revolutionary literature and/or proletarian literature are the only goals to which writers should work, Lu Xun makes no claim for any headway in that direction so far, indeed as before he dwells on the shortcomings of the movement. The 'first chapter' that he said had been written with the blood of the Five Martyrs has had no sequel.

To assess now the content of this important speech, it was typical of Lu Xun in its grudgingness. The barrier between the writer and the proletariat was not in fact more insuperable than that between the writer and the thief. The proletariat had not gone through any

supernatural transformation when they went to work in factories
(if the term is restricted to industrial workers), and some writers
lived in poor quarters alongside them. And if peasants are included
with workers in the term, then familiarity was even more possible,
as there was no shortage of new writers who had grown up in
country villages. If Lu Xun himself was able to write of country
folk and the urban poor, as he did in his short stories, then there
was no bar against his juniors doing the same, especially as Lu
Xun was from a higher social class than most of them. Ironically,
communist critics after the Liberation unanimously praised his
portrait of the poor peasant Runtu in his story "Hometown" as
catching the essence of the peasant class. But like a stern head-
master, Lu Xun was bent on reminding his pupils how hard they
still had to work.

From another point of view the speech illustrates a virtue of Lu
Xun, namely his independence. He did not allow his involvement
in the organization to fetter his freedom of expression. In that
way he was following in the tradition of the 'Shaoxing scribes' his
hometown was famous for — the astute secretaries who worked
for imperial officials but would not be their lackeys. They were
said to be always ready to roll up their bedding and decamp if
treated with disrespect or instructed to do anything against their
conscience.

Roughly six months later, in December 1931, Lu Xun swung
back to orthodoxy when he was called upon to restate his opinion
on the kind of literature demanded by the present age. The call
came in a letter from two young writers starting out on their career,
namely Sha Ting and Ai Wu (both were later to achieve considerable
eminence). They sought his advice. In his reply, entitled "Correspondence Concerning the Subject Matter of Fiction" (*Guanyu
xiaoshuo ticai de tongxin*), Lu Xun adopted a generally fatherly

tone. The most doctrinaire of his assertions was in respect of the proletariat, a to him purely notional species. He wrote:

> In the case of the proletariat who have taken up the fight, as long as what they write can become a work of art, then regardless what they write about, or what their subject matter is, it will certainly have contributory significance for the present and the future. Why? Because the authors themselves are fighters.

This represented an amazing act of faith on the part of a fifty year-old man who had made a career out of iconoclasm and the exposure of falsity. The assertion that class origin guaranteed superiority shows that he had swallowed communist theory whole. To account for his credulity we must remind ourselves that for many years he had been expressing disappointment close to despair that his 'mental fight' had had no effect. In his present position on the organized left-wing platform he was no longer a lone voice in the wilderness, he had a committed following. To keep that following he had to defend the faith.

Politically he had a right to his allegiance. His support of communism ultimately depended on whether or not to believe that the revolution in the USSR had succeeded in creating a new and better order, as it was claimed. As he had no firsthand knowledge, he had to rely on reports — and his instinct. One fact he thought of great significance that he noted in 1932 was that the USSR had exported massive quantities of petroleum and wheat in 1931, which he thought must prove that it had a thriving economy based on a contented population. (He was not to know that the grain was requisitioned, with the consequence of massive famine in the Ukraine.) He was quite aware that the USSR's detractors painted a very different picture, but he put that down to the hostility and fear of the capitalist countries, and chose to believe the favourable reports sent back from Chinese people in the USSR.

The 'instinct' came in in his predisposition to think that his enemies' enemy was his friend: since the imperialist powers (Japan as well as the Western ones) who were up to no good in China were bent on the destruction of the USSR, the USSR must be all right. In the same way, he saw in China only the Guomindang imprisoning and executing communists, which made him believe that communists must be good people. Distinguished intellectuals in the West came to the same conclusion on similar grounds.

Artistically, however, his narrowness of vision is harder to justify. He gave only reluctant approval to the two young writers' present practice of 'truly and accurately' depicting characters whom they thoroughly understood, as something that was all right if they could not do any better. Their greatest limiting factors were their upbringing (which he assumed was petit bourgeois) and their political consciousness (which he assumed must be low). Conversely, a member of the proletariat would write more meaningful literature spontaneously, because his political consciousness would be higher. Whether this hypothesis was valid could only be tested in China in the still rather remote future when workers and peasants had acquired sufficient education to manipulate the Chinese written language well. And even if the hypothesis were proved correct, it would be limiting the value of literature to its contribution to social or political progress. On the other hand, this latter consideration was not exactly new for Lu Xun. He had rarely if ever praised a work of literature simply for its aesthetic qualities.

After Lu Xun's death his class theory was implicitly denied by a Soviet author whose novel, *The Rout*, Lu Xun translated, namely A. A. Fadeyev. In his tribute made in 1949, it was the gentry-class writer Lu Xun whom Fadeyev elevated to parity with the Russian greats, not the proletarian writers in China. Why? Because of his humanism. "All the short stories of Lu Xun," Fadeyev wrote, "can touch the most important part of humanity, namely conscience, social conscience especially." And Lu Xun wrote those stories before he conceived any notion of 'the proletariat'.

If on account of being so grudging with his approval Lu Xun was not a good propagandist for the Left League, he did serve it well in denouncing its enemies. Because he hated more strongly than he loved, this was Lu Xun's element. The force of his invective can best be seen in the essay, "The Task and Fate of Nationalist Literature" (*Minzuzhuyi wenxue de renwu he yunming*) of October 1931. We have noted above that this literature intended to extol the manly virtues of the Chinese race was sponsored by the Guomindang. In his essay Lu Xun uses his usual tactic of sticking a derogatory label on his adversary at the outset, and thereafter discussing the adversary in terms of that label, as if the label conveyed their character more truly than the identity they themselves proclaimed. So here he lumps together all the literary schools unsympathetic to the Left League as 'pet hounds' of the imperialists and the government.

> Among the literature of these pet hounds, the kind that bangs drums and clashes cymbals most energetically is the so-called 'nationalist literature'. But in comparison with the visible meritorious service of the spies, police and hangmen, its writers fall far short. The reason is that they are still only barking, and have not yet got down to sinking their teeth in. Furthermore, they haven't got the guts of the drifters and desperadoes — the only drifting they do is as corpses brought in on the tide. Still, this is precisely the mark of 'nationalist literature'; this is the way they stay pets.
>
> Leaf through their publications and you will see that all kinds of people who previously paraded all sorts of ideologies have strangely enough all assembled together. Is this the giant hand of 'nationalism' that has hauled them in? Not at all. The fact is that these are drifting corpses that have been bobbing up and down along the Shanghai

Bund for ages. At first they were strung out, but when a squall blew up they floated together, piling up on each other, and due to the putrid state of each one, give out a more cloying stench.

The essay goes on to demolish certain works published in the 'nationalist literature' magazines. It is easy to think that it was powerful enough to deal a mortal blow (as some commentators claim), and it certainly outdid the competition, but one has to consider that it was published in a Left League magazine which could not be widely distributed, and would be read mainly by the converted. The general reading public would not have known of it until it was reprinted in Lu Xun's collection *Two Minds (Erxin ji)*, after the dust had settled. The 'nationalist literature' movement did disintegrate, but principally because it could not drum up enough contributions to sustain it.

Aside from its effectiveness, there is also the question of the essay's degree of venom to consider. The passage quoted is at the top of the range. If one remembers the names Lu Xun was called by his erstwhile adversaries on the left wing, it does not seem particularly out of the ordinary, but it is still very strong stuff. In fairness, though, it has to be borne in mind that there was large-scale physical carnage going on at the time, so it is not surprising that wars of words also should have waxed ferocious at times.

14

The Middle Years in Shanghai

In this chapter we pick out some of the more noteworthy things that happened to Lu Xun and that he made happen during the middle period of his 'leadership' of the League of Left-wing Writers. It may read disjointedly, but that cannot be helped. Life is not very well jointed.

Towards the end of 1931 Lu Xun wrote further articles on translation methods and principles. Several of these articles were counter-attacks on detractors who, in opposition to him, stressed 'ease of reading', mocking them for mistakes in their translations (a practice he had previously deplored). Much more courteous was his reply to a long letter from Qu Qiubai, who wrote as a comrade in arms to propose the limiting of the language of translation to what could be spoken, excluding expressions and constructions that belonged to the written language. Lu Xun made the sensible point that the target readership was not uniform, but divided according to educational level. His own 'stiff translations' were meant for the 'well educated', who could cope with the unfamiliar. Lu Xun was nonetheless willing to accept from Qu corrections to his translation of *The Rout*, as Qu had studied in Russia.

Lu Xun also resumed writing occasional *zawen* on matters that had caught his eye in the press, and got back to form as a satirist.

The most entertaining of this batch of *zawen* took the rise out of a self-satisfied report from a female Chinese student travelling in Belgium. She allegedly dispelled the delusion of the Belgians that all Chinese women had bound feet by displaying her own 'natural' feet for them to see. Lu Xun's piece was wittily entitled "Repaying the Motherland with a Foot" (*Yi jiao baoguo*). More bitter satire was evoked by the Guomindang suppression of student demonstrations against the Japanese occupation of Manchuria. By this time Lu Xun had moved into open and outright denunciation of the Chinese government. No wonder his government stipend was cut off.

At the beginning of 1932 Lu Xun had his first and only taste of war. Earlier, when he lived in Shaoxing, the town had been taken over peacefully by the revolutionaries; when he lived in Peking, warlords had fought over the city but not in the city. Now in Shanghai war came to his doorstep. The house that he rented in Shanghai was in the Japanese concession. On the evening of 28th January, columns of trucks and armoured cars rolled out of the Japanese Garrison Command across the street from him, and the attack on the Chinese City began.

The attack brought to a head the animosity between the two nations. Chinese resentment against the Japanese following their military occupations in northern China had led to a boycott of Japanese goods, which the Japanese government demanded should be lifted. After a party of Japanese monks was beaten up in Shanghai, the Japanese Residents Association had been calling for their marines to protect them. This suited the Japanese navy, which was spoiling for a fight. Incidents were manufactured as an excuse for military action, which when it came was presented as a preemptive strike against the Chinese troops in the region.

The Chinese Nineteenth Route Army stoutly resisted the

Japanese assault, and bullets and shells started flying in all directions. Two days after the conflict began Lu Xun and family took refuge in the garret of the Uchiyama Bookshop, and moved again on 6th February to another Uchiyama bookshop in the British concession where it was safer, this time taking Zhou Jianren and family with them. Lu Xun did not return to his house until the 19th March, to a scene of some destruction. His windows were broken and his house had been looted, but his books and papers were untouched. Of his personal possessions only an umbrella was missing — which goes to show how spartan his lifestyle was.

In 1932 Lu Xun compiled two new volumes of his previously published occasional pieces. In his preface to the *Two Minds* collection he stepped outside himself and indulged in a little humour at his own expense. He remarked on his habit of always talking about himself, speaking of being isolated and beleaguered, of always knocking his head against walls, as if all the miseries of the world were heaped on his head, and he were the universal scapegoat. All this he ascribed to the bad temper of the middle-class intellectual. He added, however, that he had now seen the light, which was that the future lay with the emerging working class. What he said about his faults was quite true, but a person who confesses his faults can be forgiven them. The trouble was, he never overcame them, which caused him unnecessary distress and expense of spirit. As for his new faith, that was not empty talk: it remained firm for the rest of his life. Yet, happily, that did not block out wide cultural interests, indeed his knowledge of Western as well as Chinese cultural history was quite remarkable in such an embattled individual. One is constantly surprised from glancing references in his essays by the things he knew about. We have mentioned before his purchase of books on European pictorial art that began in the 1910s, and it goes without saying that he

acquainted himself with East European literature because he
translated so much of it, but he was also familiar with Western
'bourgeois' writers. He was quite prepared, for instance, to
contribute a preface to a Chinese translation of Mark Twain's *Eve's
Diary*, and contrast Twain with Poe, Hawthorne, Whitman, W. D.
Howells and Henry James.

Leaving the Battle for Shanghai aside, Lu Xun was unsettled in
1932, despite his central position in the left-wing camp. In private
letters he talked of considering returning to Peking, and of an
invitation to settle in Japan, where his works sold well. In the
autumn he got close to accepting an invitation from the International Revolutionary Writers Alliance to visit the Soviet Union,
from where he thought of going on to Germany — in fact he
brushed up his German for that purpose. But in the end he decided
to stay in Shanghai 'to carry on the struggle'. Yet the 'struggle' was
not all-satisfying for him. He planned to write a complete history
of Chinese literature, a mammoth undertaking which would
necessarily distance him from the struggle. Again, that proved to
be only a pipe dream.

A pull in the opposite direction, towards deeper involvement
in the struggle, was his nascent friendship with Qu Qiubai, the
leading communist intellectual and translator from the Russian.
After corresponding with him on the subject of translation, Lu
Xun met him in the spring of 1932. They subsequently became so
close that Lu Xun published Qu's essays under his own name and
included them in his collections (he could not disclose their true
authorship because Qu was on the Guomindang death list). Such
permission to 'speak in the voice of the sage' was accorded to no
one else. Intimacy with Qu Qiubai grew when Qu and his wife
sought sanctuary in Lu Xun's house in December 1932. On 7th
December Qu presented Lu Xun with a wistful poem in classical

Chinese, exactly as bosom friends had signified their affection all through feudal times. Qu also made a present of a very expensive foreign-made meccano set to the boy Haiying, despite his lack of funds.

Qu was to stay with Lu Xun on two further occasions, on one of which he read all Lu Xun's published works and made a selection of his *zawen*, to which he joined a lengthy analytical preface. The selection was published in July 1933. According to their wives, Lu Xun's spirits always lifted in Qu's company, and vice versa. It would be no exaggeration to say that their relationship progressed to soul mates, as may be seen from the couplet that Lu Xun presented to Qu in March 1933:

In human life to make one close friend is satisfaction enough.
In this existence he should be cherished as another self.

In January 1934 Qu left Shanghai for the communist base in Jiangxi. He was later arrested, imprisoned, and finally shot. To mark his friend's death, Lu Xun edited Qu's translations from the Russian and had them printed in two finely bound volumes. He received copies of the first volume only two weeks before his own death in October 1936. Among those to whom he distributed them were, reportedly, Mao Zedong and Zhou Enlai.

In 1932 Lu Xun also had the singular honour of entertaining in his home a real live Red Army general, Chen Geng, who was secretly in Shanghai recuperating from wounds sustained on the battlefield (he was later arrested). Hoping that Lu Xun would weave them into a novel, Chen Geng gave him details of the communist base areas in the interior and the reforms carried out there, as well as descriptions of battles against the encircling Guomindang armies. Apparently Lu Xun listened most attentively and asked a lot of questions. He signified his willingness to write, but when it came to the point decided that without firsthand knowledge he could not do the job. The decision was a wise one, for he was in fact incapable of writing upbeat stories, and for another reason would have gone against his own lights if he wrote of things beyond his experience. Obviously the general (and, behind him, the Party) did not share Lu Xun's scruples, and was not as well up as him on the theory of the class nature of literature. In fact it was not only a matter of theory but also of performance, if we are to believe the preface Lu Xun wrote to a collection of fiction from the 'New Russia'. He said there that when fellow travellers (which is what he was) wrote of revolution and the construction of the new social order, they constantly betrayed the attitude of bystanders, whereas when revolutionaries wrote they were ever 'in the midst of it', as it was 'their business'. He would not have done either himself or others a favour by writing 'bystander' literature.

It was in October 1932 that Lu Xun composed a poem, two lines of which went down in history. They were:

> With angry brows I coldly face a thousand pointing fingers,
> With bowed head I willingly play the ox for the little children.

Mao Zedong quoted those lines at the Yan'an Forum on Literature and the Arts in 1942. Mao explained that the pointing fingers belonged to their enemies, and the children symbolized the proletariat and the masses. The ox was, naturally, the willing servant of the masses. Actually that is unlikely to be a correct interpretation, as the poem was made up impromptu in the light-hearted atmosphere of a private dinner party. The second line should more probably be read as a *contrast* to the first, that is, in public he defiantly faces the accusing fingers of his critics, but at home he submissively plays the docile ox for his little child (there being no difference between 'child' and 'children' in Chinese). Lu

Xun's son Haiying, we may recall, had just turned three at the time, and he did entitle the poem "In Mockery of Myself" (*Zi chao*). Nevertheless, Mao's interpretation could not be challenged by Chinese literary historians. As Lu Xun himself was already dead by then, he had no say in the matter.

In November 1932 Lu Xun made his second trip to Peking, in response to a telegram saying his mother was ill. In fact there was nothing much wrong with her, and Lu Xun took the opportunity to do other things. This time he was pleased by the old-world courtesy of his friends there, which he contrasted with the snobbery typical of Shanghai. Apart from renewing acquaintances, he attended on 26th November a meeting of left-wing groups organized by the Chinese Communist Party, where he reported on the situation in Shanghai. On his personal account he revealed that he planned to write a novel on the progress of the intellectual class in China between the 1911 revolution and the 1919 May Fourth movement, as the younger generation would not know much about it. This, like his projected history of Chinese literature, was a pipe dream. What it signified was his frustration over his absorption in literary politics (especially as he admitted in a private letter dated 12th December 1932 that the Left League had 'no achievements to speak of'). While Lu Xun enjoyed the taste of blood and heat of battle, he must have realized that he was not producing anything of lasting value, that he was starving his talent for scholarship and creative writing — though it is doubtful that his talent was ever suited to writing a full-length novel.

The main thing Lu Xun did in Peking was to give lectures at universities. The attendance at Peking University and Furen University was large enough, but at his lecture to Peking Normal University students the crowd was so big that the lecture had to be held in the open air on the playing field. This was when the often seen photographs of his slight figure visible over a sea of heads were taken. As he had no microphone, he was seen (because he stood on a table) but not much heard. His theme was the familiar one of the 'muddy-footed' working class invading the sphere of literature to the disconcertion of the 'leather-shod' middle class. This and all his other lectures were unscripted. Whether or not a version was published depended on an able reporter being present. If there was a serviceable text, Lu Xun revised it, and it eventually appeared in one of his collections. Two of his talks in Peking did so appear. He returned to Shanghai on 30th November.

An article Lu Xun wrote in December 1932 furnished further insights into the underpinning of his political beliefs. The point of the article was to object to a member of his own camp publishing a poem using obscene invective and threatening bloody murder, because the truth was the revolution of the proletariat only had the aim of securing its own emancipation and the eradication of classes, definitely not of killing people. Lu Xun cites in support the fact that "in Russia even the Tsar's palace has not been burned down". Like many anti-fascists in the West, he refused to believe the 'calumny' of extermination of political opponents in the USSR, the only country where the 'proletariat' had had a revolution, just as many pro-fascists accepted that the early Nazi concentration camps were benign institutions for reform by labour. He was not in a position to know, as we know now, that Lenin and Stalin's secret police sent millions of innocents to their death — and that the Tsar had been shot with all his family. Nor did he foresee that tens of thousands of 'landlords' would be executed in China after 1949.

In the new year of 1933 Lu Xun found his touch again. He turned from preaching to putting into practice the rules of engagement that he did approve as legitimate in the above article, namely that militant writers must "stop at ridicule, stop at heated vituperation, and give their sallies and abuse the polish of literature, so as to wound and destroy their enemies while scorning to degrade themselves and make themselves repulsive in the eyes of spectators". National events consequent on the Japanese encroachments in northern China, like the decision of the Chinese government to move the Palace Museum treasures south instead of defending the territory and population, and the suppression of student protests, gave him plenty of occasion to use his cutting irony and sardonic wit, most effectively while affecting a casual tone.

A new outlet for short commentaries was the "Free Talk" (*Ziyou tan*) supplement to the leading newspaper, *Shen Bao*, which had come under the sympathetic editorship of Li Liewen. From January 1933 to August 1934 Lu Xun contributed scores of articles to this supplement, under a variety of pennames. Typically these had a target in current events, but were cast as ruminations on a topic from daily life or of passing interest. They were inclined to zigzag from one item in the author's extensive storehouse of knowledge to another, in apparently random fashion, before closing in on the quarry. But there was no fixed pattern and no obtrusive dogma. Lu Xun regretted that press censorship made him temper his remarks and weaken his force, but he had no cause for regret: these short pieces display skills that no one else could match.

In the same year of 1933 Lu Xun measurably raised his status as a writer (as opposed to a polemicist) and as a man with his essay "To Remember in Order to Forget" (*Weile wangque de jinian*). This was written 'in tranquillity' on the second anniversary of Rou Shi's death. It explains better than anything else his fight against state terror. It is translated as an appendix. Since it allows Lu Xun an opportunity to speak for himself, it should come as a welcome antidote to secondary sources, including this one.

In January 1933 Lu Xun joined the Chinese Alliance for the

Protection of Civil Rights (Zhongguo minquan baozhang tong-meng), whose meetings were held at the Academia Sinica, of which Cai Yuanpei was the head. This organization was for once not Communist directed. At its third meeting Lu Xun was elected to the executive committee along with Cai Yuanpei, Song Qingling (widow of Sun Yatsen), Yang Quan (Secretary General of the Academia Sinica), Lin Yutang, and four others. The tasks of the alliance were to secure the release of political prisoners, investigate prison conditions, and uphold the freedoms of publication, speech, and assembly. Its activities were reported abroad with the help of sympathetic foreign journalists like Agnes Smedley and Harold Isaacs. It ceased activities after Yang Quan — who was a member of the Guomindang, not the Chinese Communist Party — was assassinated in June of the same year. Yang's sad end was determined by the fact that unlike Cai, Song and Lu Xun he was a key member unprotected by national fame.

While the alliance was still active, Song Qingling invited Lu Xun to a lunch she gave in honour of George Bernard Shaw, who was on a brief visit to Shanghai. Shaw had visited the USSR in 1931 and, being well impressed, had defended the communist state against its critics. On his way to Shanghai he had given a speech at Hong Kong University which according to establishment news-papers in Shanghai 'propagated communism', and Lu Xun had rushed to write a comment "In Praise of Shaw" (*Song Xiao*). Given that Shaw, an Irish socialist and scourge of capitalism, had a lot in common with Lu Xun, their encounter could have been a meeting of minds, but owing to Lu Xun not being able to speak English, a couple of photographs were about all that emerged. After Shaw's departure Lu Xun and Qu Qiubai hurried out a collection of articles, for and against Shaw, so that his visit would not be completely forgotten.

That lunch took place on the 17th February. A few days later Lu Xun met another foreigner, the American journalist Edgar Snow, who was to become very well known for his book *Red Star over China*. Snow was putting together a collection of modern Chinese literature with the aid of his secretary, Yao Ke. Seven pieces of Lu Xun's were included in Snow's *Living China*, and he wanted to check some points with the author. One of the questions Snow raised was whether there were still many Ah Qs around in China (Ah Q being Lu Xun's specimen Chinese village rascal, created in 1921). Lu Xun's sardonic reply was, "It's worse now. Now it's Ah Qs who are running the country." Afterwards Lu Xun wrote that he had a favourable impression of Snow. He lamented that some foreigners had far greater love for China than some of his compatriots.

On 20th June Lu Xun attended the funeral of Yang Quan, who had been shot down in a street in the French Settlement along with his driver. Though it was rumoured that Lu Xun was also on the hit list, he still went ahead, leaving his door key at home in case he never returned. The same day he wrote a poem in memory of this 'good man', whose like were all being killed off.

Lin Yutang, also a member of the executive committee of the Civil Rights Alliance, did not show up for Yang Quan's funeral. Lu Xun's relations with him, once very good, had been steadily deteriorating, and Lin's absence may have been a factor in their breaking up altogether. Of more general significance was the ideological divide between them. Lin had started a magazine called *The Analects (Lunyu)* in September 1932, whose purpose was to mark out a preserve for leisure reading away from the stress and strain of social, political and military conflicts by treating topics of personal interest in a humorous way. Although Lu Xun had contributed a few pieces, he had grown increasingly uneasy, and in August 1933 he wrote an article setting out his reasons for disagreement with the policy of the magazine. This article, entitled "A Year of *The Analects*" (*Lunyu yi nian*), was generously published in the magazine itself.

On the one side, the argument was that if literature is to reflect life, there should be a place for leisure reading, as almost everyone enjoys some form of relaxation. Moreover, Lin Yutang and his allies (who included Lu Xun's brother, Zhou Zuoren) could point to the tradition in China of *xiaopinwen*, the short composition for which the literati waived the rule of high seriousness in order to indulge their personal likes and dislikes. And in fact *The Analects* and its successors did prove popular.

Lu Xun disagreed. Regarding the tradition, he argued that *xiaopinwen* had also been used as a vehicle for bitter social protest. More to the point, he denied that 'humour' had any roots in China. China had only burlesque, comic cuts and jokes. 'Humour' was an Anglo-American thing engendered in the urbane atmosphere of 'round table meetings', where even slaughter and butchery could be treated as a subject for pleasantry. Accustomed now to think only on behalf of the poor, suffering and wretched in society, Lu Xun could not approve of a literature for the diversion of the comfortable middle class. His own kind of embattled literature could not be just one kind among others: it had to be *the* literature of his age.

Lu Xun followed this a few days later with a more concentrated attack. In "The Crisis of the Little Essay" (*Xiaopinwen de weiji*), he employed his customary tactic of classifying the leisure essay as 'bric-à-brac' to decorate the homes of the middle class, and discussing it thereafter solely in those terms. The compositions which, in contrast, had vitality were 'daggers and javelins'. The word 'crisis', he said, was being used in the medical sense of the turning point which led either to life or death: the 'bric-à-brac' essay had no more endurance than an opium dream.

Such was the divide which now separated Lu Xun from Lin Yutang and most of his allies and colleagues in the 1920s. Of his friends from that time he saw only Yu Dafu in Shanghai, but at the end of April 1933 Yu Dafu retreated to Hangzhou to escape the fray. However, Lu Xun did not feel alone in 1933. He enjoyed the frequent company of his close disciples Qu Qiubai and Feng Xuefeng, and they certainly helped to raise his spirits. In fact his output of essays was very high that year, and photographs taken of him then show him in fine fettle. Internal squabbles in the left-wing camp were very few (perhaps because of the mediation of Qu Qiubai), and he did relatively little translation, which left him the energy to respond to external foes and the changing times. Indeed, from 1933 onwards one can read from his essays a detailed history of his country.

By the end of 1933 Lu Xun had written off the possibility of writing any more fiction. In a letter to Yao Ke, dated 5th November 1933, he explained the reason:

> It is not because I haven't the time, it is because I haven't the ability. I've been cut off from society for many years, not in the centre of the whirlpool. Inevitably my impressions are general and superficial, and are not the stuff of good writing.

It may seem odd of him to say that he was cut off from society. What he meant was the infrastructure of society, or the 'grass roots'; he had been operating in the superstructure of the intellectual sphere. But if he was out of the running as a writer of fiction, others were coming up: he was pleased to note that there were now promising new authors. Besides which, the established author Mao Dun had published a major novel that year, *Midnight (Ziye)*, which he had positively recommended. We might add that good young essayists had come forward, too. The new talent was obvious not only in the person of Qu Qiubai, whose essays Lu Xun allowed to masquerade as his own, but also in other budding essayists, whose works, published under pseudonyms like Lu Xun's, were mistaken as Lu Xun's by hostile critics.

An interesting little insight into Lu Xun's social values is afforded in the same letter to Yao Ke. In correcting the short biography Yao Ke compiled for Snow's *Living China*, Lu Xun objected to Cai Yuanpei being called his 'friend', because Cai was senior to him by a generation. Presumably Lu Xun expected the same kind of deference to be shown to him by his juniors. To some extent that explains why he took any criticism from them as an affront.

Another interesting insight, this time into Lu Xun's old-time generosity, was given in December 1933. According to Uchiyama Kanzo, the Japanese bookseller, he had just handed Lu Xun a hundred yuan fee for an article published in Japan when a young woman approached him. Lu Xun handed the hundred yuan over to her on the spot, explaining afterwards that it was a loan to pay a bribe to get an arrested comrade out of prison. Uchiyama protested that Lu Xun had probably been duped, but Lu Xun explained that if he had the money, he had to give: "That is the Chinese custom." The woman in question was Ge Qin, a novice left-wing writer. Lu Xun never got the money back.

That did not mean Lu Xun did not avoid setting himself up as a soft touch. In an amusing reply to a letter from Cao Juren in early 1936 urging him to go to the country for a rest, he demurred on the ground that if he went back to his home district, some of his friends and relatives would have heard the story about him receiving Russian roubles as an agent of Russian communism, and would soon be on to him for a loan, anything from a few hundred to five thousand yuan. They would presume that he had come back to buy rich fields and build a mansion. Then if he happened to be kidnapped, the ransom would be set too high, and it would be curtains for him.

In the last days of 1933 an encounter took place that is worth recording. Cheng Fangwu, the former leading member of the Creation Society who had been very active in denigrating Lu Xun, and whom Lu Xun had let pass no opportunity to ridicule in return, returned to Shanghai from a communist base area in the interior to make contact with the Central Committee. As the old link had been broken, he applied to Lu Xun for help. Lu Xun agreed with alacrity, and apparently with no ill feelings. This was an indication that Lu Xun's loyalty to the Party was by then strong enough to override — or even cancel — personal animosity.

15

The Last Phase: Downhill

T he last three years of Lu Xun's life saw little change in his circumstances. He had moved to a small terrace house on the fringe of the Japanese concession and remained there, with an interruption of only one month (23rd August to 18th November 1934), when he went into hiding on the news that an assistant in the Uchiyama Bookshop had been arrested. It should be explained at this point that for Lu Xun Uchiyama's was no ordinary bookshop. He made the acquaintance of the proprietor, Uchiyama Kanzo, soon after his arrival in Shanghai, first of all simply as a customer, for Lu Xun relied heavily on Japanese material to do his translation work, which supplied a large part of his income. Some of his translations were indeed of Japanese original works, but more were from European languages (principally Russian) for which he needed the intermediary of a Japanese translation.

The close friendship with Uchiyama which ensued was useful for other reasons. As an influential person in the Japanese community whom the Chinese authorities could not touch, Uchiyama could and did provide physical protection for Lu Xun, as we have seen. But he also allowed Lu Xun to use his bookshop as a kind of post office for the reception and dispatch of secret and proscribed material, and as a safe house for clandestine meetings. From that point of view, the arrest of his assistant was truly an alarming matter. More legitimately, Uchiyama was a vital link with Japanese cultural circles. In his Shanghai years Lu Xun received an unending stream of Japanese writers, artists and academics, mostly channelled through Uchiyama. In the reverse direction, Lu Xun contributed articles to Japanese publications, composed in Japanese.

Considering the Japanese occupation of Manchuria in 1931, her control over a large part of northern China, and her attack on Shanghai in 1932, all of which Lu Xun vehemently opposed, it is on the face of it strange that Lu Xun should have maintained such close links with Japanese people. Leaving aside the usefulness of such links, as noted above, we must bear in mind that Japan was not solidly militarist and expansionist. Her civilian government at that time was relatively moderate and conciliatory in its policy towards China, and in her population at large there were liberals, socialists and communists. Lu Xun's personal standing in Japan was very high. All his major works had Japanese translations, and his readership in Japan was incomparably greater than in any other foreign country. It is quite understandable that he would not have wished to cut himself off from his Japanese following. However, Lu Xun did not mix with Japanese diplomats or military personnel, did not go to Japan, nor did he support any moves by either government, which did take place sporadically, to promote 'Sino-Japanese friendship'.

On the home front, Lu Xun continued with his by now regular programme of translating, writing essays and commentaries, promoting graphic art, and encouraging young writers. To take those in reverse order, the most rewarding of his protégés were Xiao Jun and Xiao Hong, both from Manchuria. Lu Xun edited and wrote prefaces for the novels which launched the couple's careers, viz. Xiao Jun's *Village in August (Bayue de xiangcun)*, about guerrilla action against the Japanese invaders, and Xiao Hong's *Field of Life and Death (Shengsi chang)*, which described the raw realities of life in Harbin. Xiao Jun's writing had exceptional virility, while Xiao Hong's was simply world-class.

On the graphic art side, Lu Xun lent most weight to the woodcut movement, whose patron saint was Käthe Kollwitz. Her motifs may be divined from the titles of her most famous engravings, "The Revolt of the Weavers" and "Peasant War". One of the last outings Lu Xun made was to view the All China Woodcuts exhibition on 10th October 1936, ten days before his death. There are photographs of him in animated discussion with a group of young artists. But Lu Xun did not forsake his life-long interest in Chinese prints and book illustrations, either. At great expense he had fine reprints made of Ming engravings (for stationery), purely on their aesthetic merits.

Among Lu Xun's translations in this period, the most important was that of Gogol's *Dead Souls*. Volume One of that took him about ten months to complete in 1935. He was still working on the second volume at the time of his death. Lu Xun had published at his own expense in July 1936 a volume of *A Hundred Illustrations to* Dead Souls *(Si hunling bai tu)*, which shows both his esteem for the work and his undiminished pleasure in picture books.

There was no shortage of material to fuel his topical essays. Given his credo that proletarian literature was the only kind for his age, he was apt to attack any and all alternative schools of thought that raised their heads, whether actively hostile or not. Otherwise, practically every controversy that arose attracted a comment from him. He must have spent a great deal of time reading current papers and magazines to keep abreast of the news. Indeed, one of the reasons he gave for refusing invitations to go abroad for his health was his need to have Chinese newspapers at hand so that he could respond swiftly to events. The contrast with his despondent view of a few years earlier that no one listened to what he said is complete. Now it appeared that his contribution to the formation of public opinion was indispensable. Such was the effect of leadership of the Left League on his mind.

Yet Lu Xun also wrote non-doctrinaire, good humoured essays, some at his own expense, some driven solely by human sympathy, extended to contemporaries like a film actress who committed suicide, but also more remotely to poor old Confucius, whom he envisaged bumping his way along rutted ways in his oxcart, half starved and taunted by bystanders, as he went about preaching his gospel. Here the free play of his lively mind over his subject, his graphic imagination, his wit and acumen, married to a basic honesty devoid of affectation, made firm Lu Xun's claim to be modern China's foremost essayist. We can admire the cleverness and rhetorical skills of his polemical essays, but as Fadeyev rightly saw on the basis of much less evidence than we have, his greatness is indissociable from his humanism.

Of the long-running controversies that exercised Lu Xun's mind in his last three years, space can be given to only one. Because of its long-term cultural significance, the choice falls on the question of the simplification of the Chinese language. Lu Xun's personal interest in the romanization of the written word and the formation of a common spoken language was encouraged by Qu Qiubai, whose pet subjects they were, but the question was a perennial one, and had been debated for half a century.

It goes without saying that the root of the problem was the widespread illiteracy in China. Romanization was an instrument to make reading easier for those who were denied the education necessary to master Chinese characters. Various systems of romanization were developed by foreign missionaries in the nineteenth century, some based on Mandarin (the language of the civil service, which adopted Peking pronunciation), some based on regional languages or dialects. They served the dual purpose of indicating the pronunciation of characters for the missionaries' own learning of the languages, and (hopefully) of enabling their uneducated Chinese converts to read religious tracts. The virtues of phonetic spelling were recognized by progressive Chinese intellectuals eager to promote universal education. What eventually emerged after years of debate was an agreed set of phonetic symbols (*zhuyin fuhao*), officially approved in 1918 and still in use, and in 1928 the promulgation of a National Language Romanization system, known popularly as GR. The special feature of GR was that it incorporated the four tones of Mandarin in the spelling of a word (or character), thus dispensing with tone indicators above the letters, which were fussy and often left out in printing.

The issue was taken up by left-wing intellectuals in the early 1930s. To them the romanization issue was linked to that of a 'mass language'. Their constituents were in the first instance factory workers who did not speak the Mandarin either of Peking or Nanking (the Guomindang capital), and natively spoke diverse dialects, but had evolved a common language for communication in the workplace. This common language was more composite than Mandarin, and was expected to replace Mandarin as the universal, more demotic, vernacular. The proponents of this 'mass language' favoured a form of romanization rival to GR which had been formulated with the help of Soviet linguists. This 'Latinization' had twenty-eight letters, and was claimed to be more flexible than GR. Unlike GR it did not incorporate tones in the spelling, but this was seen as an advantage, because it made it simpler to learn. Latinization was first proposed at a conference in 1931, and in the following years was promoted nationwide. The movement

culminated in a signature campaign in December 1935, to which
leading figures on the left gave their names, including Cai Yuanpei,
Guo Moruo, Mao Dun — and Lu Xun.

Lu Xun had been a member of the committee which approved
the phonetic symbols in 1918, and had taken part in the controversy
of literary language versus vernacular language in the May Fourth
period, but he did not enter the new debate on language reform
until 1934. He had by then identified the Chinese written word as
the main cause of the lack of proletarian literature written by
proletarians, but he had not proposed a solution. Now he endorsed
Latinization. In the middle of August 1934 he published a scholarly
article entitled "A Layman's View of Language" (*Menwai wentan*),

in which he gave a very intelligent (though tendentious) summary
of the function of the written character in Chinese history and the
problems of applying a uniform system of spelling in a country of
many regional languages. These problems, he opined, could
gradually be overcome by the adoption of Latinization. This well
reasoned long article was followed by more dogmatic short articles.
In September he argued that since the great majority (over eighty
percent) of the population could not read and write characters,
China had no usable written language. That prevented the
development of the working class, on whose ability the literate
class depended. He concluded that the choice was between
sacrificing everyone to the old characters and sacrificing the old
characters for the good of all. In the last essay of the series, "On
the New Written Word" (*Lun xin wenzi*) of December 1935, he
declared that the Roman alphabet outclassed simplified characters
and phonetic symbols as a means of writing. The only contest was
between Latinization and GR. GR was too complicated in its
spelling, and furthermore only spelled out the 'old characters',
whereas Latinization was not only simpler but could also write

demotic words which had no written characters. The originators of GR were remote academics, who wanted the name of reform but not the reality of reform. The article ended with the extravagant claim that Chinese literature would not have new life until it was written by people who knew only Latinized Chinese, because they would not be infected by the classical works revered by the current generation of literati.

This controversy is enlightening in showing the two sides of Lu Xun. The long essay shows him learned, shrewd, entertaining, critical but reasonably fair; and that side one can applaud. The short articles show him crusading, bigoted, and losing touch with reality. Particularly unpleasant is his resort to the unfortunately common Chinese practice of denigrating the motives of the proponents of the thing disapproved of, as in the case of GR.

With the benefit of hindsight, we know that Latinization was not found workable (the present system known as *Hanyu pinyin* is a cut-down version of twenty-five letters which can represent rather fewer sounds than GR); that 'mass language' never materialized: the present *putonghua* is Mandarin under another name; that simplified characters have had more of a take-up than any Latin spelling; and that no one (to my knowledge) has ever attempted to write a work of literature in Latinized Chinese. Though Chairman Mao himself held that Chinese characters should eventually be abolished, that has never been likely to happen, for sound political, cultural and linguistic reasons. The reduction in illiteracy has been achieved, alongside retention of Chinese characters, by the wider provision of schooling.

Having said all that, one can understand the thinking behind the position Lu Xun represented in these articles. Improvement through schooling would take a generation to bring about, and the schooling might not be provided anyway. The adult working class needed a quick and easy means to read and write in order to improve their minds, realize their potential and claim their rightful place in the front of the nation. 'Latinization' and 'Mass Language' was a well thought out (if optimistic) shortcut to achieving those ends. The weakness was, the ideas could not be put to a proper test. Experiments were tried, but there was no apparatus to put them into practice in the urban areas where an embryonic mass language was forming and had some chance of making headway. The communists controlled only rural areas, where local dialects reigned supreme — and at that time their main body was struggling for survival on the Long March. Where and when they had settled bases, the communists encouraged oral forms of literature — songs and plays, principally — among the local peasant populations, which were recorded in writing by cultural cadres. So in the end, all one can say to comfort the ghosts of Lu Xun and Qu Qiubai is, it was a try worth making.

16

‛Dissolution and ‛Death

T he clouds started to gather over Lu Xun towards the end
of 1934. It was not because the struggle against external
enemies was harder: he always found elation in taking
them on. As we know from his indiscreet private letters, his
depression stemmed from the machinations of enemies within the
gate, what he called 'maggots' in his own camp. His favourite
disciples and powerful allies in the Left League having left Shanghai,
he again felt 'the sadness of the lone warrior'. As he said in a letter
to Xiao Jun (10th December 1934), after the Left League was
founded, the 'splittism', 'big talk' and 'radical posturing' had died
down, but now the old sickness had returned. He himself was
writing less topical criticism, and his edge was being blunted,
because he could not directly confront his external enemies, only
stand sideways to them, for fear of attacks from his rear from his
'comrades in arms'. He hated those who 'wounded him from cover',
and was inclined to let them get on with it without his help. He
even suspected the same people of being in league with hostile
groups to do him down. When not secretly subverting his efforts,
they as officers of the League were 'whipping' him to work harder.

Lu Xun's falling out with the cadres who ran the League (all of
course junior to him by a generation) became more pronounced
as time went on. In June 1935 he compared Zhou Yang, the chief

cadre, to a 'generalissimo' who hides away in safety himself while
ordering his foot-soldiers out onto the battlefield to risk their lives.
In September 1935 he even wrote that he would not recommend
Xiao Jun, who had as we recall written a novel he highly praised,
to join the League, because young writers who did good work
while they were still on the fringe got 'tangled up in tiresome
squabbles' when they joined, and stopped writing. Lu Xun himself
felt as if on a chain gang, with the foreman whipping him from
behind, no matter how hard he worked. When he turned his head
to ask what he had done wrong, the foreman was all smiles, told
him everything was fine, and assured him they were getting on
splendidly together.

   As we have noted, this criticism of the League's internal affairs
was expressed in private letters: Lu Xun was not publicly rocking
the boat. But though Lu Xun avoided adding to its woes in that
way, the fortunes of the League were fading. Membership was
shrinking due to arrests and defections, and most of their
publication outlets had been stopped by the authorities, while non-
party, non-political literature outside the League was prospering.
The response to adversity of the communist cadres in charge of
the League was to operate it more like an underground political
party, tightening secrecy and discipline in its organization, and
taking decisions behind closed doors. Hence Lu Xun, ostensibly a
leader, and clearly someone the League could not do without, but
a prickly character jealous of his independence, was sidelined.
Because the leading cadres were aware that none of them had Lu
Xun's respect, they did not dare approach him directly when they
wanted to steer him either towards or away from an objective, but
attempted instead to manipulate him indirectly. Usually, however,
Lu Xun got wind of their tricks, and took them as personal affronts,
as 'shooting arrows from ambush' (his favourite phrase).

Yet if the League could not do without Lu Xun, neither could Lu Xun do without the League. Having felt out in the cold for most of his adult life, he had found a home in the League, and it was his only home. Moreover, the patron of the League was the Chinese Communist Party, which he held in so high regard that he sent a telegram in February 1936 to the Central Committee on the successful conclusion of the Long March. The telegram ended, "On you rest the hopes of China and mankind". Even if he could not advise anyone to join the League, he would not leave it himself.

As things turned out, Lu Xun was not given the option of leaving or staying. Around the turn of the years 1935 and 1936 the League dissolved itself, because of developments far beyond Lu Xun's power to influence, let alone control. On 1st August 1935 the Communist International in Moscow issued a call to the Chinese Communist Party to cooperate with the Guomindang in resisting Japan. It had the authority to do that because communism was a worldwide crusade not restricted by national boundaries. In China the Party complied by dropping, among other things, its campaigns for 'proletarian literature' and 'mass language' in order to unite all classes of the nation behind this patriotic movement. The League of Left-wing Writers was a necessary casualty. The leadership of the League typically asked a third party, Mao Dun, to pass the bad word on to Lu Xun. Initially he declared his opposition, then reluctantly agreed on condition that the League was wound up honourably with a proper declaration. In the event no declaration was made, and the League ended without even a whimper. Not a good start. But the game was not over. The question of what body, following what guidelines, should replace the League was still debatable. The dissensions on the left that opened up over this question must have warmed the hearts of all unsympathetic onlookers.

The new slogan that the cadres adopted was 'National Defence Literature' (*guofang wenxue*), and the body set up to implement it was the Chinese Writers Association (Zhongguo wenyi zuojia xiehui). In articles explaining the proposals, Zhou Yang stated that the scope of the association's work was to be broad: apart from overtly anti-imperialist and anti-capitulationist topics, they would admit works like those of Sha Ting, which described the travails of the Chinese people under the yoke of imperialism and feudalism without specifically targeting those forces. Writers of all parties and persuasions could join in, not just 'progressives'. The aim was to push the trend in recent Chinese literature on to a new stage and expand on the successes of the Left League. Zhou admitted that outside of revolutionary literature there was an extensive 'middle literature' which had more readers, yet revolutionary literature should be the driving force in the proposed literature of national 'salvation'.

On 24th April 1936 Lu Xun wrote a letter declining a formal invitation to sign up with the Association of Chinese Writers. Two days later, Feng Xuefeng called on him. This confidant of his had just returned to Shanghai after completing the Long March. His mission was to inform Lu Xun about the Party's achievements and policies. He found him in low spirits. Lu Xun told him of his 'growing distaste for people', and confessed that he would rather have the job of doorman for a rich family, as that would be less wearing on the nerves, and safe from disputes. Even Feng Xuefeng could not allay Lu Xun's doubts. He objected to traitors to the cause being welcomed back into the fold under a united front: "If to remember a grudge against an enemy is a fault, so be it!. ... Forgive past sins? What rubbish!"

A private letter Lu Xun wrote in May showed that his mood was unchanged. In it he expressed his disbelief that National

Defence Literature would produce anything. Those people would only attack those who disagreed with them as heinous criminals. In time everybody would get bored, and the movement would collapse.

In June Lu Xun took action, on the one hand instigating the issue of a manifesto for a rival body called Chinese Literary Workers (Zhongguo wenyi gongzuozhe), and on the other hand putting forward the alternative slogan of 'Mass Literature for the National Revolutionary War' (*minzu geming zhanzheng de dazhong wenxue*). The manifesto, drafted by the anarchist Ba Jin, talked only in very general terms of winning freedom for the nation, with no mention of class or party. As to the Chinese Literary Workers, the sole function of that body was to issue the manifesto: it existed only as a list of signatories, and would have no organization. Clearly, then, it was brought into being for no other purpose than to pose as an alternative to the body that supported National Defence Literature.

Lu Xun presented his arguments to the public in an article called "On our present literary movement" (*Lun xianzai womende wenxue yundong*). The reader should be warned that at this point we enter the realm of tortuous logic. Lu Xun did not oppose a literature aimed at combating Japanese imperialism, as he had been attacking Japanese imperialism for some time; and he could not reject the slogan of National Defence Literature because it had the blessing of the Party. Yet he was determined to ensure the survival of proletarian revolutionary literature, which he had been saying for years was the *only* literature for China. To complicate the matter further, Lu Xun was already gravely ill, and could only dictate his words (to Feng Xuefeng).

In his statement, Lu Xun employed the tactic of treating his own slogan, Mass Literature for the National Revolutionary War, as the main one in play, the proper successor to proletarian revolutionary literature, which was not being abandoned, simply deepening and concentrating on resisting Japan and opposing traitors to the nation. Revolutionary literature would continue its bloody struggle to oppose fascism and all reactionaries, and would not relinquish its responsibility of class leadership. It would unite the whole nation, regardless of class differences, because the standpoint of the proletarian class was identical with the standpoint of the nation. The content of the proposed Mass Literature for the National Revolutionary War should not, however, be limited to military heroics, student petitions, and the like, but could embrace practically any subject matter, because every aspect of life in China was affected in some way by the impact made by the Japanese invaders. Nor was there any need to drag a tail of dogma. Lu Xun does mention the slogan of National Defence Literature, and approves it (among others!) as serving a concrete purpose and as expedient for present needs, but the main slogan is to be his, Mass Literature for the National Revolutionary War.

We can see that Lu Xun's view here expressed is very similar in substance to that set out in Zhou Yang's articles. It differs only in emphasis, insisting more strongly on the continuity with the programme of the Left League and the continuing role of the revolutionary proletariat. But that was not a subtle difference, as Lu Xun's radicalism was emblazoned in his slogan, whereas Zhou Yang's slogan of National Defence Literature omitted any mention of 'mass' or 'revolution'. No wonder, then, that the polemic which ensued became known as 'the battle of the two slogans'.

Perhaps in an attempt to clarify the issue, Chen Xinren published an article in August 1936 stating that National Defence Literature was a component part of Mass Literature for the National Revolutionary War, which had the broader programme. This seems to be a reasonable interpretation of Lu Xun's standpoint, but he declined Chen's assistance.

In his July article Lu Xun had only been rude in passing to colleagues who differed with him. In August the dissension between them exploded into a blazing row. On 1st August, Xu Maoyong, the young former secretary of the Left League, wrote a private letter to Lu Xun, which Lu Xun chose to publish together with his long reply. As Lu Xun was still incapacitated, the reply was drafted by Feng Xuefeng and corrected and amplified by Lu Xun.

Evidently the thinking of the Party cultural cadres had moved on since Zhou Yang's earlier statement, for Xu now said that proletarian literature should not pin on a big badge and demand leadership rights, thereby scaring off allies of other classes. Lu Xun was a poor judge of character, Xu alleged, and had been led astray by bad men, like the 'mole', Hu Feng (who had been secretary of the League from December 1933 to October 1934). His views were 'mistaken', 'incorrect'.

Lu Xun was naturally furious at this 'vile youth' treating him like an old fool. At the same time he saw that Xu Maoyong was not writing solely on his own behalf, but was representing 'a certain ilk'. Lu Xun responded in kind to slurs on his supporters with a description of Zhou Yang, Tian Han and two others (Xia Yan and Yang Hansheng) jumping out of a car dressed in snappy Western suits and acting arrogantly. Xu Maoyong himself, he insinuated, frequented low brothels and gaming houses. He also disclosed that from the start the Left League had been troubled by self-styled authors — actually rootless, declassed playboys — who imported the tactics of women's jealous bickering into the organization.

Getting down to arguments, Lu Xun mainly addressed Xu's accusation that he was fomenting dissension and disunity. He insisted that he fully supported the policy proposed by 'China's present revolutionary political party' (i.e. the Chinese Communist Party) of a united front against Japan, but did not trust the people implementing the policy in the cultural sphere, and would not join the Chinese Writers Association they set up. He did not believe that body could actually unite writers, because its interpretation of National Defence Literature was itself sectarian and splittist: they were preparing the accusation of 'traitors' for those who did not join them. The leadership of the Chinese Writers Association should be in the hands of real writers, not the likes of Xu Maoyong.

To interject a comment at this point, the evidence that Lu Xun was able to adduce to back up his charge of factionalism on the part of the cadres managing the Chinese Writers Association was very weak. On the face of it, their standpoint was less sectarian and divisive that Lu Xun's, because they seemed to be extending a welcome to all and sundry. Probably Lu Xun meant that they were splitting *the left*, by alienating himself and his allies, but he could not come out and say that plainly. And, as he admitted, he had never trusted them anyway.

To continue, Lu Xun explained that his slogan of Mass Literature for the National Revolutionary War was to 'clarify' the formulation and 'correct' some explanations of the National Defence Literature slogan. His slogan was mainly directed to left-wing authors, but could also apply to all sorts of authors, as the word 'mass' could be read as 'the mass of the Chinese people', and not restricted to the proletarian 'masses'. He was not repudiating the slogan of National Defence Literature, indeed it could take priority at present, if it were stripped of its incorrect glosses. But it was not a long-term policy.

That was Lu Xun's last published word on the subject. In a private letter to Wang Yeqiu, dated 15th September 1936, he wrote even more bitterly of 'literary men' getting up to wicked tricks. When his health improved he would expose them, and then 'there will be some hope for Chinese literature'. But his health never did improve sufficiently, and he died the next month.

What this difference reveals is the difference between the inflexible moralist (Lu Xun) and the very flexible politicians (the cultural cadres). Used to giving and obeying directives, the latter could change horses easily, whereas Lu Xun had won his convictions painfully, and had invested his emotional capital in his campaigns. His orthodoxy was strong enough to resist the temptation of the Chinese Trotskyites, who scenting an ally against the Stalinist Comintern line invited him to join them in rejecting the united front and renewing the revolutionary struggle. He would not go against Stalin's Soviet Union, in which he hoped, or against 'Mr. Mao Zedong and colleagues', who had accorded him personal recognition. Yet in deciding not to join the Chinese Writers Association but 'carry on as before' in his war against 'feudalism and reactionaries', his practical policy was the same as the Trotskyites. Since at least some 'feudal and reactionary' elements were also in favour of resisting Japan, Lu Xun would find himself in the same camp as them under the National Defence Literature slogan, and that would be intolerable. 'Turncoats' who had dropped out of the League might also be welcomed under that banner. Lu Xun could be — and was — persuaded that on the level of national strategy, unity to resist external aggression was the order of the day, but on the level of personal participation he would not collaborate with hated foes. There was no reason he could see why he should not attack Japan in his way, and they should not attack Japan in their way.

Lu Xun thought that if there had to be a united cultural front, then the others should come over to him, and follow the order of a Mass Literature for the National Revolutionary War. But on that point Zhou Yang and Co. were surely in the right. In spite of Lu Xun's gloss on the word 'mass', his slogan could not be mistaken as anything other than militantly left-wing in nature. Lu Xun may have truly believed that the interests of the revolutionary masses were identical with those of the nation as a whole, but plenty of others did not think so. Besides which, his public denunciation of the underhand manoeuvring and backstabbing that had gone on in the Left League would certainly put anyone off joining any organization that was obviously successor to it.

Sadly, the bitterness of the dispute stayed with Lu Xun, and despite a slight improvement in health and revival of other pursuits, poisoned his last days. Lu Xun's last days is what we now come to.

Lu Xun believed in doctoring illness, not in living a healthy life. He had suffered bouts of lung disease since the 1920s, and had them doctored successfully, chiefly by Japanese, sometimes German, never by Chinese doctors. But advancing years, incessant cigarette smoking, and his arduous work schedule combined to lower his resistance, and his health deteriorated badly in the second half of 1935. He had difficulty in getting his breath over the winter. In the middle of May 1936 he took really ill with a fever, but his Japanese doctor could not find the cause of it. By the end of May his family and friends were so worried that through Agnes Smedley they called in an American tuberculosis specialist to examine Lu Xun, without his foreknowledge. This specialist concluded that Lu Xun's tuberculosis had reached an advanced stage. His verdict was that if he had been European, he would have died long ago: he owed his survival to stronger Chinese resistance to tuberculosis, the disease being endemic in the population. Subsequent X-rays confirmed his diagnosis. Lu Xun did not take to this doctor, and preferred to continue treatment under his Japanese one, a retired army physician. After being bedridden from 6th to 30th June, Lu Xun's condition improved enough for him to get up, but he still ran a high temperature, and had to be kept going with medicine and injections. Even when he was having fluid drained from his lungs, he still smoked a cigarette, according to his son's recollection. In several letters written around this time he mentioned his intention of going away somewhere, perhaps to Japan, to recuperate, but never did get round to it. He remained relatively optimistic, however, if we are to believe the reassurances he gave to his correspondents that his kind of illness proved fatal only to the young: to old lags like himself it was chronic, not life-threatening. In the last letter he wrote, on the eve of his death, he repeated that same message, and talked about moving house when the prices went down.

But if Lu Xun did not think he was going to go under this time round, he did realize that his life was gradually ebbing away. No doubt it was in that knowledge that he wrote an essay called "Death" (*Si*) on 5th September. The essay concluded with his 'last wishes', addressed to his family, in lieu of a legal will. The provisions were:

> Do not accept a penny from anyone for my funeral — old friends excepted.
> Hurry up and put me in my coffin and bury me, and have done with it.
> Do nothing in the way of commemorating me.
> Forget me, and take care of your own lives — if you don't you are really idiots.
> When the child grows up, if he is not talented he can find a little job to earn a living. On no account should he pretend to be a writer or artist if he is not up to it.
> Don't believe promises.
> Don't have anything to do with people who wound others but oppose retaliation and preach tolerance.

Finally, Lu Xun says that he has considered the European deathbed rite of forgiving and asking forgiveness, but declines to follow it. He has made too many enemies, he says; they can carry on hating him, and he will not forgive one of them.

Taken in isolation, these last wishes seem very bleak, not to say misanthropic, but the last three are a backwash from his disenchantment with the double-dealers and poseurs in literary circles. The first four, though phrased unusually bluntly, are not uncommon sentiments. The tone of the major part of the essay is in fact quite detached and relaxed, and in places humorous. Being a materialist, he did not look forward to an afterlife, but he expressed neither fear of nor wish for death, only the composed attitude of 'we shall see what we shall see'.

Xiao Hong, the young woman writer from Manchuria we have mentioned, was a houseguest at the time Lu Xun was bedridden in 1936. She throws a fascinating sidelight on him in her reminiscence published in October 1939. She writes:

> When he was ill, Lu Xun did not read papers or books, just lay peacefully. But there was a little picture he put by his bed and looked at constantly. Before he fell ill, he had shown that picture to everyone along with a lot of others. It was as small as a cigarette card. It depicted a woman in a long skirt running along with her hair streaming out behind her in the wind. On the ground beside her there were little red roses.
>
> As I recall, it was a coloured woodcut done by a Soviet artist. Lu Xun had lots of pictures — why did he choose that one to put by his pillow? Xu Guangping told me she didn't know either why he habitually looked at that one.

Obviously Lu Xun sought solace in the picture. Inevitably he must have entered imaginatively into its world — to find what? A release from his own surroundings, no doubt. Even if the artist was Soviet, it was no specifically Soviet utopia that was depicted, more like some pre-Raphaelite vision. Supposing it had been the romantic Anglophile poet Xu Zhimo who cherished such a picture, there would have been nothing surprising about it, in fact athletic maidens running in the wind are typical of his imagery, but none of Lu Xun's professed tastes account for his attachment. If the picture represented a fantasy that he often indulged, he kept it very private. In the end, we have to confess, like Xiao Hong and Xu Guangping, that we cannot even make a good guess.

The last times Lu Xun left his house were to go to a woodcut exhibition on 8th October, as we have noted, and to the cinema on the 10th, to see a Soviet film based on Pushkin's *Dobrovsky*. As Lu Xun had written to friends in March 1936 "My only pleasure now is to go to the movies, but sadly there are few good ones," he was fortunate in that he enjoyed this one. He recommended it in two letters he wrote the same day.

After letting up for about three months, Lu Xun's disease struck again. In the early morning of 18th October, after a restless night, he had great difficulty in getting his breath. He struggled to write a note to Uchiyama Kanzo (unnecessarily, as Xu Guangping volunteered to deliver the message orally) apologizing for having to break their 10 a.m. appointment, and asking him to send his doctor round. The doctor's injections brought temporary relief, and Lu Xun was able to question Xu Guangping about what was in the morning papers, but then he had to retire to bed. That day he could take only a little milk. He passed away at 5.25 a.m. the next day, 19th October.

An announcement of his death was issued the same day and carried in the main Shanghai evening newspapers. Lu Xun's corpse was transferred to the Universal Funeral Parlour for viewing in an open coffin (donated by Song Qingling). On the first viewing day (20th October) 4,462 people queued to pay their respects and sign the book of remembrance. The hall was filled with wreaths and funeral banners. On the 22nd the long funeral cortege wound its way along streets lined by police out from the International Settlement, through the Chinese quarter to the Universal Public Cemetery (Wanguo gongmu), where the coffin was lowered into the grave, draped in a white flag on which the words 'The Soul of the Nation' (*Minzu hun*) were inscribed in black. In 1956 Lu Xun's remains were transferred to Hongkou Park. His name on the tombstone was written by Chairman Mao. By that time Lu Xun had been made a modern icon, for reasons we will go into next.

17

Epilogue

Very soon after Lu Xun's death a big operation was mounted to collect and publish all his writings. This resulted in his *Complete Works (Lu Xun quanji)* in twenty volumes coming out in 1938. Glowing tributes were appended to the collection, including one by Cai Yuanpei; the homage paid was to a great man of letters, an outstanding scholar, a 'genius'. The *Complete Works* was reprinted in 1946, and subsequent new editions ensured that his total *oeuvre*, from his student apprentice pieces to his mature works, his translations, diaries, and letters, were always available to researchers all over China to produce a continuous stream of articles and books on him. Needless to say, the individual volumes which made up the collection were also separately kept in print.

If that served to keep alive the Lu Xun word, attempts were also made to keep alive 'the Lu Xun spirit', for instance by the launch in Shanghai in 1939 of a magazine called *The Lu Xun Trend (Lu Xun feng)*. The purpose of the magazine was not to imitate or idolize Lu Xun, but to emulate his fighting spirit — to be courageous, forward-looking and steadfast in adversity. Meetings were also held on the anniversary of his death to pay tribute to him. While the war against Japan was pursued, Lu Xun was claimed as much as great patriot as great writer. The way to canonization was not cleared until all the media in China came under control of the Chinese Communist Party after 1949.

The political purpose of canonization in the communist book was to shape the model of an intellectual who made his way from the feudalism of the Qing empire through the chaos of proto-democratic reformism in the republican period to the inevitable conclusion of adherence to communism. To qualify as model, the intellectual would have to be of acknowledged eminence, to have shown strength of character, and to have written a lot on social questions so that his words could be quoted. Given these pre-requisites, the publicity machine could take over. The model's human failings and weaknesses would be deleted, and elevation achieved by a number of ploys. Those ploys would include selective citation, highlighting those words and deeds that conformed to the desired image and ignoring or explaining away those that did not; presenting all his decisions as bold and resolute, with his moral authority quelling opposition; giving him sole credit for any meritorious joint enterprise; getting people who had known him in his lifetime to render purely flattering witness to his nobility; emphasizing tireless endeavour and self-sacrifice; and, particular to communism, stressing his poverty and love for the toiling masses. All those techniques were indeed used in Lu Xun's case, and the 'accepted view' of him so formulated could not be challenged. Only very recently has it become possible to publish anything derogatory of him.

Presuming that any cause has to have its heroes and martyrs, and Chinese communism has its fair complement, the question is, why was Lu Xun elevated so high above the others? Was he in fact that much more admirable than other contenders for sainthood? If we take away the mantle of posthumous mythology, was he in his lifetime really a great man? If so, what distinguished him from his contemporaries?

There are objective measures of his eminence: the sales of his books, the crowds attracted to his public lectures, and the length of his funeral cortege. The heart of the matter, however, is how far he measured up to the title accorded him by the funeral banner, 'the soul of the nation'. It goes without saying that those who gave him that title were his supporters, and there were others who thought of him as the devil's disciple, but if we attempt to exercise the judgement of history, should we on balance accept or reject the claim? To discuss the question sensibly, we have to reduce it to realistic proportions. All nations are divided, and so cannot have one 'soul'. Even the wisest cannot be right on every issue, so we cannot confuse 'soul' with faultless judgement. What we are really talking about is having the good of the nation at heart, and consistently and courageously speaking out on matters of conscience, in a way that coincided with the general popular will.

If we were Lu Xun himself, we would say that the proof of his stand coinciding with the general will is that his stand roused the wrath of the authorities, who were bound to be in the wrong. Using the more objective measure of political history, in the last decade of his life Lu Xun came to support the Chinese Communist Party against the Guomindang, and it is undeniable that in that period support for the Chinese Communist Party grew and support for the Guomindang diminished. It is also undeniable that when it came to civil war in the late 1940s the victory of the Red Army was made easier by large bodies of Guomindang troops *defecting* with their commanders to the communist side. Whatever the sins of the Chinese Communist Party after it came to power, there is no doubt that its victory was welcomed by the majority of the Chinese people.

The most important aspect, though, is the moral struggle. A substantial number of Lu Xun's topical essays were directed against

manifestations of cruelty and inhumanity, or as we would say
nowadays violation of human rights, and against suppression of
civil liberties. As a simple category of protest that puts him on the
side of the angels, but does not make him special, because plenty
of other people, including the 'proper men' he treated with hostility,
did the same. If his words were more pungent and his protests
more skilfully and effectively made, that still does not radically
alter the picture. What does mark him out is his severe and
unrelenting analysis of the dark side of the Chinese character, not
— this is the crucial point — in a detached way, dissociating himself
from this dark side, but just the opposite: painfully probing the
recesses of his own psyche, as a Chinese himself. To tell people
unpleasant truths about themselves does not of course immediately
endear you to them, but their recognition of those truths does
earn respect and eventually their admiration. As a small token of
that recognition, tales are told about readers suspecting, quite
wrongly, that they were the models for characters satirized in Lu
Xun's short stories, which betokens recognition of those traits in
the self and in others. And, staying with the short stories, it is a
sign of Lu Xun's association with those character faults that his
narrator typically either condones them or seems unaware of them
— though as author he naturally transcends that level and both is
aware of them and laments them.

Lu Xun once claimed that he dissected himself more ruthlessly
than he dissected other people. Such introspection is taken to an
extreme in the self-punishing and self-destructive visions in his
Weeds prose-poems, which were unparalleled in Chinese literature.
His baring of the soul was quite different from the 'confessional'
literature of the early Creation Society, which was reader-directed
and not altogether truthful. But his habit of self-examination is
plain too in his sometimes startlingly frank admission of weakness

and prejudice in his essays and reminiscences, as when he admitted his writing in Guangzhou had been 'pussy-footed' because he was scared to death by the bloodletting, and in his piece on Rou Shi that we have translated. Though he still had his blindsides, and was stubborn and petty and arrogant at times, in the end he did try to be honest about himself, and that kind of honesty did much to redeem his faults.

Lu Xun was no philosopher. His thoughts as he set them out were systematic only within the confines of the short essay. If protracted his expositions tended to expose loopholes and inconsistencies. He was very well informed, but his positions were taken instantly and instinctively. In that way he was more sensitive as a sounding board than a philosopher who fits his perceptions into his scheme of things. To adopt a common expression, Lu Xun was 'thin skinned'; in other words, his nerve endings were close to the surface. He himself spoke in 1935 of the writer's duty to be 'a reflexive nerve'. His own nervous system had of course been formed by personal experience, but also by much common experience. He had played several different roles in his life, at different levels, in different climates, and he drew on a deep well of collective memory through his wide reading. Therefore, taking into account also his superior powers of articulation, one could fairly make the case that Lu Xun represented the 'Chinese mind' in responding to events as well as, and probably better than, any of his contemporaries — insofar as it is possible for any individual to do so.

One other vital factor has to be considered, and that is Lu Xun's persistence in struggle. Right from childhood he had been attracted by the image of the warrior. He had been delighted to be recruited to the band of boys who as part of a ghostly ritual that preceded a country play galloped on horseback to a cemetery and threw spears into a grave mound. And of all the strange creatures pictured in *The Classic of Mountains and Seas,* his favourite was Xing Tian. Xing Tian was headless, and 'used his nipples as eyes and navel as mouth'; he is pictured as 'dancing with shield in one hand and battleaxe in the other'. Evidently the figure of the warlike Xing Tian impressed Lu Xun, because he mentioned him several times in his mature essays. Otherwise, we have seen that Lu Xun liked to cut a martial figure as a cadet, and had been disappointed at being assigned to a career below decks in the engine room. Had there been a prospect of him standing on the bridge and steaming at the enemy with guns blazing, he might have stayed in the navy, and died in some glorious action.

After Lu Xun converted to 'mental fight' in Japan, he had to find new inspiration. No Chinese hero seemed to fill the bill. The European 'Mara' poets briefly served their turn, but Lu Xun was not a poet, and he was anyway mainly relying on second-hand knowledge of them. The fighter *par excellence* that he discovered was Friedrich Nietzsche, in the role of the prophet Zarathustra. The example of Zarathustra sustained Lu Xun though his 'sloughs of despond' when he felt isolated, misunderstood and spurned, because Zarathustra willingly submitted to similar adversity, willingly undertook to 'go under', in order to prepare the way for the coming of a better humankind. Like Zarathustra, Lu Xun did not expect to succeed, but would not spare his enemies, and would go down fighting. Zarathustra said, "I love only what a man has written with his blood. Write with blood, and you will experience that blood is spirit." That could well have been Lu Xun's motto. The mature Lu Xun did not embrace Nietzsche's ideas, but he did embody more than any other prominent Chinese intellectual the spirit of Nietzsche. Of course, he had to live in the real world, and he was not going to recklessly put his life on the line, yet he did go on brandishing his 'shield and battleaxe' to the end of his days in what he thought was a good cause, and ultimately in the best interests of his country.

As to how Lu Xun would have regarded his canonization for political purposes, we already have an indication in his 'will' that we have quoted. A further clue comes from Nietzsche again. In Part Two of *Thus Spoke Zarathustra*, Zarathustra tells his disciples of a nightmare he has had. He dreamt he was a guardian of tombs. Down in the vaults a roaring wind arises, and casts up a black coffin before him. "And amid the roaring and whistling and shrilling the coffin burst and spewed out a thousandfold laughter. And from a thousand grimaces of children, angels, owls, fools, and butterflies as big as children, it laughed and mocked and roared at me. Then I was terribly frightened; it threw me to the ground. And I cried in horror as I have never cried. And my own cry awakened me — and I came to my senses."

Zarathustra's most loved disciple offers a comforting interpretation of the nightmare. "Are you not yourself," he says, "the wind with the shrill whistling that tears open the gates of the castle of death? Are you not yourself the coffin full of colorful sarcasms and the angelic grimaces of life? Verily, like a thousandfold children's laughter Zarathustra enters all death chambers, laughing at all night watchmen and guardians of tombs and whoever else is rattling with gloomy keys. You will frighten and prostrate them with your laughter; and your power over them will make them faint and wake them. And even when the long twilight and the weariness of death come, you will not set in our sky, you advocate of life. New stars you have let us see, and new wonders of the night; verily, laughter itself you have spread over us like a colorful tent ..." and so on. Zarathustra is not amused. He promises to show this disciple "a sea in which he can drown". Then "he looked a long time in the face of the disciple who had played the dream interpreter and he shook his head."

Lu Xun's life and thought instructs us that he would have likewise rejected the optimistic 'spin' put on his legacy, the glorification of him as creator of a brave new world. Rather would he, like Zarathustra, have regarded with horror the 'black coffin' that was opened in the Cultural Revolution (1966–1976), when his words were used to persecute decent people who had become political enemies — as indeed Nietzsche would have regarded with horror the use to which his words were put by the Nazis.

For all these reasons we can come down on Lu Xun's side, and allow that to call him 'the soul of the nation' in and for his time was not a gross exaggeration.

The Chinese nation is not now as it was then. The Communist Party governs, as Lu Xun thought it would, but believers in communism are a dying breed. The goal of 'wealth and power' set in the second half of the nineteenth century still drives the nation's will, but consumerism threatens to obliterate the cultural wealth that Lu Xun drew upon. His works, sixty-six years after his death, are not nearly as approachable as they once were. That applies particularly to his essays, not only because they have to do with 'battles long ago', not only because of their numerous cultural citations and quotations that now have to be footnoted, but also because of the language they were written in, which sometimes reads as a translation either from classical Chinese or from a foreign language. The younger generation of Chinese readers find the task of reading his essays, with a few exceptions, rather intimidating.

Lu Xun's fiction survives better, both in its original form and in adaptations for stage and screen. A notable example is a successful adaptation of the "Kong Yiji" story of the pathetic derelict scholar to the form of Zhejiang opera. Continuity is in any case ensured by the inclusion of his stories in school syllabuses. How far they are still read with pleasure is an open question. On the whole short stories wear less well than novels, as novels are lengthy enough to create their own imaginative world, while short stories have to tap into an existing one. Some of the limited dramas enacted in the short story may be universal and timeless, but nevertheless certain evocations and associations that the author's words give rise to — and that therefore play a key role in creating tone and atmosphere — are lost or changed with the passing of time. That problem is magnified when the short story is translated into a foreign language. Such is the gap between Chinese and Western history and culture that echoes are not heard, and the surface is either too featureless or too strange. For those who are willing and able to reconnect with Lu Xun's world, however, the resonances of his short stories are very strong. The critical consensus is still that they are genuinely the best that modern China has produced.

Sketches of Lu Xun's Literature

Battlecries (Nahan)
[Also translated as *A Call to Arms*. Published 1923. Fourteen stories written 1918–1922.]

The reputation of this collection of sundry items rests on a handful of stories to do with village and humble urban folk. The exception is the first story, which is untypical artistically but important thematically. "The Diary of a Madman" (*Kuangren riji*: the title is taken from Gogol) presents the realization that behind the façade of 'virtue and morality' that China prided itself on lay the barbaric reality of man eating man — a realization so disturbing that it could only come to a 'madman'. The madman's diary records a classic medical case of persecution mania, which culminates in the conviction that people in the street want to eat him, and a fear that he himself has unknowingly eaten human flesh. But set against these 'delusions' are the many instances he cites of cannibalism in ancient history and current life which are undeniable fact, so there is no mistaking the author's message that insanity is sanity. The stories that followed, however, owed their success as works of literature to the deletion of any overt message and the suppression of any show of sentiment on the part of the author. As classical Chinese literature was given precisely to extravagant expression of sentiment, this was itself a mark of modernity.

The story "Medicine" (*Yao*) in fact picks up one of the examples of 'man-eating' cited by the madman, namely the use of fresh human blood — from a public execution — to cure consumption, the consumptive being the young son of a poor teahouse owner. The succession of events is presented in four scenes without interlinking commentary. First, the collection of the blood-soaked bun at the execution ground; next, the triumphant return to the teahouse; third, the arrival of the blustering rogue who set up the trade in blood; lastly, the meeting of two bereaved mothers in a paupers' graveyard a year later — the one whose son had uselessly consumed the blood, the other whose son, a revolutionary, had provided the blood. The story is credible and told as real, but over it is laid a veil of symbolism that extends its significance.

"Kong Yiji" has no symbolism. Its power to affect derives from the *lack* of emotion on the part of the narrator, who recounts with indifference the pathetic story of the old failed scholar who on his descent to the human scrap heap is treated with derision by the vulgar patrons of the wine shop that he frequents. His only epitaph is the slate which marks his unpaid wine bill: 19 coppers.

"Hometown" (*Guxiang*) is much more complex in its plan. Here the narrator is difficult to separate from the author himself, as the experiences described closely resemble Lu Xun's own on his return to Shaoxing in 1919. Actually it is a cleverly composed reflection on memory deceived and dreams dissolved. The pivotal figure is the peasant Runtu, whom the narrator had played with as a boy, and whom he now finds drained of vitality by the severity of the demands made on him as provider and father. In their youth Runtu had opened up to the inhibited son of the gentry a new world of healthy living and spontaneous pleasure, but in adulthood the class barrier reasserts itself, and their relationship is awkward. Moreover, Runtu has suffered moral as well as physical decline. The subtlety of the story lies in little of this being spelled out, and the bruising, lamentable facts of life not being presented indignantly, in the form of social protest, but being absorbed into the subjective consciousness of the narrator.

"A Slight Disturbance" (*Fengbo*, also translated as "A Storm in a Teacup") is an amusing treatment of the pigtail theme on the village level. The rumour (around 1917) that the emperor has been restored to the throne and pigtails are required again comes to a remote village. It causes consternation to the family of the boatman who has cut his pigtail off, and exultation in the local 'scholar' who has kept his. When two weeks pass with nothing happening, everything returns to normal. This story prepared the ground for Lu Xun's major work of fiction, "The Authentic Biography of Ah Q" (*A Q zhengzhuan*, also translated as "The True Story of Ah Q"), which started life similarly as an 'entertainment', serialized in a newspaper.

Ah Q is a homeless odd-job man in a village typical of the Shaoxing region. The "Q" is claimed to be the initial consonant of his name when romanized, used because the author pretends he cannot determine his real name. This opens up the interpretation that Ah Q could be anybody — or everybody: and indeed that is how he is cast, as the unlovely Chinese Everyman. He is seen first in a series of humiliating encounters, which he is nevertheless able to rationalize to himself as 'moral victories'. When this consolation fails, he falls back on the ancestral 'capacity to forget'. Eventually he is undone when his sexual longings are stirred and he makes an indecent proposal to a respectable amah. He is forced to leave for the nearby town.

Some months later Ah Q returns to his village with money in

his purse and goods to sell. His fortunes plunge again when it is discovered that he has run away with the booty of a robber band for whom he has been keeping watch. His last moment of glory comes with the Xinhai Revolution (1911), when he drunkenly proclaims himself a revolutionary, and strikes fear in the villagers by singing martial songs. But then the local gentry dash the cup from his lips by also 'joining the revolution', and driving him away with blows from their sticks. At this point Ah Q loses the initiative and his role changes from a brainless, bullying scoundrel to that of an uncomprehending victim. He is blamed for a burglary he did not commit, condemned to death, paraded through the streets in an open cart, and shot. By now the village notables have been shown to be every bit as contemptible as Ah Q, and even more detestable. So, being small fry in comparison, Ah Q becomes pathetic.

The tone of this novella is heavily ironic, irony being the best protection against surrendering to outrage on the one hand, and pity on the other hand. In this respect, and in other ways too, Lu Xun made use of a technique he had learned from the Slavic authors he had read and translated as a student in Japan. Like them he belonged to a numerically tiny internationally-educated, reformist intellectual class who felt surrounded by an inert, feudal-minded populace whom ignorance had left without understanding of themselves or of their fellow men. Sympathy is practically unknown to the characters in this and the other stories; neither is it displayed by the author. All the same, there is an underlying current, if not of a common bond between author and creations, then of common bondage. Perhaps that is why the best stories continue to vibrate after reading.

Wavering (Panghuang)

[Also translated as *Hesitation* and *Wandering*. Published 1926. Eleven stories written 1924–1925.]

The title of this collection presumably refers to the theme shared by several of the stories of a generation of men who had received a modern education and imbibed high ideals backsliding, compromising, opting out, or even totally betraying their former principles. The setting has shifted from the country village to the city, and the issues dealt with are the contemporary ones of the mid-1920s.

"The New Year's Sacrifice" (*Zhufu*) is a link with *Battlecries* in that the inset story is of an unfortunate peasant woman, but the narrator is an educated man who seals her unhappiness by confirming what he knows to be her superstitious fears. Readers have understandably been struck more by the harrowing story of Sister Xianglin, whose ill fortune (her baby son is carried off by a wolf) is compounded by the malicious and salacious gossip of her 'friends' and rejection by her employers; actually, however, the author gives equal attention to the well-meaning but weak-minded narrator who lets her down.

More central to the collection are "In the Wine Shop" (*Zai jiulou shang*) and "The Lone Wolf" (*Guduzhe*, also translated as "The Misanthrope"), in which the narrator is hardly more than a device to make known the stories of two 'superfluous men', as the type was known in Russian literature. Both are composite pictures of intellectuals of Lu Xun's generation, whose personal histories in fact have similarities with Lu Xun's own. Perhaps he conceived of them as what he himself might have become had he remained an unknown schoolteacher in his home province. Lü Weifu of "In the Wine Shop" is a lapsed reformist of the sensitive and sentimental kind, who likens himself to a fly that flies off when disturbed, but only completes a small circle before returning to its starting place. Wei Lianshu of "The Lone Wolf" is eccentric and erratic; he is still an active radical when first seen, but he loses his job as a schoolmaster because of his critical journalism; at the end of his tether, he makes an abrupt about-face, and joins a general's staff as an adviser. Having cynically gone over to the enemy bag and baggage, he spends the last year of his life in falsehood and dissipation until he succumbs to tuberculosis.

The male protagonist in "Remorse" (*Shangshi*, also translated as "Regret for the Past") is also a failure, though in this case in the private context of a love affair. Many strands are woven together in this naïve affair: commitment and cohabitation based on fashionable Western ideas of romance; the disapproval of society; the harsh realities of life on the breadline; enchantment turning to resentment; honesty versus deception; and more besides. The outcome is that the pair break up and the girl dies shortly afterwards. The young man resolves he will in future take 'forgetfulness and falsehood' as his guide, like the others we have seen. This story was written in the middle of Lu Xun's own love affair with Xu Guangping, and no doubt reflects his own doubts and fears, but it is not autobiographical, and broaches matters that apply to any intimate relationship that turns sour. Its bent is psychological rather than sociological.

Psychoanalysis of a deliberately Freudian kind spotlights the chief character in "Soap" (*Feizao*). Reverting in this story to his overtly satirical mode, Lu Xun undermines the pretensions of a priggish husband and father to a purely charitable interest in a grimy but comely young woman whom he has seen begging in the street. The cake of scented soap he subsequently presents to his wife was obviously bought with the beggar in mind, as his wife is sharp enough to twig. This is probably the most sheerly enjoyable of Lu Xun's stories: cleverly structured, with a lot of subtle touches, it is funny without being facetious, and, unusually, ends well.

The prize for the most perfect composition in the collection, however, should go to "A Public Spectacle" (*Shizhong*, also translated as "A Warning to the Public"). It has no story to speak of, and the few words spoken are disjointed. It consists only of a scene on a hot and dusty street in the capital. A policeman parades a convicted felon to public view, as a form of punishment and deterrent. A crowd quickly forms round them, and latecomers jockey for position. The purpose of the spectacle is not served. No one can read the characters that state the felon's crime, and when one spectator does look him in the face, it is he who is discomposed, not the felon. All that is achieved is discomfort from the press of bodies. The piece can be read as Lu Xun's commentary on, literally, the Chinese 'man in the street', a dramatization on a lesser, domestic level of the news picture he had seen in Japan of an unfeeling Chinese crowd witnessing an execution of one of their own. But there *is* no commentary in the story, which is why it works so well.

The pain and passion of *Battlecries* is not evident in *Wavering*. The author is more contemplative and analytical. His main theme is disillusion. Consequently the stories have been much less cited than the classic statements of position in *Battlecries*. The one exception is the inset story in "The New Year's Sacrifice" of the tragically victimized Sister Xianglin. It seems, though, that statement of position was ultimately more important to Lu Xun than perfecting the art of the short story, for he wrote no more, preferring to speak plainly through the medium of essays.

Weeds (Yecao)
[Usually translated as *Wild Grass*. Published 1927. Twenty-three 'prose-poems' written September 1924–March 1926.]

This collection is important because it is an expression of Lu Xun's unique genius: no one else in China could have written anything like it. Nor could Lu Xun have written it at any other time than what he did. His state of mind is described most plainly in a sentence he wrote to Xu Guangping in the midst of writing *Weeds*: "My works are too dark, because I just feel that 'darkness and nothingness' are 'reality', but I obstinately want to fight a desperate war against them."

There is no unity in this collection. A few pieces present apparently ordinary scenes or episodes from his own experience; one is written entirely in verse, another as a dramatic sketch; a sequence of seven start with "I dreamed ..."; others are disembodied visions. In their diversity they resemble Lu Xun's earlier experiments with the genre, a series of six very short pieces published in 1919 under the general title "Soliloquies" (*Ziyan ziyu*); in fact two of the *Weeds* pieces grew out of this earlier work. The "Soliloquies" were jejune and immature, and Lu Xun had no wish to preserve them. The *Weeds* he unhesitatingly gathered and published.

By the mid-1920s other Chinese writers had produced collections of prose-poems. Lu Xun also had a German translation of Baudelaire's *Petits poèmes en prose*. But his own *Weeds* owed likeness to none of them so much as to Turgenev's *Poems in Prose* (1882). Lu Xun was certainly well acquainted with Turgenev — his brother says they read everything of his they could get hold of while in Japan — and may have read Liu Bannong's translation of four of Turgenev's prose-poems published in 1915. Though it cannot be proved that he had read the whole collection, the similarities in type are remarkable. Turgenev's pieces are also very mixed and varied. They range from scenes from everyday life, through encounters with strange, symbolic figures in empty landscapes (some confessedly dreams, some not), to allegories, parables and legends, and also include veiled attacks on real persons. Lu Xun's pieces have a similar mixture: like weeds, they seem to have seeded themselves. Turgenev's pieces are most memorably dark and nightmarish, in his case due to awareness of approaching death; Lu Xun's are much the same: predominantly eerie, surreal and frightening, with the difference that his terror may be allied to exhilaration. There is, however, little correspondence in content.

The most quoted piece in *Weeds* is 'The Passer-by" (*Guoke*), the one that takes the form of a dramatic sketch. A nameless traveller comes upon a nameless old man and young girl outside their isolated hut. They converse in enigmatic fashion. The traveller detests the regions to the east through which he has passed, and must go on to the west, where the old man tells him there are graves, but the young girl insists there are wild flowers. The girl offers him a cloth to bandage his feet, but he refuses it because he cannot owe her such a heavy debt. The passer-by stumbles off, and darkness closes in behind him. The traveller is obviously embarked on a quest, as he hears voices that impel him on, but he cannot share the vision of flowers that the girl offers, nor will he, by accepting her 'alms', involve her in the desolateness which is all he can see ahead. The old man has also heard the same voices as the traveller, but has lapsed into passivity. In contrast, the traveller can neither stand still nor turn back.

"The Passer-by" can thus be seen as a dramatic enactment of the state of Lu Xun's mind that he described privately to Xu Guangping. Its framework may well have been inspired by Nietzsche's *Also Sprach Zarathustra*. The prophet Zarathustra, we recall, was the ultimate obstinate traveller. He went down from his mountain to share his vision, was beaten and reviled, was nowhere understood, yet still carried on. Lu Xun started writing about Nietzsche in 1907, and translated the prologue to *Zarathustra* in 1920. Interestingly, Lin Yutang presented him with his own translation of the episode from *Zarathustra* called "On Passing By" (*Zouguoqu*)

on Lu Xun's departure from Xiamen. Apart from the coincidence of the title, however, there is no similarity between the two episodes in content or language. But there is some resemblance to Zarathustra's first encounter on coming down from his mountain. He meets an old hermit in a forest, who like Zarathustra once "loved man", and who counsels him to stay and find his satisfaction in the forest also. Zarathustra rejects his advice and passes on.

In the 1930s Lu Xun dismissed Nietzsche on the ground that his way led to madness. Judging by the more grotesque of his 1925 'weeds', those framed as dreams, he seemed in danger of ending up the same way. The strange thing is that he exposed his torment so willingly to public view. Or indeed that he should have been tormented to such a degree at all. His domestic frustrations were acute, it is true, but they could not account for the apocalyptic quality of the dream visions. Perhaps the answer is that rather than being modernist, as most critics see the prose poems, they are in spirit a reversion to antiquity. That is to say, the extreme to which Lu Xun goes was licensed by the example of the sainted, or possessed, poets of the *sao* school, who despaired of the world to the extent of frenzy. The *Songs of the South* (*Chu ci*) anthology, which collected their fabulous imaginings, was not only a favourite of Lu Xun, but also a revered classic. Because of that, in China you were not deemed to be truly demented if you wrote as if you were demented. All the same, *Weeds* did not start a trend.

Zawen

A *zawen* as a distinctive form of literature is a topical commentary that is critical and combative. Straightforward diatribe or plodding reasoning do not make for a good *zawen*. As defined by Lu Xun's example, good *zawen* variously include the elements of satire, caricature, figures of speech, analogies, and other kinds of artfulness recruited to buttress an argument. In tone *zawen* may be mild and calm, or bitter and passionate, or more often a combination of those opposites. To Lu Xun's critics, his *zawen* compositions were indeed summed up in the formula 'cold sarcasm plus heated invective'.

Topical commentaries were published in great numbers in Republican China, the peak period being roughly from 1925 to 1937. Their platforms were the weekly magazines and newspaper supplements that burgeoned in that period. As any expression of opinion was usually followed by a rebuttal, running battles were a common occurrence. It was from this kind of journalism that Lu Xun derived a large part of his income in his Shanghai period, and it was also this kind of journalism that went to form his popular image.

Lu Xun's *zawen* were not better argued than those of his competitors and adversaries, but they were more effectively composed. Lu Xun's superiority in debate derived from the following sources:

1. From his training in Chinese classical rhetoric, 'rhetoric' being used here in the Aristotelian sense of skill in presenting an argument. Unlike his younger adversaries, Lu Xun had practised writing the 'eight-legged' examination essay (*baguwen*), which was designed precisely to test verbal and argumentative skills and ingenuity, and on his own behalf he had read widely in freer classical disputation. On occasion he resorted to a modern version of the 'eight-legged essay'; more often and more broadly he utilized the rhetorical tactics of past masters.

2. From his own mordant wit and protean invention. He had a talent for summing up the arguments of adversaries in a snappy way that exposed them to mockery while retaining a core of accuracy. He coined new terms and concepts, made innovations

in form — some pieces being written entirely in figures, some as dramatic sketches. He inherited from Chinese parabolic literature a fondness for animal metaphors. By such means he enlivened his surfaces. In manipulation of words, he commanded the whole range of the Chinese language from the classical to the modern demotic.

3. From his encyclopaedic knowledge of Chinese and Western literature and history. His capacious memory enabled him to pick an 'old saw or modern instance' out of the air when needed.

To the common perception, Lu Xun's *zawen* consisted too much of personal attacks. Because people now read only Lu Xun and not his opponents' work, they do not realize that in the overwhelming majority of cases his personal attacks were in response to personal attacks on him. Nevertheless, his ripostes tended to be more wounding and insulting than the attacks he received, and injuries and grudges were never forgotten (though he was generous enough to apologize when he was mistaken). While it is not true to say, as his defenders do, that in individuals he was merely attacking *types*, it can be fairly argued that he saw in them — his fellow writers, scholars and intellectuals — the people who in their compliance with, if not actual support of, the men in power made his country the mess it was. He extremely rarely had a good word for his equals, his generosity and compassion being reserved for the poor, the humble, the unfortunate. As we have seen, 'fair play' was not part of his vocabulary, and he positively enjoyed the rough and tumble of controversy.

Having said what made Lu Xun's *zawen* stand out, it must be noted that they had their faults, too. He was frequently unable to rein in his inclination towards banter, facetiousness, and ostentatious cleverness.

Central though Lu Xun's contentious *zawen* were to the public perception of him, it would not do to lump all his non-fictional compositions together as *zawen*. He also wrote conventional essays, which expressed his thoughts about right and wrong, good and bad, truth and falsehood, and virtue and vice in a more contemplative way. These rose above the heat of battle, took a long view, and ultimately were more important than his *zawen* in establishing his intellectual credentials.

To Remember in Order to Forget

The purpose of translating this essay is to let Lu Xun speak for himself. In it he reveals more of himself as a man than I have done in my biography. It also offers a rare insight into the kind of life he and his young comrades led, on the fringes of the law, as members of the Left League. There is no attitudinizing here, no histrionics; the essay is written so plainly that it would be almost blasphemy to doubt its sincerity and truthfulness. Perhaps indeed it would have given more satisfaction artistically if the diction had not been so plain, but Lu Xun was deliberately disciplining himself, and I have tried to do likewise in translating it.

For a long time now I have been thinking of writing something in memory of a number of young writers. The reason is quite simply that for two years I have been suffering from a sense of outrage, and it still does not let up. I hope by this means to shake off my outrage at one go, and find relief. To put it plainly, I want to forget them.

At this time two years ago, that is on the night of the 7th or morning of the 8th of February 1931, our five young writers were done to death together. The Shanghai newspapers did not dare, or did not wish, or did not bother to carry that news; only in the *Literary News* was there a veiled reference. Then in Number Eleven

(25th May) there appeared a piece called "An Impression of Bai Mang" by Lin Mang. This is a passage from it:

> He wrote quite a lot of poems, and translated some of the Hungarian poet Petöfi. When Lu Xun, the then editor of *The Torrent*, received a contribution from him, he wrote to a arrange a meeting, but Bai Mang did not like to meet celebrities, so the upshot was Lu Xun himself made the effort to call on him, and encouraged him as best he could to take up literature as his work, but he found he could not sit writing in his little cubby-hole, and went his own way once more. Before long he was arrested again....

Actually, this story of our relationship is not accurate. Bai Mang was not so bigheaded: he did come to my lodgings, though not because I demanded that we meet. I was not so bigheaded either as offhandedly to summon a contributor who was quite unknown to me. The occasion of our meeting was very routine. The contribution in question was "The Life of Petöfi", which he had translated from the German, so I wrote for the original text. This biography was printed at the head of Petöfi's collected poems, and couldn't easily be sent by post, so he brought it along personally. To look at, he was in his twenties, with regular features, and very dark skin. I've forgotten what we talked about; I only remember he said his surname was Xu, and he came from Xiangshan. I asked him how come the lady who took letters for him had such a strange name (I've forgotten in what way it was strange). He replied that it was her fancy to use a romantic name, something he didn't altogether go along with. That's all that remains with me.

That night I made a rough comparison of the translation with the original. Apart from a few mistakes, I found he had deliberately mistranslated one thing. Apparently he didn't like the expression 'national poet', and substituted 'poet of the popular masses' for it. The next day I received a letter from him, saying he regretted coming to see me. He had said a lot, but I had said very little, and that coldly. He felt he had been put down. I replied, explaining that not to say much on first encounter was ordinary human nature, and telling him he should not make changes to the original to suit his own likes and dislikes. Because his book had to stay with me, I sent him two collections of my own, asking him to translate some more poems for the readers' reference. He did indeed translate some, and brought them round in person. That time we had more to say than before. This life and the poems were later published in Volume Two, Number Five of *The Torrent*, which was its last number.

I remember the weather was hot the third time we met. Somebody knocked on the door, I went to open it, and it was Bai Mang. But he was wearing a thick padded gown, and his face was covered in sweat. We both burst out laughing. Not till then did he tell me he was a revolutionary, and had just been let out of prison. His clothes and books had all been confiscated, including the two books I had given him. The gown he wore had been borrowed from a friend. Since he had to wear something that came down to his ankles, and had no lighter gown, he had to put up with sweating. I imagine this was the occasion that Liu Mang referred to, when he "was arrested again".

I was very pleased that he had been released, and made haste to pay him the fee for his contribution so that he could buy himself a plain lined gown, but at the same time was pained at the loss of my two books: falling into the hands of gaolers, it was casting pearls before swine. Actually the two books were extremely ordinary. One was a collection of Petöfi's prose, the other a collection of his poems. According to the German translator, he had assembled the collections himself, and no such complete ones existed even in the author's homeland of Hungary, yet being printed in Reclam's Universal-Bibliothek, they could be bought anywhere in Germany, at the price of under one yuan. But to me they were treasures, because I ordered them thirty years ago from Germany through the Maruzen Bookshop, when I had a passion for Petöfi. Because they were so cheap I was afraid the shop assistant would be reluctant to handle the order, and I placed it very nervously. Afterwards I carried them around with me, but enthusiasms change with the times, and since I didn't plan to translate anything of his myself, I decided to make a present of them to this youth who had a passion for Petöfi, as I had had then. That would be a good home for them. So, not wanting them to go astray, I had Rou Shi deliver them personally. Imagine them falling into the hands of the 'three chevron men'[1] — what an injustice!

2

The reason I did not invite contributors to meet me was not entirely out of modesty. In large part it was also to avoid bother. I knew from long experience that young people, especially young writers, were almost all very sensitive, and esteemed themselves highly. A careless word could easily be misunderstood, so I was inclined to avoid them. Since I was even afraid of meeting them, even less did I dare give them jobs to do. Yet there was someone in Shanghai then, the only one I dared not only to laugh and joke with, but also to have do some private jobs for me, and that was Rou Shi, the person who delivered the books to Bai Mang.

---

1. Police sergeants of the International Settlement, so called because of the three chevrons worn on their sleeves.

I do not know when and where I first met Rou Shi. I think he said that he attended my lectures in Peking, in which case it would have been eight or nine years ago. Neither do I remember how it was we started to mix socially. In any case, he lived in Jingyun Lane, only four or five doors from my lodgings, and somehow we became sociable. It was probably at our first meting that he told me that his surname was Zhao and his given name Pingfu. But then he got onto how overbearing the big gentry were in his home region, and how one of them took a fancy to his given name, and wanting to use it for his son, told him not to use it himself. So I suspected his original name was another 'fu' character, meaning 'good fortune', which would have appealed to that gentryman. He came from Ninghai in Taizhou, which one could guess from his Taizhou-style stubbornness. He was unworldly with it, a combination that reminded me sometimes of Fang Xiaoru,[2] who I think must have been rather like him.

He hid himself away in his digs, working at his writing, both creative literature and translation. After a good many days of keeping company, we found we hit it off well, so he got together some like-minded youths, and we set up the Morning Blossoms Society. The aim was to introduce East and North European literature, and import foreign graphics, because we all agreed that we should lend support to a plain and robust kind of literature and art. Subsequently we published *Morning Blossoms Trimonthly*, *Modern World Stories*, and *Morning Blossoms in the Garden of Art*, which all followed that line. The only exception was *Paintings*

---

2. Fang Xiaoru (1357–1402), also from Ninghai, was an imperial tutor who refused loyalty to a usurper of the throne, and was executed along with all his clan in punishment.

of Koji Kukiya, which was published to smoke out the self-styled 'artists' of the Shanghai Bund, and expose the paper tiger Ye Lingfeng.[3]

But Rou Shi had no money. He borrowed over two hundred yuan to start printing for the society. Besides buying paper, most of the manuscript reading and odd jobs like running to the printers, preparing illustrations and proofreading, were in his hands. But he was usually dissatisfied with the results, and he frowned when he spoke of them. His early works all have a pessimistic tone, but the reality was quite different: he believed people were good. When I sometimes got round to talking about how deceitful people were, how they sold out their friends, how they were bloodsuckers, the sweat would glisten on his forehead, his short-sighted eyes would go round in consternation, and he would protest, "Could that be true? Surely it's not as bad as that?..."

However, the Morning Blossoms Society folded up before long, for reasons I won't go into. Anyway, Rou Shi's idealistic notions took a big hammering. His efforts had gone for nothing, and on top of that he had to borrow a hundred yuan to pay the bill for paper. After that he was less disbelieving about my philosophy that 'the human heart is treacherous', and sadly he would now sigh, "Could that be true?..." All the same, he still believed that people were good.

At that point he sent the little remaining stock of the Morning Blossoms Society that reverted to him to the Tomorrow Bookshop and Guanghua Bookshop, in the hope of getting back a few coppers, and set about translating for all he was worth, in order to pay his

---

3. Ye Lingfeng (1904–1975) had antagonized Lu Xun in 1928–1929 by publishing cartoons and articles satirical of him. Lu Xun thought he was artistically a poor imitator of Koji.

debts. The results were *Short Stories from Denmark* and Gorki's novel *The Artamovs' Business*, which he sold to the Commercial Press. But I think his manuscripts may have gone up in smoke in last year's warfare.

Gradually his unwordliness underwent a change, and he finally ventured to walk along the street with friends or fellow natives of Ninghai of the female sex, but still he kept a distance of at least three to four feet from them. This was a bad practice, because when I happened to run into him I would suspect that any attractive young woman three to four feet in front or behind, or to the left or right of him was a friend of his. Yet when I walked with him he would close up on me, to the point of propping me up, because he was afraid of me being run over by a car or trolley bus. For my own part, I was nervous at him taking someone else in hand with his short sight. So it was we both scrambled along, in a pother the whole way. Therefore I rarely went out with him unless I had no choice: it obviously put a strain on him, and so put a strain on me.

Of his own free will he took up responsibilities under both the old and the new moralities, as long as the purpose was to help others, not himself.

In the end, he made a decisive break with the past. He once told me plainly that the content and form of works ought to have a new direction. I said, I'm afraid that's not going to be easy. If someone is used to using a knife, how can you ask him to use a club? His answer was simple and clear-cut: You just have to learn!

Those were not empty words: he really did start all over again. He brought a friend to see me then — that was Miss Feng Keng. After some days of talking I found that she and I were at cross purposes. I suspected her of having a romantic streak in being in too much of hurry to notch up results. I also suspected that Rou Shi's new plan to write a big novel had been her idea. But I also

232   *The True Story of Lu Xun*

suspected myself: perhaps Rou Shi's blunt answer to my earlier question had made me conscious of the weakness of my own stand, which was in fact an argument for indolence, and unconsciously I had made her the target of my resentment. That would mean I was in no way superior to the oversensitive and self-important young writers I was afraid of meeting.

Her constitution was weak and she was not at all pretty.

3

I didn't discover until after the League of Left-wing Writers was set up that the man I knew as Bai Mang was the same person as the poet Yin Fu who published in *The Pioneer*. I took along a book to a general meeting to give to him, a German translation of an American journalist's account of his travels in China. The idea was simply to enable him to practise his German, nothing more profound than that. But he didn't turn up, so I had to get Rou Shi to pass the book on to him. Soon afterwards, though, they were both arrested, and my book was confiscated, ending up like the others in the hands of the 'three chevrons' lot.

4

Tomorrow Bookshop wanted to put out a periodical, and got Rou Shi's agreement to edit it. The bookshop also wanted to publish my translations, and they got Rou Shi to approach me about royalties. So I made a copy of the contract I had with the Beixin Bookshop. He stuffed it in his pocket and left in a hurry. That was on the night of 16th January 1931. I could not have foreseen that this would be the last time I would see him, that in fact it would be our final parting.

The next day he was arrested at a meeting. He still had my contract with my publisher in his pocket, and I heard that the authorities were on my trail. The contract was plain and aboveboard, but I did not want to go somewhere where nothing was plain and aboveboard to explain myself. I remember that *The Tale of Yue Fei* tells of a venerable monk who was about to be arrested by an agent of the prime minister. As the agent, named He Li, neared the monastery gate, the monk took up the meditation posture and 'ascended to heaven', leaving behind the immortal words, "He Li approaches from the east, I depart towards the west". This was the best way of escaping from the 'sea of sorrows' that the slavish mind could imagine. In default of a knight at arms riding to the rescue, it was the coolest solution. Not being a venerable monk, I haven't the option of release into nirvana. On the contrary, I am still attached to my life. So I made myself scarce.

The same night I burned old letters from friends, and moved to a boarding house with my wife and child. Not many days afterwards, rumours were rife that I had been arrested, or killed, but there was little news of Rou Shi. One story went that he had been taken to the Tomorrow Bookshop, where they asked if he was an editor; another story went that he had been taken to the Beixin Bookshop, where they asked if he was Rou Shi. He was handcuffed, which showed the case was serious, but what the case was, nobody understood.

I have seen two letters that Rou Shi wrote while in custody to a fellow native of Ninghai. The first went like this:

> Yesterday I was brought with thirty-five fellow prisoners (seven women) to Longhua Prison. In the evening they put us in chains, which is a new departure for political prisoners. As this case implicates so many people, I won't be released very soon, so I hope you will look after my bookshop business for me. Things are all

right at the moment, and I am learning German with Yin Fu. You can tell Mr. Zhou [Lu Xun] that. He is not to worry, we haven't been tortured. The police and security people have several times asked me for Mr. Zhou's address, but how would I know? Please don't worry. Regards,
Zhao Xiaoxiong. 24th Jan.

On the back of the letter is written:

I need two or three tin rice bowls. If you can't get in to see me, please leave the things for me, Zhao Xiaoxiong.

He was the same as ever, wanting to study German and get ahead. He still was concerned for me, too, like when we walked along the street together. But some things in his letter were mistaken. The chaining of political prisoners did not start with him. He had too high regard for the ways of officialdom. He thought they always had been civilized, and only descended to cruelty with them. Actually it was not so. Sure enough, his second letter was very different. His wording was very distressed, and he said Miss Feng's face was all swollen up. Unfortunately, I didn't make a copy of that letter. The rumours then multiplied, some saying he could be bailed out, some saying he had been transferred to Nanjing, none at all reliable. At the same time I got more and more enquiries by letter and telegram about my own safety. Even my mother far away in Peking got sick from worrying. I had to write to put them right one by one. That went on for about twenty days.

As the days grew colder, I wondered if Rou Shi had a quilt for his bed. If not, we had one. Had he received the tin bowls or not?... But suddenly we got reliable information that he and twenty-three others had been shot on the night of the 7th or morning of the 8th of February at the Longhua Garrison Command. Ten bullets had entered his body.

So that's how it was!...

Late one night I stood in the yard of the boarding house, surrounded by heaps of junk. Everyone was asleep, including my wife and child. My heart was heavy: I had lost a very good friend, China had lost a very good young man. From out of the depth of bitterness I retrieved my composure. And in composure old habits took over. I put together the following lines:

> I am used to pass spring in long waking nights.
> I shelter my wife and child, my hair turning grey.
> In my dreams the blur of a kind mother's tears.
> On the city ramparts flies a new chieftain's banner.
> They turn my friends into ghosts, dreadful to witness.
> Angrily I face the rows of swords and contrive a poem.
> I can say the poem to myself, but no one will take it.
> Moonlight clear as water falls on my dark gown.

The last but one line turned out not to be true. Eventually I wrote the poem out and sent it to a Japanese songwriter.

However, in China there truly was nowhere to publish it: all outlets were sealed as tight as a tin can. I remember Rou Shi had gone back home at the end of the year and stayed there quite a time, for which he was severely criticized by his friends. He said to me indignantly, his mother was now completely blind, and since she wanted him to stay on a few days, how could he just turn round and leave? I knew that his blind mother doted on him, and how earnest Rou Shi's heart was. When *Northern Dipper* was launched [September 1931], I wanted to write something on Rou Shi, but could not; I could only choose one of Käthe Kollwitz's woodcuts, entitled "Sacrifice", which depicted a mother sorrowfully offering up her son. I was possibly the only one to know it was a memorial to Rou Shi.

Of the four other writers who met their end with him, I wasn't acquainted with Li Weisen, and Hu Yepin I had met only once in

Shanghai and chatted with briefly. More familiar was Bai Mang, alias Yin Fu: he had written to me, and sent me manuscripts, but no trace of those can now be found. I think I must have burned the whole lot on the night of the 17th, though at the time I didn't know Bai Mang was among those arrested. But his copy of *Poems of Petöfi* is still with me. Leafing through it, I find very little, only a translation of "Wahlspruch" (Maxim) written in ink alongside the original:

> Life is truly worth treasuring,
> And the value of love is even higher.
> But if the cause is freedom,
> I will cast both aside!

On the inside page is written "Xu Peigen", which I assume was his real name.[4]

5

On this day two years ago, while I was taking refuge in a boarding house they were going to the execution ground. On this day one year ago, while I was fleeing to the British Concession to the sound of cannon fire, they were already buried in an unmarked grave. Only on this day this year am I sitting as before in my own lodgings. Everyone is asleep, including my wife and child. Again my heart is heavy: I have lost a very good friend, China has lost a very good young man. From the depth of my bitterness I have retrieved my composure, and in composure old habits have taken over again, and I have written the above.

---

4. Actually Xu Peigen was the name of his elder brother.

If I write any more, there will be no place in the China of today to publish it. When I was young I read Xiang Ziqi's "Thinking of Past Times",[5] and was annoyed by the way he had barely begun before he came to an end. Now I understand, though.

This is not the young writing in memory of the old, as it should be. In the last thirty years I have witnessed the spilt blood of many young persons mount up in waves and overwhelm me, so that I cannot breathe. All I can do is use brush and ink in this fashion, to make as it were a small hole in the encrusted surface, and suck in some lame breaths of air. What kind of a world are we living in? The night is long, the way is long; it would be better if I forgot, and spoke not. Yet I know that there will come a time when they will be remembered and spoken of again, if not by me, then by others....

7th–8th February [1933]

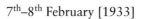

5. This composition of Xiang Ziqi (A.D. 227–272) comprised only 156 characters. It was written in memory of his friends Ji Kang and Lu An, who had been killed by Sima Zhao, the ruler of the kingdom of Wei.

Sources

Not surprisingly, the written sources for Lu Xun's life are in Chinese, and the material vestiges of his existence are in China. Taking the latter first, there are three locations to visit in order to get a firsthand impression of his surroundings. Working from north to south, the small house with walled yard in the Fucheng Gate district of Beijing where Lu Xun lived with his wife and mother in the mid 1920s has been preserved and the site expanded to include the Lu Xun Museum. Apart from having extensive displays of photographs, manuscripts, table models of buildings, and so on, this museum is the chief archive for written material relating to Lu Xun. In Shanghai one can see the terrace house in which he died in 1936, and now there is a big museum for him in Hankou Park. The most interesting exhibit there is a continuously running short film of his funeral cortege. In his birthplace, Shaoxing, the three Zhou clan mansions and his schoolhouse have been restored, and further displays are mounted in the associated museum. As the urban environment has changed beyond recognition since Lu Xun's day, these physical remains and reminders help one to understand the everyday realities of our subject's life.

Reverting to written sources, comparably solid information on places and people has been provided by local historians: for example, the books put out by the Shaoxing Lu Xun Museum, including Zhu Min et al., *Lu Xun zai Shaoxing* (*Lu Xun in Shaoxing*, 1997), and in the north *Lu Xun zai Beijing* (*Lu Xun in Beijing*, 1996) by Liu Lihua and Zheng Zhi. Intimate knowledge of Lu Xun naturally comes from the persons closest to him. On his early life the most knowledgeable source is Lu Xun's brother, Zhou Zuoren. In 1957 he published *Lu Xun de gujia* (*Lu Xun's Family Home*) under the name Zhou Xiashou and *Lu Xun de qingnian shidai* (*Lu Xun's Youth*) under the name Zhou Qiming. The third brother Zhou Jianren contributed *Lu Xun gujia de bailuo* (*The Decay of Lu Xun's Family Home*) in 1984. Lu Xun's common law wife Xu Guangping published *Xinwei de jinian* (*Comforting Memories*) in 1951 and *Guanyu Lu Xun de shenghuo* (*On Lu Xun's Life*) in 1954. His lifelong friend Xu Shouchang published *Wangyou Lu Xun yinxiang ji* (*Impressions of My Late Friend Lu Xun*) in 1947, along with other books. Many more reminiscences are included in the six-volume *Lu Xun huiyilu* (*Memories of Lu Xun*) put together by the Beijing Lu Xun Museum in 1999. Most recently Lu Xun's son, Zhou Haiying, has published *Lu Xun yu wo qishinian* (*My Seventy Years with Lu Xun*, 2001).

Primary sources are Lu Xun's diary, included in the sixteen-volume *Lu Xun quanji* (*Complete Works of Lu Xun*) of 1981, his correspondence in the same collection and, less reliable, his own retrospective essays. The annotations in *Complete Works* are very helpful across the board. Also indispensable is the *Lu Xun nianpu* (*Year-by-year Chronology for Lu Xun*) in four volumes compiled by the staff of the Beijing Lu Xun Museum (1981–1984).

Since the 1980s writers have dug into aspects of Lu Xun's private life that previous accounts skated over, particularly his sex life and his rift with Zhou Zuoren. Among those that cover the former matter are Li Yun, *Lu Xun de hunyin yu jiating* (*Lu Xun's Marriage and Family*) of 1990, and Ma Tiji's two books, *Lu Xun shenghuo-zhong de nüxing* (*The Women in Lu Xun's Life*) and *Lu Xun xinzhuan* (*A New Biography of Lu Xun*), both published in 1996. Huang Qiaosheng's *Dujin jiebo: Zhoushi san xiongdi* (*The End of Trials and Tribulations: The Three Zhou Brothers*) of 1998 covers the latter matter, as does Duan Guochao's *Lu Xun jiashi* (*Lu Xun's Family Background*), also 1998.

Lu Xun has also been written about in English and other European languages, but to my knowledge there is as yet no independent full biography (there is a French translation of an adulatory Chinese one). The concentration has understandably been on his works. Probably the most biographical detail is contained in William Lyell's *Lu Hsun's Vision of Reality* (Berkeley, 1976), which goes into Lu Xun's home background to explain the genesis of his fiction. ('Lu Hsun' is the way Lu Xun's name was formerly spelled.) Tsi-an Hsia's *The Gate of Darkness: Studies on the Leftist Literary Movement in Shanghai* (Seattle, 1968) and Wang-chi Wong's *Politics and Literature in Shanghai: The Chinese League of Left-wing Writers, 1930–36* (Manchester, 1991) deal among other things with Lu Xun's part in literary politics in Shanghai. Leo Ou-fan Lee's *Voices from the Iron House: A Study of Lu Xun* (Bloomington, 1987) contains biographical information along the way. Like the others mentioned it is worth reading to gain an all-round view of our author, as is the volume Lee edited, *The Legacy of Lu Xun* (Berkeley, 1985). The book by James Pusey mentioned in this biography is *Lu Xun and Evolution* (Albany, 1998). John Fitzgerald's *Awakening China* (Stanford, 1996) provided precious information on Guomindang organization. The quotations from Nietzsche are translated by Walter Kaufmann in *The Portable Nietzsche* (Penguin Books, 1976 edition).

For English translations of Lu Xun's works, first mention must go to Yang Xianyi and Gladys Yang's *Selected Works* in four volumes, first published in Peking 1956–1960, with several new editions. More latterly William Lyell translated Lu Xun's fiction in *Diary of a Madman and Other Stories* (Hawaii, 1990) in a style that would be more appreciated by American readers. Translations of individual stories and essays are scattered about, as in my anthology, *The Chinese Essay* (Hong Kong, 1999; London, 2000).

On a personal level, I have over the years enjoyed conversations with Mr. Wang Dehou, formerly deputy head of the Beijing Lu Xun Museum. The conversations have been somewhat one-sided, as he is vastly more knowledgeable than me, but he is good humoured enough to overlook the disparity.